The Corrupted Land

FRED J. COOK

The
CORRUPTED
LAND

THE SOCIAL MORALITY OF
MODERN AMERICA

THE MACMILLAN COMPANY: *New York*

FIRST PRINTING

The Macmillan Company, New York

Collier-Macmillan Canada, Ltd., Toronto, Ontario

Library of Congress catalog card number: 66–11102

Contents

The Corrupted Land

A Way of Life

DOUGLAS WILLIAM JOHNSON was looking for work on March 10, 1961, when sheer chance elected that he should become a symbol of life in the corrupt society.

Johnson was a fifty-year-old Negro janitor in Los Angeles, a man who had felt the pinch of poverty. On this particular March day, he drove with his wife, Helen, thirty-eight, out to an apartment house that was under construction to try to get the job of cleaning up the debris. The superintendent he had to see wasn't at the site, so Johnson climbed back into his station wagon and started home.

So far he had performed only the most routine of actions on this most routine of days, and almost certainly the great American public would never have heard of Douglas William Johnson if, on that drive home, he had not spotted a bulky canvas bag lying in the road, almost in the path of his car.

Thinking the bag just possibly might contain something useful, Johnson stopped, picked it up and tossed it into the back of his station wagon. Then he got behind the wheel again and drove off, not bothering to examine his find. His wife, more curious, squirmed around in her seat, reached back and picked up the bag. It was sealed, but it bore a tag. Mrs. Johnson read what the tag said, then turned to her husband.

[9]

"Do you know what you've picked up?" she asked. "There's two hundred and forty thousand dollars in that bag!"

"No!" Johnson exclaimed—and started to shake all over.

Explaining his reaction later, he told reporters:

"I was knocked off my feet. I never dreamed I'd have my hands on anything like that."

In this Douglas Johnson certainly differed from most Americans. Abundant evidence would seem to indicate that most of us dream constantly of getting our hands on something just like that, but for the great majority the dream remains divorced from reality. Only for Douglas Johnson, by a whim of fate, had the dream come true. What should he do?

Examination of the bag showed that its valuable contents consisted of bills of relatively small denominations, the kind that are not easily traced. Johnson was a part-time maintenance man; he had a wife and three sons to support—and here this virtually untraceable king's ransom had fallen into his lap. Douglas Johnson wouldn't have been human if he hadn't been tempted.

But he thought about it and came to a quick decision.

"I thought if I kept that money I'd never be able to look my three kids in the face again," he explained afterward with the simplistic imagery of a bygone age when a man had stature and was supposed to be responsible for his acts.

This basic decision made, Johnson acted according to the dictates of pure and simple honesty. As soon as he reached home he telephoned a friend, a former Chicago policeman, to find out whom he should notify about the money; the friend advised him to call the Federal Bureau of Investigation. Johnson did. In minutes, four FBI agents were at his door.

What had happened was this: A Brinks Inc. armored truck had been taking fifteen bags of money from the United California Bank to the Federal Reserve Bank. The bags had been piled high at the rear of the truck. One apparently slid off the pile, hit a horizontal inside handle that released the door and fell into the street. A guard inside the truck at the time was sitting facing forward, updating his records, and didn't notice the loss. Not until the truck had proceeded for some distance did the driver,

Robert Downs, happen to glance back and see the loose door. Then there had been the very devil to pay.

Scores of police and FBI agents had begun to canvass the streets along the truck's route when Johnson telephoned and said in matchless understatement:

"I've got something here you folks might be looking for."

So concluded the first act in the saga of Douglas Johnson, an honest man who had decided quite simply that he should return the fortune he had found—the fortune that did not belong to him. What happened next speaks volumes about the ethics of our times.

Brinks paid Johnson a $10,000 reward for his honesty. The reward was certainly generous, and Johnson just as certainly deserved it. All the elements for a happy ending seemed to be present. But this was not to be. A little more than a month later, the Associated Press, in an article carried by newspapers from coast to coast, revealed the surprising and shocking sequel.

The deed that should have made Douglas Johnson the happiest of men had made him the most miserable. If we truly believe in the principles of honesty to which we give such fervent lip service, Douglas Johnson's stellar performance should have made him the hero of the hour; instead, it had made him the most despised, ridiculed, and harassed of men.

Crackpots wrote obscene letters to him, neighbors sneered at him, fellow workers needled him, schoolmates taunted his sons. The universal theme was that Johnson had proven himself the world's greatest boob by returning that $240,000 once he had it in his hands. The taunts became too much for his oldest son, Richard, sixteen, who on one occasion ran away from home, returning hungry and disillusioned after a few days.

"The kids kept saying things to me," he explained. "All the time, they were saying my father was dumb, and a fool and stupid. . . . I just couldn't stand it."

Johnson himself said it was "nice" that Brinks had given him that $10,000 reward, but he added:

"I can't leave the house to get work without someone throws

it all up to me and calls me a fool. Can't be on the job without someone says, 'Why you need work? You had $240,000.' And now it's hurting my boys. . . .

"That money? It's not worth anything. It has made me a poor man.

"I wish I'd never seen any of it. I wish we'd let that money sit in the street and rot. I wish we'd thrown it down a sewer or burned it. . . ."*

This tragedy of the honest man pilloried on the unfaith of a dishonest age inspired novelist Nelson Algren to write Douglas Johnson a letter bitterly satirizing the reverse morality of our times:

It is one thing to get caught doing something crooked, but the man who snitched on himself for doing something innocent, as you did in returning $240,000 in small bills to the Brinks Express Co., makes me wonder not only whether you are worthy of the name of an American, but even whether you can call yourself an honest janitor.

Where were you when millions of Americans felt their blood pound with pride in Charles Van Doren, replying to reporters who asked him if he intended to give the money back, "No"—*in thunder!*

Where were you when James C. Hagerty advised us on television that the moral of the U–2 incident was "Don't get caught"?

I regret, for your sake as well as my own, that in this crisis you did not think along the same lines as Mr. Ike Williams, former lightweight champion of the world, thinks now. When congratulated recently by Mr. Estes Kefauver on having turned down a $100,000 bribe in return for throwing a fight and offered the hope, by Senator Kefauver, that in time he would be glad he had resisted the temptation, Mr. Williams replied that he would regret turning it down the rest of his life.

I believe you have not only deprived yourself of a contented existence by returning money that belonged to you as much as to anybody else in the free world, but have struck at the very foundation of our society.

For shame, Mr. Johnson, for shame.

* An almost identical incident happened in North Philadelphia in early March 1965—except that this time there was no Douglas Johnson. A Brinks truck, picking up money from banks, lost a bag containing $40,000 in the street. Brinks spokesmen cited the example of Douglas Johnson and urged the finder to come forward, but this time no one rushed to return the $40,000 and a widespread police search was instituted.

I

Douglas Johnson's experience illustrates a fundamental truth about modern American society: it is a society in which money has become its own ethic—and so a society in which the morality we practice is virtually the reverse of the morality we preach.

In this society, possession justifies any means of attainment. As H. L. Mencken wrote about Vice-President Charles G. Dawes: "His ethical ideas are simple and devoid of cant. He believes that any man deserves whatever he can get." Dawes was representative of a business class, always sizable and influential on the American scene, that nevertheless had not in his day threatened to become universal.

America has always had its full share of bold buccaneers swashbuckling across the landscape in pursuit of individual booty; but in past epochs its national standards, the ideals to which the great mass of its people adhered, were set by the Protestant ethic with its faith in hard work, in thrift, in truthfulness, in honesty, in honor. In those past Americas, the buccaneers might be successful, but they still would be stigmatized. A Jay Gould or a Jim Fisk might amass millions, rig the stock market, and engineer the virtual collapse of the national economy; but their deeds did not set a standard the public felt free to ape. Wealth could always command power, but not respect. Today it commands both.

One reason it does is that the practices of a Jay Gould or a Jim Fisk have become institutionalized. The individual pirate has yielded place to the predominant corporation. A Serge Rubinstein is so rare he becomes a remarkable curiosity upon the American scene—a scene that is typified, not by him or his ilk but by General Motors and American Telephone & Telegraph and Standard Oil. The Rockefellers, though still infinitely potent as individuals, no longer represent in their persons an entire industry as the original John D. Rockefeller did; they have become submerged behind the façades of their innumerable corporations and foundations. This is a relatively new world—a world of infinite and impersonalized bigness in which the institution, not the man, sets the standards. And so it has become a world in which the man who adheres to the standards of his institution—or adopts them for his own in private life—has the perfect exculpation for deeds that, in another context and another time, might have shocked his individual sense of propriety.

The result is that the America in which we live has become a profoundly different nation from the America in which our middle-aged and older generations were born. We recognize this instinctively and are disturbed by it. But we are frequently at a loss to identify the precise nature of the change or to plumb its causes. An illustration of both the concern and confusion that are hallmarks of our time was provided by the 1964 Presidential campaign. Senator Barry Goldwater, an extremist of the right, charged recklessly to one of the most decisive repudiations in American political history; but, in the process of thrashing about for a telling issue, he latched onto the theme that we as a people are confronted with a great moral crisis. Of all the elements of an unelevating campaign, this was the one, pollsters found, that seemed to strike a responsive chord in the American people. Their common sense prevented them from buying Goldwater's simplistic contention that President Lyndon B. Johnson was at the root of all evil; but they felt, without at times quite knowing how or why, that our society was indeed suffering from a debilitating moral malaise.

Just what is this difference that we feel but cannot identify? Is it true that America today is suffering from ethical rot? And if so, to what degree? Perhaps we can find some clues by contrasting the present with the past, by examining the standards of an earlier time that was not without its own moral and ethical problems.

The post-Civil War period in America was definitely such an age. It was the era of the robber barons, an epoch when the vast resources of an enormously wealthy continent were being opened, in one heady rush, to man's exploitation. There were mighty forests to be despoiled, leaving a denuded land; incredible mineral resources to be discovered and looted; far-flung railroad systems to be stretched north and south, east and west, threading the continent. It seemed at times as if the entire nation were caught up in a gold-rush orgy—and the corruption was incredible.

President Ulysses S. Grant, the victor over Robert E. Lee, sat in the White House and presided over as deplorable an administration as the nation has known. A general by trade and an innocent in the ways of politics, as most generals have been, he sheltered under his hero's mantle a looting horde whose depredations were to set the tone of national political life for decades to come. It was common practice for railroad magnates, in cooperation with other vested interests, to buy up entire state legislatures. When young Theodore Roosevelt first took his seat in the New York state assembly in 1882, he found the entire legislature dominated by what the press of the time publicly called "the black-horse cavalry," legislators who were unabashedly on the payrolls of huge corporations. It was common practice for an unscrupulous legislator to introduce a "reform" measure, of which nothing more would be heard, simply so that he could hijack the threatened special interest into paying him a cushy bribe. There can be little question that ethical standards, both in business and in politics, had never been lower.

And yet, under the scum that covered so much of the upper surface of life, there was vigor and there was health. The age that was tarred with scandals was an age that also bred some of the doughtiest fighters and reformers in American politics, men like Theodore Roosevelt, the elder Robert M. (Fighting Bob) La Follette, and George W. Norris, the father of the Tennessee Valley Authority. These and others like them were to spearhead a reform movement the influence of which was to be felt throughout the first four decades of the twentieth century. It could hardly have been a sheer accident of history that such men sprang into being. Nor was it. Though they came from different backgrounds, such leaders were very much the products of a society that, at its base, had still not been corrupted by the excesses at the top. Some of the features of this society were recalled years later by Senator Norris in his autobiography.

Norris was born on a poor Ohio farm. His older brother died of wounds incurred in the Civil War during Sherman's march from

Atlanta to the sea. Norris was left with his mother and six sisters to share what he called "the heritage of an Ohio farm." And what was that heritage? Norris described it in these terms:

When finally the estate was settled, my share was $132; but the money that came to me was the least of my heritage.

There on that farm I lost all fear of poverty. I learned to live most simply, and I learned to get a great deal of joy out of work. It never occurred to me in those years that lack of money was of any consequence. I grew up to believe wholly and completely in men and women who lived simply, frugally, and in fine faith. . . .

There were weeks when there was not a cent in our home. At that time the clothing I wore, and for some years to come my clothing, was handed down to me from others who had outgrown it. It was a great occasion for rejoicing when mother had the good fortune to sell one of the huge walnut trees on the farm for lumber for a few dollars.

Wants were few; no one in the community possessed money, it seemed, and the lack of it in all families made them unconscious of poverty. . . .

The essence of that life was perhaps capsuled by Norris in a single anecdote:

There was that warm spring afternoon when mother, who had been busy throughout the entire day, called to me to assist her in planting a tree. She had dug a hole, and she wanted me to hold the seedling upright while she shoveled the dirt in around its roots and packed it tightly. I looked up at her, and it came to me she was tired. The warmth of the afternoon and her exertions had brought small beads of perspiration to her brow.

So I said to her:

"Why do you work so hard, mother? We now have more fruit than we can possibly use. You will be dead long before this tree comes into bearing."

The little farm was well stocked with fruit. It had its apples, its peaches, and its sour cherries.

Her answer was slow to come, apparently while she measured her words.

"I may never see this tree in bearing, Willie," she said, "but somebody will."

That was the unselfishness of the pioneer era.

Its thought was not solely for itself.

In its planting of the fields it derived the satisfaction of growing things. Its planting was not only for the present but the future.

Such were the times, such were the people—the times hard for most, the imprint of the frontier still indelibly upon them; the people, hard-working, frugal, largely self-sufficient and independent, their own labor supplying most of their wants and giving them a pride in building and creating for the future, their lives not so dependent upon money that money could ever become for them an end in itself. It was, clearly, a different age from ours, and these were a different people.

In the completely moneyed society, a man is considered a fool if he doesn't cheat. The attitude finds perhaps its clearest expression in the annual national contest to see who can gyp Uncle Sam most on income taxes—and get away with it.

Treasury officials have estimated that, each year, some $25 billion of taxable income goes unreported, and most of this represents a deliberate defrauding of the government—and of other taxpayers. Cheating on taxes has become almost a national pastime, and few persons apparently experience any feelings of remorse unless they get caught. Doctors and dentists pocket cash, domestic servants who work one day a week for five or six different employers just forget to report their earnings, the proprietor of the small store doesn't put every sale in the till, and waiters and waitresses stash away their tips without accounting to Uncle Sam.

The brashness and the widespread scope of some of these tax frauds have been chronicled by Philip M. Stern in *The Great Treasury Raid*. One doctor kept a large fishbowl in his office and advised his patients: "Three dollars in the fishbowl or I'll bill you five dollars." A dentist was discovered who had $27,000 in cash filed away among his patients' X rays. Any number of taxpayers have claimed fraudulent deductions for their pets—dogs, donkeys, cats, and birds. One former movie and TV actor listed six nonexistent children as dependents. And Philippe of the Waldorf, who received some $300,000 in gratuities and kickbacks from caterers, was convicted for failing properly to account for his loot and pay taxes on it. Such incidents have been so perpetually repeated that they have become a commonplace of our time—and so set it apart, in stark contrast to the mood of the 1880s, when the lack of strict honesty in matters of a few dollars, or even a few cents, was enough to trouble the conscience.

Today, as Douglas Johnson's experience showed, we would be all too apt to greet such refined scruples with derisive scoffs. The man who is so meticulous in his honesty now seems to merit not respect but scorn, for his instinct runs counter to the prevalent practices of his age—he simply "isn't with it." And this, in the final analysis, is the hallmark of the corrupt society.

2

Just how important in any evaluation of our times is this question of ethics?

Chief Justice of the United States Earl Warren devoted himself to this issue in an address that attracted national attention in November 1962. Speaking at the annual awards dinner of the Jewish Theological Seminary in New York, he said:

"In civilized life, Law floats in a sea of Ethics. Each is indispensable to civilization. Without Law, we should be at the mercy of the least scrupulous; without Ethics, Law could not exist. . . ."

The core of Chief Justice Warren's thesis was that a sharp distinction must be drawn between the wrongs with which the law can deal and that much greater ocean of human conduct that the law cannot possibly legislate, that must be left to the collective conscience of man. Law, he explained, cannot make every moral decision for man. To do so would "reduce men to automata, incapable of making their own moral decisions and defeating the very purpose of civilization itself." The courts cannot compel love or friendship; they cannot legislate mercy; they cannot "outlaw selfishness or greed, or avarice, or cowardice, except in a few particularly gross manifestations. . . .

"Therefore, Society would come to grief without Ethics, which is unenforceable in the courts, and cannot be made part of Law. If there were no sense of love in families, if there were no sense of loyalty, if friendship meant nothing, if we all, or any large proportion of us were motivated only by avarice and greed, Society would collapse almost as completely as though it lacked Law. . . .

"There is thus a Law beyond the Law, as binding on those of us who cherish our institutions as the Law itself, although there is no human power to enforce it. . . .

"In the Law beyond the Law, which calls upon us to be fair in business, where Law cannot command fairness; which bids us temper justice with mercy, where the Law can only enforce justice; which demands our compassion for the unfortunate, although the Law can only give him his legal due, each of us is necessarily his own Chief Justice. In fact, he is the whole Supreme Court, from which there lies no appeal. The individual citizen may engage in practices which, on the advice of counsel, he believes strictly within the letter of the law, but which he also knows from his own conscience are outside the bounds of propriety and the right. Thus, when he engages in such practices, he does so not at his own peril—as when he violates the Law—but at the peril of the structure of civilization, involving greater stakes than any possible peril to himself."

Chief Justice Warren suggested that each industry, each trade union, even college administrations and political parties invite "ethical counselors" to sit at their elbows when crucial decisions are to be made. He conceded that those in executive capacity might have qualms about seeking ethical advice, lest it become a roadblock to cherished projects. "But what in fact is the alternative to such discouragement of what is contrary to the public good, or the long-range good of mankind, or to simple compassion for the individual?" he asked. "Is it to proceed headlong as we are proceeding now, deifying Success as the sole goal in life, and constantly putting greater emphasis on quantity rather than on quality in what we achieve?"

On the other hand, the Chief Justice said, if we can accept moral guidance in our actions, "we will have taken a giant step toward bringing ourselves closer to the idea to which men have been striving since the origin of the species. We will also, I believe, be doing much to prevent the moral decay of our community, a decay similar to that which has proven fatal to all earlier great empires and civilizations."

3

Chief Justice Warren's analysis of the ethical dilemmas of our time sparked a brief nationwide debate. There was general agreement with his eloquent statement of the problem and considerable disagreement with his proposed remedy. Obviously it would be impossible to station an ethical counselor at the elbow of every man, yet just as obviously what was most needed was a strengthening of the ethical concepts of every man to create a more wholesome national climate. Dr. James W. Fifield, Jr., pastor of the First Congregational Church of Los Angeles, was one who saw the ultimate issue in these terms.

"Man is a sovereign soul," said Dr. Fifield. "He is endowed with a conscience which grows with use and stultifies when ignored by nonsovereign souls who let others do their thinking for them— and follow like puppy dogs instead of measuring up to their own inherent stature as free men. . . .

"If we live up to our own ethical understanding, we will find that understanding increased. If we rely on others to be our consciences, our consciences will atrophy.

"No 'expert on ethics' can be as expert as the sovereign-souled individual. . . . We don't need anyone to tell us the difference between right and wrong. What we need is the faith, courage, and strength to do the right we know."

Dr. Fifield's analysis, though it accurately emphasized the responsibility of the individual, ignored as virtually all such analyses have ignored the patent reality of our era: in the mass society twentieth-century technology has created and daily intensifies, Dr. Fifield's "sovereign-souled" individual has become almost an anachronism. To measure up to "their own inherent stature as free men" men must be free, but man today is becoming steadily less free, more of a cipher in the mass forces that dominate and mold his time.

The crux of the American ethical dilemma lies in the fact that we live in delusion, blind to current and obvious realities. We live, for example, with the myth of the "free-enterprise" system when, in reality, for the vast majority of Americans, our enterprise is no longer free. The small tradesman whose store was his empire, the artisan whose skill was his wealth, the farmer who owned his acres and was greatly self-sufficient—these were the stalwarts of the nineteenth century's free-enterprise economy. They could and did rely largely on themselves; they owed fealty to no man. Today they are a vanishing breed. This is the age of the vast multibillion-dollar corporation; it is, increasingly, the age of the computer and automation. It is an era in which individual initiative finds it increasingly difficult to survive, for survival increasingly depends upon the acquisition and utilization of the ever more complex and ever more costly machinery of the technological revolution. The result has been not just that the individual has been driven into a corporate existence, but that the small corporation has been driven into the larger. This irreversible thrust toward the creation of ever more awesome structures of power has featured the entire post-World War II era. In the single decade 1950–1960, there were more than a thousand major business mergers, and the result is that well over two-thirds of the nation's entire industry—transportation, manufacturing, mining, and utilities—today is controlled by a relative handful of a few hundred corporations. Analysis of 1960 census figures showed that 40 per cent of all the millions of men and women employed in manufacturing worked for just 361 firms. This is indeed the world of the mass society—a world in which man becomes steadily the dependent creature of vast organizations, and so a world in which inevitably his individual will and conscience weakens if it does not, as yet, completely atrophy.

Most dramatic in this saga of the shrinking American is the story of the farmer. The world of Senator Norris' youth, the world of the Ohio farm on which men and women could live "simply, frugally and in fine faith," has been perhaps the greatest casualty of modern technology. Farming is no longer an individual, but a massive, enterprise. The family farm of a few hundred acres cannot be worked as efficiently or as economically as a vast spread of thousands of acres, tilled, sprayed, and tended by mammoth

and costly machines. As a result, the number of farms has shrunk
—and their size has increased. In 1920, we had 32 million
farmers, 30 per cent of our population. But the Census Bureau's
Statistical Abstract of the United States disclosed in 1962 that we
now have only 15 million farmers, a scant 8 per cent of our
population. In other words, in decades in which our population
(105 million in 1920) has nearly doubled, the farm population
has shrunk by more than 50 per cent—and still, with modern
mechanized methods of farming, we are producing enormous surpluses of food in a process that is steadily driving more families off
the farm.

As with the farmer driven from his acres, so with other Americans driven from their crafts. If one excepts the dwindling millions
who still live on the farm, census figures show that more than 80
per cent of the rest of us depend for our livelihoods upon the
weekly corporate paycheck. The influx of workers from the farms
to the cities, the concentration of hired hands on corporate payrolls, have led to significant changes in the distribution of population. We are today predominantly an urban-suburban nation—so
much so that projections of current population trends indicate
that, by the mid-1970s, some 80 per cent of us will be concentrated
in huge, sprawling metropolitan areas.

Such are the dimensions of the mass society. It is a development
that has nothing to do with political ideologies. It is the forced
and inevitable result of the current scientific-technological revolution that, for epochal change, dwarfs completely the upheavals
caused by the industrial revolution of the last century. Yet we
have stubbornly refused to gear our thinking to altered circumstance. We cling with the fanaticism of the religious bigot to the
shibboleths of "free enterprise" and "rugged individualism." We
refuse to recognize that today we live, not in an individualistic
society but in a corporate collectivism. We refuse to acknowledge
that we live not in a world of free enterprise and free competition,
but in a world of mass corporate structures and administered
prices. And so we fail to see that, by persistently mouthing for our
guidelines slogans of the past that no longer have validity in the

power-packaged present, we only compound and intensify the dimensions of our ethical dilemmas.

It is not that the truth is difficult to perceive, but that we have been too obdurate to see. More than a decade ago, Robert S. Lynd, the Columbia University sociologist and author of *Middletown,* perceptively analyzed this dichotomy in our lives and indicated where it would lead. He wrote:

Middle-class individualism has tried the novel and precarious experiment of hanging a large society together primarily by $'s. This formula evoked prodigies of energy in an era when men moved out more or less single-handed over an empty continent. No need was felt to view this thin, spreading web of national life as in any important sense a collective enterprise. As a matter of fact, liberal democracy never envisaged, was not equipped for, the stating of positive collective purposes. Where we were going as a whole society was seen as the sum of our private short-run aims; to take care of longer-run goals "progress" was manifestly "happening," and we had only to throw the reins on the nag's back and let him move ahead.

Such a theory of society may work in small communities living a basically self-controlled existence. But today we are a society of 150,000,000 people [Lynd was writing in 1951] living a highly interdependent urbanized existence with extreme divisions of labor. We are, in fact, a collective society in our functional interdependence, and national and personal welfare depends upon increasingly coordinated action to predefined collective ends. But our institutions and associated traditions, stemming from the middle-class break-away from centralized controls, have deterred us from attempting to state, let alone to implement, the potentials and conditions of the positive use of democratic power for democratic ends. As a result we still plunge along on the theory of "each for himself and God for all of us, as the elephant said as he danced among the chickens."

The elephants, "both rogue and semi-tamed," Lynd wrote, had grown and

luxuriated in the green pastures of power left vacant by democracy. Today we as a nation, our Congress and our institutions are afraid of, and thrown into a posture of deference before, these private powers— organized business, organized professions, organized labor, organized patriotism, organized religion. [The result had been the development of a racket society, its goal exemplified in the scramble of each man to grab a piece of the racket for himself.]

This cumulating "racket" quality of private power in American life defeats all efforts to strengthen the democratic process. Not only are private interests increasingly manipulating public opinion and diverting attention from democratically important issues with such false slogans as "The free-enterprise system is the basis of all our democratic freedoms"; but, ultimately more dangerous, all of us are being psychologically turned against such rationalizing steps as national economic planning by the contagious preoccupation with "getting a break," cutting in on a racket of our own. We tolerate and secretly approve breaches in the strict rule of law or in "democracy" because we so passionately hope to escape our social fate through "getting to know the right people" and thus "getting in on something good."

4

If one day in our life and times could be said fairly to illustrate the racket quality of American society Robert Lynd had described and the ethical problems Chief Justice Warren had defined, no better day could be selected than July 6, 1962. On that day, in Washington, the McClellan Committee, wading to its armpits in the Billie Sol Estes scandal, heard how two Agriculture Department employees had solicited and accepted bribes, making certain that the money would be paid in cash. Both Washington and New York were concerned about a book, *Calories Don't Count,* whose sales had reached the neighborhood of two million copies under the august auspices of Simon and Schuster. In Jersey City, police uncovered a second hoard of Joseph Vincent (Newsboy) Moriarity, the lifelong bookie who had defied their vigilance so successfully that he had become the living proof of the truth that crime does so pay. After Moriarity had been finally packed off for a short stay in prison, police had uncovered two caches—one in the trunk of an old abandoned Plymouth, the other in an unused garage—that totaled $2,421,850 in cash. Up in Boston and also in New York, detectives were trying to unravel a deft financial swindle involving the disappearance of $100,000 two New Jersey businessmen had been inveigled into putting into a safe-deposit box under the misapprehension that it would grow magically in a get-rich-quick gold-smuggling scheme. The businessmen, of course, had had no ethical qualms about enriching themselves through a shady plot; they had been shocked only by the discovery that *their* gold had become the source of someone else's riches. Capping all, in New York, both the Citizens Union and the City Club of New York were horrified at the prospect that Supreme Court Justice J. Vincent Keogh might collect his $20,000 annual pension even though he had just been convicted of taking a $22,500 bribe to fix a federal-court sentencing. (The courts would later rule that Keogh, no matter what he had done, was indeed entitled to his pension.)

A moment's reflection on this *dramatis personae* and their deeds lends some italic emphasis to both Robert Lynd's description of the racket society and Chief Justice Warren's definition of ethical problems. Represented here were neither the normal types of wrongdoers nor the common categories of crime. Holdup, robbery, burglary, physical assault, murder—did not appear on the calendar of this particular day. And the people—two civil servants, a passel of blind law-enforcers, a distinguished publishing house, two wealthy businessmen, a highly placed judge—were not certainly the kind who appear on the docket in Night Court. Were they not, on the contrary, the very types most representative of the best in our society? The very ones who are supposed to set our standards?

Quite obviously, in every case there had been only one standard —success. Success as measured solely in the terms of money.

There had been, for example, nothing illegal in the conduct of Simon and Schuster in publishing *Calories Don't Count*. But what about its ethics? In Washington, a spokesman for the Food and Drug Administration angrily denounced the book's main thesis; calories, he said emphatically, do so count. He charged that the book was a concoction of "false and misleading statements" and that before it was published advance copy had been sent to a Florida land-development company so that sections could be inserted promoting the sale of safflower-oil capsules. The government had obtained a court decree against false claims being made for these "Calories Don't Count" capsules.

Equally revealing—and perhaps even more disturbing—was the performance in Washington where the two petty bribe-takers in the Billie Sol Estes case bared their conduct and their consciences to the McClellan Committee. As long ago as the early 1940s sociologist Ruth Benedict had perceptively noted that our society was changing from one dominated by a traditional, individualistic ethic to one that might be described as a how-do-we-look-to-others ethic. Already, man was abandoning any inner guideline for his conduct, and he was looking around him, taking his own personal poll. He was deciding that if "everyone is doing it" it must be all right. Ruth Benedict made the point that this change in attitude represented a profound and significant development; our whole society, she wrote, was becoming no longer a "guilt" culture but a "shame" culture. In other words, we no longer deeply and sincerely felt guilt for our misdeeds, but if we were caught and exposed we had to pretend that we did. So were devised certain rites of punishment and expiation, the ritual of publicly baring one's soul in shows of debasement and remorse, exercises from which the ethical backslider could emerge in perfect self-delusion, cleansed and purified—and essentially unpunished and unchanged. It would be difficult to find a more perfect example of this procedure, in itself expressive of the hypocrisy of our ethical attitudes, than the sideshow staged by the McClellan Committee on this July day of multiple revelations.

Billie Sol Estes, as all the nation knew at the time, was the big wheeler-dealer from Texas who had built a financial empire on a quicksand of illegality and had decorated its portals with the industriously collected autographs of some of the most eminent politicians in America. At the core of the Estes operations was an illegal manipulation of cotton acreage. Farmers are allowed to plant only so much cotton and are fined if they exceed their allotments; under federal regulations, it is illegal for them to transfer or sell their rights to plant cotton acreage. Estes flouted both the policy and the law. He bought up unused cotton allotments all over the Texas and Oklahoma landscapes, and the McClellan Committee on this Friday in early July 1962 learned just how a couple of small-fry Agriculture Department employees, whose duty it was to put an end to such shenanigans, had found their rewards, instead, in helping further the Estes scheme.

The Agriculture officials were Arthur D. Stone, fifty-five, and Louis N. Dumas, fifty-six. Dumas was county office manager for the Agriculture Stabilization and Conservation Committee in McIntosh County, Oklahoma; he earned $7257 a year. Stone was his deputy at a salary of $5070. When the Billie Sol Estes scandal exploded, both Dumas and Stone were questioned by Federal Bureau of Investigation agents; both denied any dealings with Estes or his representatives. Subsequently both men were questioned by investigators for the McClellan Committee; again both denied all.

Fortunately for the committee, there was a third party who was not so reticent. He was Parnell E. Biggerstaff, a former land agent for Estes. A chunky, round-faced man whose aplomb was so unruffled by the lights and the marble columns of the Senate Caucus Room that he didn't hesitate to call Senators "you fellas," Biggerstaff testified that he had hardly registered at the Western Motel in Eufaula, Oklahoma, in the early summer of 1961 before there came a knock, knock, knocking at his door. Only, instead of Poe's Raven, he found on the doorstep two human visitors, Dumas and Stone.

They represented themselves, said Biggerstaff, not as Agriculture Department officials but as men who had cotton allotments to sell. Biggerstaff, cautious, told them that he wasn't buying cotton allotments; he was just selling Estes' Texas land to Oklahoma farmers who had cotton allotments on the chance that they might be willing to "lease" the land back to Estes. All perfectly legal, he assured them. One thing led to another, and on a return visit some weeks later, after each side had felt the other out, Dumas offered to "help" Biggerstaff in his chore of finding farmers with the right cotton credentials. Biggerstaff, no novice when it came to the generous impulses of the human heart, asked Dumas and Stone bluntly if they wanted to make a deal.

Dumas, according to Biggerstaff, protested righteously:

"Listen, we aren't going to make no deal. We are going to help you."

All right, said Biggerstaff, but after the "help" had been delivered, "What do I owe you?"

"If your boss is the man we hear he is or believe he is, he can show his appreciation when we get through," Dumas said unctuously. Then he added: "Be sure it is cash."

On the basis of this fine meeting of minds and high intentions, Dumas and Stone subsequently gave Biggerstaff the names of Oklahoma farmers with cotton allotments who might be good Estes prospects. In return, Biggerstaff expressed Estes' appreciation in cash—$1640.80 in a plain envelope. Dumas and Stone split. Cash, they evidently figured, could not be traced, but this cash left a trail behind it. It had been drawn from Estes' accounts by a check, dated August 1961, and the Estes records listed the payments as "commissions" to Dumas and Stone. Unaware of this telltale bookkeeping, Dumas and Stone neglected to report their windfalls on their 1961 income tax returns, an oversight they were busy rectifying by filing supplementary returns when they appeared before the McClellan Committee.

Testifying in shirtsleeves, the agitated Agriculture Department officials finally admitted all. Stone was almost in tears. Explaining his motives for his previous lies on two occasions to federal investigators, he protested: "I was simply scared and didn't know what to do. It had been bothering me quite a bit."

The evidence would seem to suggest that it only began to bother him quite a bit when it became apparent that he wasn't going to get away with it, but Senator John L. McClellan, the Arkansas Democrat whose voice rasps up and down the spines of union malefactors, was in this case a compassionate and understanding interrogator.

"I think you realize you made a mistake," he told Dumas and Stone. "I don't believe you are bad people. You are the victims of a much bigger scheme, a get-rich-quick scheme. You've been caught in this trap and have no one to blame but yourselves."

This chivalrous summary seemed to ignore the fact that Dumas and Stone had set the trap, baited it, and then walked into it of their own free and eager will. But none of this, of course, mattered. Senator McClellan, an astute man, understands his times. Dumas and Stone weren't to be blamed. They weren't "bad people"; they were good guys really—solid, free-enterprise Americans who weren't really responsible for their individual actions because they were just little cogs in a gigantic conspiracy that was much too big for them. That they were free-will cogs, that they weren't shoved or pushed but asked in, affected not the degree of their responsibility or the ethics of the case. Pity, not blame, was their lot. As Mary McGrory wrote in her syndicated column, "having been confessed and absolved, they went off," and nobody seemed to be aware that they by their testimony—and McClellan by his treatment of it—had limned a significant dimension of the moral crisis in modern America.

5

A society that could scorn a Douglas Johnson for his honesty and absolve the cupidity of a Dumas and Stone is a society flirting with disintegration. It is a hypocritical society, one that loudly professses in words the ethics it has abandoned in deed. It is a society in which man has ceased to count, even to himself—or to believe that he can count, even to himself—and so it is a society in which everyone is absolved for everything, for no one has any individual stature or individual responsibility. Only the mass, impersonal forces have that.

Erich Fromm has written that the great humanist thinkers of the eighteenth and nineteenth centuries, our ideological ancestors,

thought that the goal of life was the full unfolding of a person's potentialities; what mattered to them was the person who *is* much, not the one who *has* or *uses* much. For them economic production was a means to the unfolding of man, not an end. It seems that today the means have become the ends, that not only "God is dead," as Nietzsche said in the 19th century, but also man is dead: that what is alive are the organizations, the machines; and that man has become their slave rather than being their master.

In general, our society is becoming one of giant enterprises directed by a bureaucracy in which man becomes a small, well-oiled cog in the machinery. The oiling is done with higher wages, fringe benefits, well-ventilated factories and piped music, and by psychologists and human-relations experts; yet all this oiling does not alter the fact that man has become powerless, that he does not wholeheartedly participate in his work and that he is bored with it. . . .

The "organization man" may be well fed, well amused and well oiled, yet he lacks a sense of identity because none of his feelings or his thoughts originates within himself; none is authentic. He has no convictions, either in politics, religion, philosophy or in love. He is attracted by the "latest model" in thought, art and style, and lives under the illusion that the thoughts and feelings which he has acquired by listening to the media of mass communication are his own.

He has a nostalgic longing for a life of individualism, initiative and justice, a longing that he satisfies by looking at Westerns. But these values have disappeared from real life in the world of giant corporations, giant state and military bureaucracies and giant labor unions. He, the individual, feels so small before these giants that he sees only one way to escape the sense of utter insignificance: He identifies himself with the giants and idolizes them as the true representatives of his own human powers, those of which he has dispossessed himself. . . .

Yet, as Joseph Wood Krutch has pointed out in another penetrating analysis, what really matters—and must always matter—is man, the stature of man.

"I hold that it is indeed inevitable," Krutch wrote, "that the so-called social conscience unsupported by the concept of personal honor will create a corrupt society. But suppose that it doesn't? Suppose that no one except the individual suffers from the fact that he sees nothing wrong in doing what everybody else does? Even so, I still insist that for the individual himself nothing is more important than this personal, interior sense of right and wrong. . . . It is impossible for me to imagine a society composed of men without honor.

"We hear it frequently said that what present-day men most desire is security. If that is so, then they have a wrong notion of what the real, ultimate security is. No one who is dependent on anything outside himself, upon money, power, fame, or whatnot, is or ever can be secure. *Only he who possesses himself and is content with himself is actually secure.* . . ." (Italics added)

What follows is a study of a society in which man has lost himself, in which he has surrendered his inner identity and honor to the organization, the group; a society in which, as a consequence, his guidelines derive not from inner conviction but from the performances of the mass power structures to which he belongs; a society that absolves him, the individual, because he is so tiny and so insignificant that he can hardly be blamed for his own acts, especially when "everybody else" is doing the same or much worse. It is a society that justifies man's biting man, man's biting the organization hand that feeds him—even man's biting his own self. This, then, is a picture of our times, an age in which virtually everyone gets bitten.

∽ 2 ∽

The Great Electrical Conspiracy

IN AUGUST 1956, a Very Important Person was ostensibly enjoying a little vacation in the cool air of Camp Keystone at North Bay, a plush small island resort in the province of Ontario, Canada. The VIP had a comfortable cabin; the wind rustled in the trees, water lapped gently against the shore. The surroundings were idyllic for a gentleman of means to take his ease and revivify himself by communing with nature.

But more than placid communing was taking place at Camp Keystone this August. Down the road a piece there was another cabin. Here a number of obviously Very Important Persons were gathered. For them, too, the soft breezes blew, the lake water gurgled, the cool night air and the cool drinks offered balm to the soul. Yet the men inside the cabin seemed impervious to such blessings. They were engaged in heated and earnest debate.

From time to time, one VIP would split off from the group, leave Cabin No. 2 and trek up the road to that other cabin where the solitary vacationer communed with the great outdoors. The visitor usually arrived considerably out of breath, for the men in Cabin No. 2 had left their track and bellhop days far behind them. Between pants, however, the courier would inform the Solitary One of the trend of discussions in Cabin No. 2.

Like an Oriental potentate, Mr. Solitary would ponder for a

moment upon the news his visitor had brought, then he would speak crisply and incisively, giving his own views on the matter. As soon as these had been uttered, his visitor would depart, scurrying up the road to Cabin No. 2 as swiftly as his shortened breath and unaccustomed legs would carry him. These strange and protracted maneuvers continued until finally a decision was reached between the solitary VIP in Cabin No. 1 and the gaggle of VIPs in Cabin No. 2. The result: consumers all over America were going to have to pay a hefty 10 per cent more for heavy electrical industrial-control equipment.

The solitary sojourner in Cabin No. 1, according to some of the other participants in this strangely divided conference, ultimately dictated the decision, for his was the mightiest voice of all the voices at North Bay. He was General Electric Vice-President W. F. Oswalt, general manager of mighty GE's industrial-control department. His fellow conspirators in the cabin down the road were representatives of the small, tight ring of major electrical manufacturing companies that have a stranglehold on business across the length and breadth of the American continent. And so the price decisions they reached in this clandestine conclave at North Bay would be accepted by the American consumer because the American consumer had no choice; this small group of men and their companies—they and they alone—controlled the product and set its price.

But why, one might ask, had W. F. Oswalt, the real power figure in the group, remained aloof from the discussions in Cabin No. 2? Why had he been at such pains to participate only by Organization Man messenger and remote control? The answer was simple. General Electric, the corporate giant that dominates the electrical industry, is loud and voluble in its espousal of the free-enterprise system. It had made fierce noises in paper directives, admonishing its executives that they were not—no, never—to participate in such an anti-free-enterprise enterprise as price-rigging.

This note of hypocrisy, implicit in the contrast between GE's pretensions and its actions, seems an appropriate motif on which to begin this account of one of the most colossal business con-

spiracies in American history—a conspiracy that made a mockery
and a myth of free enterprise and that raised the most profound
questions, still largely unrecognized and unanswered, about the
bedrock ethics of the American system.

I

As the government was later to show, the rigging of prices
and the manipulation of business and contracts were conducted
with a conspiratorial guilt reminiscent of the gangsters who met
at Apalachin. Distinguished executives in the $100,000-a-year
bracket, with their Brooks Brothers suits and suave Organization
Man veneer, went running around the country, hiding their iden-
tities under code numbers and false names. General Electric was
No. 1; Westinghouse, No. 2; Allis-Chalmers, No. 3. A telephone
call from "Joe Number One" meant that the man from General
Electric was on the wire.

Whenever possible, the conspirators used pay phones for price-
rigging talks, since these are free from wiretaps and calls from
them cannot easily be traced. When written communications had
to be exchanged, the data were typed on a plain sheet of paper,
folded into a plain envelope and sent to the conspirators' homes,
never to their business addresses where secretaries might open the
communications and read more than was good for them. When
the price-riggers had to get together for tête-à-têtes, they traveled
to designated rendezvous and registered under assumed names so
that later there would be no written record to connect them with
the guilty mission. In the morning, if they breakfasted in a hotel
dining room, they breakfasted alone, giving no evidence of contact
with those other guests in Brooks Brothers suits with whom they
had huddled the night before. Once back in their home offices,
they jiggered their expense accounts, again to avoid the telltale
written record, putting in vouchers for a trip to Pittsburgh, for
example, when in reality they had been in Atlantic City.

The rigging of the economy of an entire nation in a vast field
like the electrical business is naturally a complicated task, and the
necessity was constantly arising to hold more and more of these

Big-Business Apalachins. Eight meetings were held in 1958, thirty-five in 1959. During the course of a conspiracy that ran from 1951 through most of 1960, the swankest of hotels and motels, obscure bars, and posh country clubs came to know the furtive men in the conservative pin-stripe suits. They conferred in a Milwaukee bar known as "Dirty Helen's"; at the magnificent Skytop in the Poconos; at the Traymore and Haddon Hall hotels in Atlantic City; at the Cherry Grove Inn near Haddonfield, New Jersey; at the Barclay, Roosevelt, and Statler in New York; at the Penn Sherwood in Philadelphia; at the Homestead in Hot Springs; at the Treadway Inn in Rochester; at the Union League Club in Chicago. The list goes on and on.

The result of these conspiracies, as the government later charged and the conspirators themselves admitted, was to allocate the heavy-electrical business of the country and jack up prices to unconscionable levels. In the field of power-switchgear assemblies, for example, it was determined exactly how much of the available market each firm was to get. Originally General Electric was allotted 42 per cent of the business, Westinghouse 38 per cent, Allis-Chalmers 11 per cent, and I-T-E Circuit Breaker 9 per cent. Subsequently, when other members of the conspiracy in other electrical lines wanted to extend their business into this particular field, it became necessary for General Electric and Westinghouse, in order to keep peace in the fraternity, to cut back on their percentages of over-all business to make room for the newcomers.

In setting prices, a couple of different devices were used. On the more routine, run-of-the-mill items of equipment, all of the conspiring firms pegged prices at figures that were identical to the last penny. So was established a uniform market price, and the consumer had no choice except to take it or leave it. On larger items, like huge power turbines whose cost might run high into the millions of dollars—items on which bids would be asked and the competition in a free-enterprise economy ordinarily should be keen —the conspirators would meet and decide in advance which firm, according to the allotted business percentages, was due to get "position." The victor having been decided by the cartel, the price would next be determined. The "lucky" bidder would then submit a bid just a little below the high plateau on which all its supposed rivals obligingly pegged their prices. This practice became known inside the industry as "the phase of the moon," and when the "phase of the moon" became right for a certain company, it harvested the plums of connivance.

These plums were truly luscious fruit. The secret cartel dictated the price on every item of electrical equipment from the ordinary light bulb and $2 insulator to gigantic, multimillion-dollar turbine generators. Prices on generators rose 50 per cent from 1951 to 1959—a period during which wholesale prices of all commodities were rising only 5 per cent. In 1959 and 1960, the Senate Small Business Committee charged that Westinghouse had bilked the Navy by a 900 per cent overcharge for one type of gear assembly, while on another contract General Electric battened on prices 446 per cent too high. What the total booty came to, no one will probably ever know. In a painful process that has now dragged on for years, prominent members of the conspiracy have been disgorging to swindled customers some of their ill-gotten millions; but almost certainly what they disgorge will only be a percentage of what they raked in. Only this much seems certain: by allocating business, fixing contracts, and rigging prices, some of the most powerful corporations in the land stuffed themselves with hundreds of millions of dollars in excess profits on a gross business of some $8 billion. In the process they traduced the faith to which they pledged lip-service allegiance. In place of their cherished free enterprise, they arrogated to themselves the power to allocate territories and apportion business, to banish competition, to crush any rash interlopers, to ban and keep off the market cheaper devices that might threaten the products and self-interest of members of the entrenched conspiracy.

Yet, with the astigmatism of self-interest run amok, the princeling executives of the conspiring corporations looked upon themselves as the stalwart champions of free enterprise, and they saw no incompatibility between their deeds and their pretensions. They all admitted that they knew they had been violating the law—specifically the Sherman Anti-Trust Act, which prohibits just such conspiracies in restraint of trade—but their attitude was that this law, really the bulwark of America's free-enterprise system, was an anachronism. This may indeed be true; but, if it is true, it is only because the free enterprise the law has endeavored to preserve is itself an anachronism. For the modern businessman to admit so much, however, would be to open up a veritable Pandora's box of horrors, and so these masters of the executive suite, although they fractured the law at every conspiratorial meeting they held, still had to maintain to themselves and the public that they stood for the same principles the law stood for. Listen to this self-justifying quote from one of the leaders:

"No one attending the gathering was so stupid he didn't know the meetings were in violation of the law. But it is the only way a business can be run. It is free enterprise."

The author of this classic definition was Fred F. Loock, president, general manager, and sales manager of the Allen-Bradley Company of Milwaukee, Wisconsin. Loock told the U.S. Senate investigating committee headed by the late Estes Kefauver that he had been meeting with competitors since 1919. He argued that such private arrangements were necessary to insure a profit and to keep out the "tin knockers"—his term for fly-by-night operators who "put up a shack and sell controls" at ruinous prices.

"If we are all to get down to the level of tin knockers," he declared, "there would be no progress in our industry. You cannot get research and development with red ink."

This was the justification. It was not entirely without reason.

At the outset of his hearing into "administered" prices—the polite term for industry price-rigging—Kefauver was told by a succession of expert economists that administered prices are a necessity in a modern industrial economy. In essence, the experts agreed, "They are here to stay, and there is nothing much to be gained by trying to pretend otherwise."

The economists pointed out that, unless price levels were established by agreement, it would be perfectly feasible for one or two industry giants (say, General Electric and Westinghouse) to launch price wars so ruinous they would destroy all competition. The giants would be hurt, too, but their resources and wealth are so enormous they could take the beating, assured that in the end they would capture for themselves an unbreakable nationwide monopoly. Then, of course, they could price as whim and avarice dictated.

The picture the economists painted raises inevitable and obvious questions—but questions that nobody was interested in acknowledging should even be asked. If "administered" prices are indeed vital to the healthy functioning of the economy, by whom should they be "administered?" By the very businesses most interested, whose primary concern must ever be to price as high as practicable in the sacred cause of the largest possible profit? Or by some impartial arbiter (almost inevitably an arm of government), acting in the general public interest?

This last suggestion is, of course, anathema to big business. The idea that government should fix prices, that it should in any way regulate business, always produces anguished screams that this is socialism, it is communism, it is dictatorship—it means, in fine, the death of "the American way." That government should have a role is the thought we mustn't think, and this explains perhaps the pertinacity with which business adheres to the myth of free enterprise, even when by secret conspiracy it is demonstrating it no longer lives by the ideal it so vociferously champions.

In any event, here was the resolutely unfaced issue that was the specter in the background throughout the tortuous course of the great electrical conspiracy. Senator Kefauver, having obtained a glimpse of the dilemma no good free-enterprise American wants to face, shied away from a deeper probe. Business refused to acknowledge even that a dilemma existed. And so we were left in the end with a hypocrisy—the pretense that free enterprise, a system that everybody by action has disowned, was still a viable goal, our most precious and inviolate heritage.

2

What sort of men could flaunt such unabashed double standards?

They were, as they said themselves, Organization Men. They were men who had surrendered their own individualities to the corporate gods they served. Though they knew that their acts were illegal, not to say unethical, though the shady maneuvering at times

affronted their sense of decency, not one found it possible to pro-
nounce an unequivocal "No." Price conspiracies had been the
norm of the business long before they rose to positions of power,
and as young men, scrambling hard up the ladder, they had come
to accept such clandestine rigging as "the way of life." Good Organization Men all, they did not question too deeply, they did not
fight too vigorously; they merely got into the swim of things and
rigged as hard as the next fellow.

The pattern and the pressures stood clearly revealed in a series
of interviews some of the guilty high executives, under a pledge of
anonymity, gave to *The Wall Street Journal.* One of the defendants, a most vigorous defender of "the system," put into clear
focus the application of Chief Justice Warren's dictum of ethics
versus the law.

"One of the problems of business is what is normal practice,
not what is the law," he said. "If it's normal practice, it's ethical—
not legal, but ethical."

It obviously had never occurred to this executive that an individual must have an ethical sense and be guided by it; to him,
ethics meant that what "everybody was doing" must be right.
Deluded by this conception of ethics, this particular executive, even
in the aftermath, felt no sense of guilt. His only reservation was
that the conspiracy, once embarked upon, had gone too far; it had
been "wrong to allocate business," he felt, but he still found
nothing wrong about rigging prices because "the customer buys
total value, in which price is only one significant factor."

This man seemed not to consider that a cartel able to set its
own prices would hardly be ungenerous with itself or that such a
cartel, flaunting such make-or-break powers, also would ultimately
determine questions of quality and product. The inevitable raw
deal for consumer and public—and the whole economy of the
nation—did not register with this executive who defended corporate practice as an ethic superior to the law.

Some of his colleagues were more sensitive to the implications
of their deeds, but even the most sensitive maintained that the
individual was helpless to resist the mass corporate pressures. One
man, for example, had drifted almost by accident into the price-

rigging cabal. Originally, he had kept records for his company on competitive bids, and he had become "amazed at how close together the sums were." Later, his superiors let him in on the secret and introduced him to competitors with whom he was to fix prices. Much disturbed, he finally worked up the courage to broach the subject to his boss.

"The boss readily admitted there had been meetings to stabilize prices," he said. "But he said my predecessor had gone too far, and he didn't want me to go so far."

This worried executive had been indecisive about what course he should follow. "When I was first convinced this was going on, I thought it was very wrong," he said. "I thought of going to them and saying I didn't want the job. But by that time I had been doing the job for some weeks. And then I didn't know whether I was just being naïve. I thought maybe this was the normal thing."

A third executive explained to *The Wall Street Journal* that he had come into the business as a young man possessed of a blind corporate faith. It never occurred to him to question the ethics of his own company; he never thought about the illegality of price-rigging because, obviously, whatever the company did must be right. He was curious only about the reasons for it, and these were explained to him.

"It was pointed out to me," he explained, "that this is the only way to run a heavy-electrical-goods business. This is the way of life. It was necessary, or so I thought, to prevent a chaotic market. There was a well-known high executive who had been fixing prices for years—it was latrine knowledge.

"These people above me were damn fine citizens and I had developed quite a respect for them. Why should I question them?"

When he achieved the status of price-rigger himself, he was proud. "I'd seen others doing it, and now they were entrusting it to me," he said. "Keeping the market stable—that was a big task." When he began to meet with competitors, he explained to his wife that there was "a certain risk involved" and "she accepted it as part of my job." It was the necessary route to promotion and prosperity; but, in time, even for this blindly dedicated Organiza-

tion Man the shady devices to which the fixers had to resort began
to humiliate and to worry him.

"I'd be making phone calls from phone booths," he said, "and
I'd get unsigned letters in the mail. There'd be calls for me at
home."

Sometimes the whole disreputable procedure plunged him into
a blue funk. Then—"I'd get up at three in the morning and go
downstairs and get a drink. I'd have to think things over."

With all his thinking, though, he never asked for a showdown.
He never worked up the courage to go over the heads of his immediate superiors to headquarters, which in its directives was
proclaiming a no-price-fixing policy. He explained:

"The tendency is for executives, who get stock options, big
salaries, pensions and so on, to accept the facts of life going on
around them. It is very hard to quit when you get a big compensation, and it's also tough to be a nonconformist under such conditions."

This, then, was the atmosphere prevailing in the world of the
Organization Man. How it worked out in detail in the career of
one man and one company is perhaps best shown in the story of
Clarence E. Burke, fifty-five, the $70,000-a-year general manager
of GE's High Voltage Department. A smallish man, about five feet
six, with delicate-looking hands, Burke described GE in his testimony before the Kefauver Committee as "the company I loved,"
and he gave this analysis of himself:

"I guess I am an Organization Man. I felt I had to go along
with the price-fixing scheme or I couldn't get promoted in the
company. I always felt guilty about it, yes, but I felt I had to go
along."

Burke had joined the heavy-equipment division of GE in 1926,
fresh out of the Georgia Institute of Technology with a B.S. degree
in electrical engineering. The heavy-equipment division was the
oldest and most important of GE's branches, the foundation stone
on which the whole sprawling corporate structure had been built;
it accounted for 25 per cent of sales. Burke advanced through the
ranks and by June 1, 1945, when he was transferred to Pittsfield,

Massachusetts, as sales manager of distribution transformers, he was tabbed as a rising young executive of great promise.

He had scarcely become established in Pittsfield when he became involved in the preliminary collusion that was to lead finally to price-rigging. Those were the closing days of World War II, days in which the much-hated Office of Price Administration presumed to tell businessmen what they could charge for their products. Business was intensely unhappy about such governmental interference with the pure competitive laws of the free-enterprise system, and it was determined to get rid of OPA just as soon as it could. In the meantime, it had to live with this odious, un-American bureau. And so Burke's boss, H. L. (Buster) Brown, called him in and told him to attend a meeting of the National Electrical Manufacturers Association in the Penn-Sheraton Hotel. After the regular session, he was to meet with competitors and discuss how the industry could best unite in pressuring Washington to jack up OPA ceiling prices.

This, for Burke, was the beginning. Big business and an unsympathetic press soon decapitated OPA, despite the persistence of shortages. But did the disappearance of OPA restore the competition of the free-enterprise system? Did it put an end to price-fixing? It did not. All that happened was that the restraining hand of government was removed from price-fixing and virtually *carte blanche* power was put into the hands of the private interests that stood to profit by gouging the most that they could out of the market.

The price-fixing discussions in which Burke had become enmeshed went merrily on. General Electric, under its guiding genius of the period, Charles E. Wilson, had issued a directive forbidding such collusion, but Buster Brown assured his boys that this guideline, issued in fear of antitrust prosecution, didn't apply to the *kind* of thing that *they* were doing. He "assured us," Burke subsequently told *Fortune,* "that Antitrust would have to say we *gouged* the people to say we were doing anything illegal. We understood this was what the company wanted us to do."

In 1946, GE's lawyers became concerned because the federal government was making antitrust noises, and they made a tour of the individual plants, putting everyone on notice. There were to be absolutely no more discussions with competitors on prices. In GE parlance, this period of enforced withdrawal from the price-rigging conspiracy became known as "going behind the iron curtain"; but, even curtained, the Pittsfield shut-ins were not left entirely in the dark. Their understanding competitors thoughtfully telephoned them the details of their price agreements, and so, in effect, the price conspiracy operated much as before. Then, after a period of nine months, the curtain was suddenly lifted.

"Word came down to start contacting competitors again," Burke recalled. "It came to me from my superior, Buster Brown, but my impression was that it came to him from higher up. . . . That is when the hotel meetings got started."

One difficulty in determining just where such abrupt and mysterious shifts of policy originated—and an invaluable protective device, insulating top executives like Charles E. Wilson and his successor, Ralph Cordiner—was the corporation's rigid "one over one" hierarchy. Each executive had direct contact only with the man immediately above him on the ladder; he never jumped up three or four rungs to discuss a vital problem with the executive who had to decide it. Every recommendation went up and every order came down through this rigid "one over one" chain of command. As a consequence, what a man knew about policy depended upon what his immediate boss told him; he could only assume that his boss had *his* orders from *his* immediate superior and so on, all the way to the very top. But he had—and this was to be vital later —no direct and positive evidence of how much the top knew or didn't know, how much it did or didn't approve.

This was a fine distinction that didn't trouble Burke at the moment, for he had no qualms, no doubts, that he was carrying out company policy set on high, no matter what paper directives might say. Not even the accession of Cordiner to the control of GE in 1950 greatly shook his faith in the necessary two-facedness of GE policy. Cordiner had a reputation as an advocate of the school of free and unrestricted competition, and one of his first acts as president was to read all junior executives a riot act about the antitrust laws and the evils of price-rigging. The words sounded good, but the policy remained unchanged. The overt policy of GE was one thing; its actual, *sub rosa* policy was evidently the very opposite, for the price-riggers continued to rig happily away. In fact, Burke got his next promotion because the simpleton who had held the office before him had taken the Cordiner admonitions seriously and had refused to rig any longer.

In September 1951 Burke was boosted into the post of manager of all switchgear marketing, including circuit breakers (the industrial version of the house fuse—devices as much as 40 feet long, 26 feet high and weighing 85 tons—designed to cut off the flow of electricity when it reaches a dangerous voltage). Burke was interviewed for his new position by Robert Tinnerholm, who left him with a very definite impression as to how it had all come about.

"I was to replace a man who took a strictly religious view of [price-rigging]; who, because he had signed this slip of paper [the GE directive forbidding rigging] wouldn't contact competitors or talk to them—even when they came to his home . . . ," Burke explained. Apparently this surly treatment of the opposition conflicted with GE's image of the way a good GE executive should conduct himself, for Burke said it was made clear to him he was being given this important boost precisely because he wasn't burdened with such silly scruples. "They knew I was adept at this sort of thing," he explained. "I was glad to get the promotion. I had no objections."

Burke's new boss in the switchgear division was Henry V. Erben, an important man in the GE hierarchy, the executive vice-president, apparatus group, which meant he was the No. 3 man in all GE.

"He was saying then," Burke recalled, "that he had talked to Cordiner about this policy, that Cordiner was not pleased with [the idea of conspiring with competitors], but that he, Erben, had said he would do it in a way that would not get the company into trouble. And I'd been told by others that Erben had said things like this earlier than that."

This was as clear an expression of the prevailing winds on the rarefied GE summit as any executive could expect to get under the "one over one" remote-control system. Burke was satisfied, and he was soon meeting with the marketing executives of Westing-

house, Allis-Chalmers, and Federal Pacific. Also, under Erben's
instructions, he began to indoctrinate the men under him into the
intricacies of price-fixing.

"Erben's theory," Burke explained, "was to live and let live,
contact the competitors. He gave us that theory at every opportunity and we took it down to other levels and had no trouble
getting the most innocent persons to go along. Mr. Erben thought
it was all right, and if they didn't want to do it, they knew we
would replace them. Not replace them for that reason, of course.
We would have said the man isn't *broad* enough for this job, he
hasn't grown into it yet."

Corporate hypocrisy probably never found more vivid expression than in this sequence. Here was GE proclaiming holy virtue
at the Cordiner summit—and here was an executive who tried to
keep his word and live up to the proclaimed policy being bounced
out of his job for his effort, his successor selected precisely because
he had no such scruples; here was a whole echelon of lower
executives being trained to perform the very deeds high-level
policy ostensibly proscribed and disavowed, with the threat, obvious if not blatant, that if they didn't go along they would be
judged not *broad* enough, not capable enough for advancement in
GE. In the whole picture, there was only one consoling thought:
the Organization Man sometimes earns for himself the ulcers he
deserves.

Having surrendered his soul to the corporation, having let it
mold his every thought and belief and dictate his most vital decisions, the corporate executive who has been rewarded for obeisance by promotion to a post of key responsibility now finds himself
in a veritable pressure cooker. He must produce ever more business, ever greater profits. The sensational performance of last year
must be topped by an even more sensational performance this year.
"All we got from Lexington Avenue," Burke later recalled, "was
'get your percentage of available business up; the General Electric
Co. is slipping.' "

Cordiner admittedly is a hard driver. His "asset is stretching
men," one GE executive has remarked. If a man couldn't meet the
quota set for him, he was finished—and he knew it. All along the

chain of command, under this kind of inflexible driving, the pressures became so intense as to be almost unbearable. Executives, faced with the incessant demands for ever more profits, felt that there was only one way to reach the profit goal and save their own hides—meet with competitors and jack up the prices the public had to pay.

Clarence Burke later put it this way:

"We did feel that [price-rigging] was the only way to reach part of our goals as managers. Each year we had to budget for more profit as a per cent of net sales, as well as for a larger percentage of available business. My boss, George Burens, wouldn't approve a budget unless it was a 'reach' budget. We couldn't accomplish a greater per cent of new profit to sales without getting together with competitors. Part of the pressure was the will to get ahead and the desire to have the good will of the man above you. He had only to get the approval of the man above *him* to replace you, and if you wouldn't cooperate he could find lots of other faults to get you out."

Under such unremitting pressure, Clarence Burke became a changed man. "He used to be a hail fellow well met," a colleague subsequently told *Fortune,* "until he was put under this great pressure for profits. Then he simply shrank into himself; everything got to be cold turkey with him—without any warmth at all."

3

Life in the world of the price-riggers was complicated by, of all things, a simple question of honor. As with thieves, so with the connivers. They could all get together and reach solid price agreements in defiance of the law of the land, American free-enterprise philosophy, and the stated public policies of their own companies; but the difficulty was to get everybody to keep his word. These were all gentlemen, of course—and high-salaried ones. But almost every time one turned around, it seemed, some blackguard in the group was falling out of his chair at the Union League Club and yielding to temptation. Somebody was always trying to snatch a luscious contract to which he wasn't entitled by trimming a few percentage points off the agreed price. The throat-cutting among the corporate gentlemen got so bad that by May 1953 Clarence Burke, by then promoted to general manager of high voltage, one of GE's three new switchgear departments, decided to get out. Through the rest of 1953 and 1954, GE boycotted the price-rigging cabal.

The effect soon showed on its ledgers. The year 1954 was a bad one for business. Sales slumped for the first time during the Cordiner regime, dropping nearly $176 million. Worse, profits as a percentage of sales remained well below the 8 per cent figure established by Charlie Wilson. The reflection on Cordiner and his right-hand man, Robert Paxton, then executive vice-president for industrial products, was obvious. And the heat that had been applied before to boost sales was almost like a breeze from the Arctic compared to the torrid pressure-cooker temperatures now.

What this fierce stoking of the fires did to the men on the executive chain who were in direct range of the blast is perhaps best illustrated by the experience of Burke's over-all boss, George E. Burens. Burens, like Burke, was fifty-five, but he had been cast in a far different mold than the usual GE executive. Unlike most, he was not a product of the Ivy League, but of the wrong side of the tracks. He had grown up in a relatively poor neighborhood on Cleveland's East Side, and he had quit junior high school at sixteen to join GE as a laborer in the lamp-development laboratory. He had become a foreman, then a clerk; he had battled his way slowly up the chain of command; and he had arrived finally at the $127,000-a-year eminence of GE vice-president and general manager in charge of the switchgear and control division. Of all the price-riggers, Burens was the one who retained his stature as a man; he was a rough, tough, independent fighter who hated the very idea of price-fixing and was dedicated to the belief that the way to run a business was to go out and battle the competition in a war of quality and price.

Yet it was Burens who, in midsummer 1955, called Burke into his office and told him they were going to have to resume meetings with competitors.

Burens didn't tell Burke where the orders came from, but W. V.

O'Brien, who filled in for Burens while he was vacationing in Europe, told Burke that Paxton (soon to become president of GE when Cordiner moved up to chairman of the board) had ordered all hands to "stabilize" prices. This was the suave Organization Man's word for price-rigging. Paxton was later to insist that he was the most misunderstood of men, that he had never authorized or had knowledge of such dreadful deeds, and that whatever his boys did they did on their own in absolute violation of company policy. Be that as it may, the prevailing idea in GE—and it is amazing how many executives caught it at about the same time— was that it was the wish of their corporate lord and master that they should rig again. And so rig they did.

For a time the pressure on prices, which had tumbled as much as 40 to 45 per cent off book, was eased, and everybody was happy. But it seemed it was impossible to run a gentlemanly conspiracy among gentlemen—and have everybody remain a gentleman. There was always some greedy blackguard who couldn't resist temptation. In this instance, the culprit was Westinghouse. One of its executives broke the gentlemen's agreement by offering Florida Power & Light Co. a concealed discount; General Electric got wind of the deal and matched the price. Soon the throat-cutting was cosmic, and prices were being slashed as much as 60 per cent off book.

There was, naturally, the very devil to pay. The lush profit world to which the electrical giants had become accustomed was taking an unholy beating, and there was, it seemed, just one way to stop it—to get back into the price-rigging game and to try to make certain this time that every gentleman in the jungle behaved like one. Only George Burens disagreed. He had hated price-fixing from the beginning; he had tried it only under orders, only because he had to, and now he bucked like an angry steer at the prospect of starting the practice all over again.

Burens had the support of his departmental general managers— Burke, H. F. Hentschel and Frank Stehlik—all of whom were disillusioned about price-rigging. But it seemed as if these four formed a small island of dissidents in the great ocean of GE. Everybody else wanted to get those prices and profit margins up, and there was a whole series of angry explosions before Burens was finally bludgeoned into line.

The first of these brutal tugs of war came in early summer 1958, when Burens attended a dinner for all apparatus-division managers in New York. Arthur F. Vinson, group manager and executive vice-president, the new and powerful No. 3 man in GE, presided over the affair and kept significantly silent during what turned into a "Beat Burens" free-for-all. The other division managers, incensed at Burens because, so long as he continued the price war, it was difficult for them to rig, ganged up on him. They accused him of wanting everything his own way, of not being "nice" to his competitors, of keeping up a competition that was driving prices down all along the line. Why couldn't he be "nice"? Why couldn't he "stabilize" a little? Vinson (who was later to deny any knowledge of price-rigging) sat through it all and only he knows what he could have thought the boys were talking about.

Burens, furious at the gang-up to which he had been subjected, went back to his headquarters in Philadelphia. His mood had much to do with what followed. The annual business-review meeting of big and medium GE brass was coming up shortly at the Philadelphia Country Club, on July 30 and 31, 1958. Vinson and Paxton, now president of GE, represented top management; Burens, as the ranking GE executive in the Philadelphia area, was host at the kickoff dinner. This turned into an affair no one present ever forgot, for Burens committed the cardinal indiscretion for an Organization Man: he locked horns with the president.

A general discussion of prices and policy touched off the fireworks. Burens argued fiercely that the only way to run a business was to keep quality up, get costs down, and price products at just a fair margin above costs. Price levels then would be genuine, and there wouldn't be so much fat on the bone that some chiseler could break one of those gentlemen's agreements, trim his price, and still make a mint on a large contract. Burke vowed later that he heard Paxton reply: "But that doesn't get you optimum prices."

The debate didn't end with the cocktails. It continued right through the dinner hour, and it got rougher as it went along. Stehlik said later that Paxton kept criticizing Burens' outlook, kept telling him he was a factory man and didn't understand marketing, kept arguing that prices had to be higher and discounting from book by one division was bad because it undercut all prices. Stehlik got the impression that Paxton didn't like anything about the way Burens was running his division. The angry clash stilled all merriment at the table, made the diners embarrassed and silent. In this hush, Stehlik heard Burens growl: "I guess I'll be fired to-morrow." Paxton told him icily: "Perhaps you will."

At the other end of the table, Hentschel, the third of Burens' managers, was sitting beside Executive Vice-President Vinson. Vinson was paying close attention to the head-knocking at the head of the table and at its peak Hentschel later recounted, Vinson turned to him and remarked: "That's the way we lose vice-presidents."

Paxton's explanation of all this afterwards was simply that Burens had gotten drunk and abusive. "He was drinking Scotch and ginger ale," Paxton said with a shudder, adding that he thought this "a pretty poisonous mixture." All that had happened, he insisted, was that he had discussed price strategy in very general terms, and suddenly Burens, fueled up on Scotch and ginger ale, became abusive. It was very distressing, but Paxton, a charitable man, had decided to forgive Burens.

Burens' own version was that the discussion had developed just the way Burke, Stehlik, and Hentschel all said they heard it. After the dinner, Burens added, he saw Vinson privately and told him he was resigning; he was through with GE. Vinson placated him, urged him not to do anything rash, advised him to go home and sleep on it overnight. The next day, Paxton himself told him to forget the whole business, to wipe it completely out of his mind as if it had never happened. Burens was still stubbornly bent on resigning, but again Vinson, the peacemaker, argued him out of his intention and persuaded him to stay. It was for Burens a fateful decision; only by resigning could he have avoided the trap that now closed on him.

The jaws of the trap snapped shut, according to everybody but Arthur Vinson, at what must certainly be considered one of the most mysterious luncheons ever held in an executive suite. According to Burens, Burke, Hentschel, and Stehlik, this event took place sometime after the Philadelphia Country Club confrontation, probably between August 1 and September 13, 1958. They all insisted that on a day during this period—a day they could not later pinpoint—Arthur Vinson came to Philadelphia, had lunch with them in Dining Room B, told them he had fixed up everything with Westinghouse, and ordered them to begin rigging again. According to Arthur Vinson, it never happened; he wasn't even in Philadelphia during this period.

Clarence Burke's recollection was explicit. He was in his office when he got a telephone call to join Vinson and Burens in Burens' office. There Burens asked him to tell Vinson about his experiences in price-rigging. Burke did. He told the No. 3 man in GE, he insisted later, that price-rigging never worked, somebody was always double-crossing GE by cutting book prices, and one of the worst offenders had been Westinghouse. "Well, that confirms what I've been telling you," Burens remarked to Vinson. But Vinson would not be put off. "I know it will work," he said. He added that he had a guarantee from Westinghouse, that Westinghouse admitted it had been a bad boy in the past, but "they have learned their lesson." Westinghouse, he said, was "more interested in making a profit than they are in regaining leadership, and they promised me it will work."

Burens still demurred. According to Burke, Vinson got red in the face and said: "Well, it's got to be done."

On this note, they left Burens' office and went to Dining Room B to join Stehlik and Hentschel. This was an executive dining room, but on this day it was blocked off, reserved for this one exclusive group of five executives—a very rare occurrence. According to Burke, Stehlik was considered a problem child in the organization because he had never rigged and was obstinate about starting; for this reason among others, Burke wanted Stehlik to get the word directly from Vinson about what had to be done. Vinson, however, with everybody present, seemed to prefer to talk in generalities.

"All during lunch we talked about price stability," Burke later told *Fortune,* "and I tried to get Art to say the same thing he had in Burens' office, but he wouldn't volunteer anything. Finally, I said, 'Art, these competitors of ours have been calling us up recently.' He looked at me as if he could have hit me, and Burens said quickly, 'Yes, Art, what do you think we ought to do?' Vinson said we ought to talk to them, but he said don't let it get below the general managers' level."

This was the decision that set off another price-rigging spiral. It lasted for two more years, and then finally there came the explosion—public exposure of all these devious dealings and a scandal that rocked the business community.

4

One thing the great electrical conspiracy definitely proved: the American people need the Tennessee Valley Authority, if only as a guide to the honesty and ethics of big business. TVA, of course, has long been anathema to the business community; it represents to businessmen unfair government competition in the realm of the electric-power industry—why, it is an experiment in socialism, that's what it is! But without TVA the giants of the electrical industry might never have been exposed, and the millions of dollars they mulcted out of the economy of the nation would still fatten their balance sheets.

The role of TVA in the exposure of the electrical swindle was fundamental. The authority had watched with deepening suspicion as prices of electrical equipment zoomed some 50 per cent (on some items nearly 80 per cent) in a few short years. In early 1959 transpired the event that transformed TVA's suspicions into virtual certainty. The authority asked bids on a 500,000-kilowatt turbogenerator. When the competition was opened, TVA was astounded to find that a reputable British firm, C. A. Parsons & Co. of London, had underbid mighty General Electric and Westinghouse by more than $5 million. The Parsons bid was for $12,095,800. General Electric, which apparently had "the phase of the moon" working for it, had bid $17,563,000, and Westinghouse, cast in the role of predestined loser, had made the GE bid seem reasonable by pegging its price at $17,633,000.

Now, federal agencies are not permitted to buy outside the country unless the domestic bids exceed foreign offers by more than 6 per cent. TVA, leaning over backwards in an effort not to offend the business community, had permitted domestic manufacturers a 20 per cent margin, but in this case the discrepancy was more than double that, a whopping 46 per cent. So TVA awarded the turbogenerator contract to Parsons.

The outcry in the business community couldn't have been louder if some heathen had spit on the flag. The American companies actually sought to have the Parsons contract set aside, contending that "national security" was involved in keeping up our industrial capacity. One GE vice-president argued that foreign manufacturers could underbid our sterling American businesses because of "substantially lower wage rates and competitive facilities."

The hypocrisy of these arguments was quickly exposed. The International Union of Electrical Workers, computing the labor involved in the turbogenerator contract, concluded that "if GE and Westinghouse had gotten their labor completely free, they would have had difficulty in competing with the Parsons bid." TVA's studies showed that our tariffs adequately compensated for any wage differential; yet the Parsons firm could pay the tariff, defray heavy shipping costs across the Atlantic, agree to pay damages in the event of delay in delivery (which General Electric and Westinghouse refused to do)—and still undersell the American firms by more than $5 million. In the light of these incontestable facts, the award to Parsons was ratified.

The commotion that had been caused, however, led directly to exposure. Reporter Julian Granger, of the Knoxville *News-Sentinel,* wrote a series of articles, based on TVA's records, exposing dramatic evidence of persistent price-rigging by U.S. firms bidding for TVA contracts. Senator Kefauver and his investigating committee took up the trail as a result of Granger's articles, and the U.S. Attorney General's office went to work. In Philadelphia, grand juries began to study the case, and evidence quickly piled up. Working for the government was the basic fact that the conspiracy had been too vast and too long-enduring for perfect secrecy. Too many persons had intimate knowledge of its details, and not all of them were going to risk perjury indictments for the cause. Some began to talk; others, hearing this, talked too; and soon the probe snowballed to the point where several grand juries had to be kept in almost continuous session to handle it.

On February 16, 1960, the grand juries began to grind out indictments. Before they finished, twenty-nine companies and forty-five executives had been haled before the bar of justice in the largest criminal case ever developed under the Sherman Anti-Trust Act. At first, the defendant corporations donned the mantle of righteousness; they were truculent, injured innocents. Their lawyers demanded bills of particulars from federal prosecutors—and promptly got them. The bills were so detailed, so specific that they spread on the record vital facts about the conspiracy that otherwise might have remained secret; they were so convincing that even the highest-paid corporation lawyers in the nation could see no way out except to cop pleas.

They tried first to get the government to accept *nolo contendere* pleas, a weasel-worded legal device that means "maybe we did, maybe we didn't, but we won't bother to fight it if you say so." Robert A. Bicks, the hard-driving boss of the antitrust section of the Attorney General's office, stood stanchly against any such compromise, and Attorney General William Rogers took the virtually unprecedented step of filing a personal brief with the court, insisting on outright guilty pleas in all of the major cases. Judge J. Cullen Ganey, the presiding federal jurist, listened to the arguments and then gave the individual and corporate defendants this choice: they could plead guilty or go to trial. They pleaded guilty.

Now arose the vital question: What kind of punishment would be meted out? Judge Ganey, known as a fair and compassionate jurist, wouldn't actually send any of those distinguished, $100,000-a-year executives to jail just like common criminals, would he?

The answer was given in Philadelphia Federal Court on Monday, February 6, 1961, a cold and snowy day. No more suave and distinguished group of defendants had ever appeared before that bar. They looked like what they were—the well-groomed masters of the executive suite, their shoes mirror-shined, their conservative suits flawlessly pressed. Judge Ganey looked down sternly from the bench and, almost with his first words, the chill in the courtroom matched the chill outside.

"This is a shocking indictment of a vast section of our economy," the judge said, "for what is really at stake here is the survival of the kind of economy under which this country has grown great, the free-enterprise system. These men and these corporations have flagrantly mocked the image of the economic system . . . and destroyed the model which we offer as a free-world alternative to state control and eventual dictatorship."

Judge Ganey conceded that the government had not been able to develop enough positive evidence to convict the men at the very top of the corporate power structure, the Cordiners and the Paxtons, but he added:

". . . In a broader sense, they bear a grave responsibility for the present situation, for one would be most naïve indeed to believe that these violations of the law, so long persisted in, affecting so large a segment of the industry and finally, involving so many millions upon millions of dollars, were facts unknown to those responsible for the conduct of the corporation. . . ."

Accordingly, he said, the corporations would be subject to heavy fines.

Turning to the individuals, the judge stared at them silently for a moment out of cold blue eyes. He was convinced, he said, "that in the great number of these defendant cases, they were torn between conscience and an approved corporate policy, with the rewarding objectives of promotion, comfortable security and large salaries—in short, the organization or company man, the conformist, who goes along with his superiors and finds balm for his conscience in additional comforts and the security of his place in the corporate setup." This, the judge said, might explain their misdeeds, but it did not exculpate them. Those "with ultimate responsibility for corporate conduct, among those indicted," were going to jail.

The words quickly assumed a personal impact when the first defendant was called for sentencing. He was John H. Chiles, fifty-seven, a small man with gold-rimmed glasses, a vice-president and general manager of Westinghouse, a Senior Warden of St. John's Episcopal Church in Sharon, Pennsylvania. His lawyer pleaded that "no further punishment is necessary to keep these men from doing what they have done. They are not grasping, greedy, cutthroat competitors. They devote much time to their communities. My client is not only Senior Warden of his church, he is vicepresident of his United Fund drive. He is the benefactor of charities for crippled children and cancer victims. He is a fellow of a distinguished engineering society." Judge Ganey looked down and pronounced sentence—thirty days in the Montgomery County Jail.

The other defense attorneys fought desperately to spare their clients similar fates. Three GE executives were among the principal defendants—George E. Burens, who had fought so hard against rigging; Lewis J. Burger, forty-eight, the man who had succeeded him in charge of the Philadelphia GE office before the scandal broke; and William S. Ginn, forty-five, a $135,000-a-year vicepresident of GE, the man long considered heir to Cordiner's mantle. In arguing for clemency for the three, their attorney put the blame squarely on GE, saying:

"There is such a thing as business compulsion, as corporate coercion, and this, sir, does not require some superior official coming in and saying, 'I direct you to do thus and so.' There is such a thing as atmosphere, there is such a thing as knowing acquiescence in a situation."

Judge Ganey, pointing to one of the defendants, stressed that he was high in the hierarchy of GE, manager of an important division. And he asked: "Did he have any degree of judgment in the doing of the things which he must have known were wrong?"

The defense attorney hesitated only momentarily, then replied:

"True enough, I suppose he could have said, 'No, I will not participate in this.' But then I think that belies the corporate reality which does exist in America today. . . . In my submission, he would not have been able to continue his job in the company."

Here Robert Bicks, the chief government prosecutor, interrupted:

"Your Honor, we are unable to answer what would have happened had any of these men decided definitely to live within the law and fight it out with their superiors because, to the best of our knowledge, none of the men in this case tried it or did."

Clarence Burke, of course, had seen what happened to a predecessor who tried it; that gentleman's head had been lopped off. But nobody was recalling this now. GE especially was not recalling it. The GE attorney jumped up, quite indignant, and told the court that he could not let the suggestion stand "that the conduct was compelled and directed." GE was "distressed," he said, that its explicit regulation against violating the antitrust laws had been disobeyed by the defendants. Judge Ganey commented drily that it seemed GE policy "was honored in its breach rather than its observance."

Burens, Berger, Ginn, all drew thirty-day sentences. They were soon joined by C. I. Mauntel, sixty, Westinghouse division sales manager; John Marvin Cook, vice-president of Cutler-Hammer; and Edwin R. Jung, sales vice-president of Clark Controller.

It took Judge Ganey two full working days to impose all the fines and sentences. When at last it was over, the twenty-nine guilty corporations had been fined $1,787,000, seven of their executives had been sent to jail, and forty-four of their executives had been fined $137,500. Twenty-one received suspended prison terms and were placed on probation for five years. Among the corporations, the penalties fell heaviest on GE and Westinghouse. GE was fined $437,500, Westinghouse $372,500.

The business community was shocked to the soles of its custom-made shoes. It was understandable to businessmen that jails might appropriately receive the Mafia leaders who met at Apalachin— but not businessmen, not these leaders of their communities. And yet, as Attorney General Robert Kennedy later noted, in a conspiracy that spanned a decade and affected the entire economic life of the nation, far more than seven jail sentences would have been justified—and for much longer terms than a mere thirty days. The two-bit thief is much more severely punished. Typical was an Asbury Park, New Jersey, case that occurred only a few months after Judge Ganey sentenced the electrical conspirators. A man who stole a $2.98 pair of sunglasses and a $1 box of soap was packed off to jail for four months—four times the sentence imposed on executives whose illegal machinations had cost the American public literally hundreds of millions of dollars. Contrasting such sentences, one might justifiably conclude that, horrified though the business world was, its distinguished representatives had actually escaped with little more than slaps on the wrists.

And the men at the top did not get even this.

At one point during the prosecution, the government had believed that it could carry the war into the rarefied inner sanctum of GE. Burens, Burke, Stehlik, and Hentschel had testified before a federal grand jury about the luncheon in Dining Room B at which, they said, Arthur Vinson had told them explicitly that they must rig. The grand jury had indicted Vinson. This indictment implicated the powerful No. 3 man in GE, the man who was the direct link to Paxton and Cordiner; if it had stood up, there was no telling where the trail might lead. But the indictment did not stand up.

Vinson challenged it and forced the government to back down. He produced records from the Philadelphia office to show that there were only eight days in the critical August–September period of 1958 when Burens, Burke, Stehlik, and Hentschel could all have been present for luncheon in Dining Room B. Then Vinson, from his New York office, brought forth written memoranda and records to indicate that he had been there on each of those eight days, establishing for himself an alibi. The government, it seems, had goofed in the preindictment period by relying solely on the testimony of the four GE executives and not trying to corroborate it with written records from the Philadelphia office. Now, when such records were sought, they either weren't to be had or they showed nothing.

Burens, Burke, Stehlik, and Hentschel (who by this time had all been fired by a righteous GE) sought to get their day-by-day letter books to establish the date of the luncheon, but their own former subordinates told them regretfully that the books just could not be found. Books for prior years and subsequent years, yes; but not those vital books for 1958. When the four men tried to get the records for Dining Room B to see who had signed for the luncheon check, they were told that there were no records for any such luncheon. When the FBI finally managed to subpoena the company chauffeur's records, to see if a company car had picked up Vinson, the records showed nothing that would substantiate the Vinson visit. Burens, Burke, Stehlik, and Hentschel went to Washington and took a FBI lie-detector test; they all passed with flying colors, a performance that government attorneys found infinitely persuasive. Vinson refused to take such a test; he was content to rely on the ironclad written record he had established. And this in the end won the battle for him. The government dropped the indictment, halting its probe at the very door of the throne room of GE. It was an outcome that left the corporate summit legally unscarred.

5

Such were the revelations; such the punishment or the lack of it. In almost any perspective, the great electrical conspiracy was a watershed case in the ethics of our times. Both the business community and the general public recognized it as a development colossal in its scope and historic in its implications. But just what were those implications? What ethical judgment should be rendered on the conduct of some of the most powerful executives in America? What, really, had been learned? And what had been changed?

To ask such questions is to plunge into a mire of confusion. On virtually every level of American society, the principal development was bewilderment. So wedded are we to our myths that our minds are shackled in confronting facts. We cannot admit the plain truth before our noses, and the result is hypocrisy and a kind of intellectual and ethical schizophrenia.

Nowhere was this split personality exhibited to clearer view than on the stratosphere of the corporate summit. On the one hand, the top men of General Electric and Westinghouse reacted with the shock convention demands; on the other, they demonstrated a contradictory determination to act as if nothing of earthshaking moment had happened. Convention demanded that the proper obeisant noises be made before the holy shrine of free enterprise, but businessmen themselves often expressed the emphatic belief that the great electrical conspiracy really had amounted to nothing more than "a motorist driving at 35 miles an hour in a 30-mile zone."

President Mark Cresap of Westinghouse conceded that the price-rigging disclosures had been "very disturbing to me," and he urged all good Westinghouse men "to carry out our jobs—in every respect—with honesty and integrity, to live within the law of the land." At the same time, he said, he would not dismiss or demote any of Westinghouse's price-rigging executives. They had not acted for "personal gain. They acted in the belief, misguided though it may have been, that they were furthering the company's interest. . . ." Furthermore, Cresap said, each of the faulty Westinghouse execs was "a reputable citizen, a respected and valuable member of his community and of high moral character." Logic hardly endorses such smooth reconciliation of the incompatible.

General Electric exhibited no such tenderness toward executives who had labored so excessively if misguidedly in its behalf. It was shocked, righteous, utterly holy, and it fired out of hand its executives who had had the misfortune to draw sentences. GE's chairman Ralph J. Cordiner condemned the price-riggers for "a deliberate violation of General Electric directive policy and of the expected high standards of our corporate way of life." But then he turned around in a speech to some 600 Wall Street security analysts and tried to belittle the seriousness of what had happened. "We don't think anybody's been damaged," he said at one point. He also said: "We don't think anybody in the Federal Government has been damaged. . . . We don't intend to be responsive to suits [for damages]. We intend to resist any such suits. . . . I've yet to encounter the first man who said, 'Cordiner, we've got a complaint, we've been damaged.' . . . There is not much that can be done to correct what has happened. The issue is to correct what happens in the future."

This business of correction turned out to be extremely difficult in the free-enterprise economy to which the electrical industry was so devoted; for, even while the great electrical conspiracy case was pending in court, there were multiple indications that in the practical world of business nothing had changed. On December 14,

1960, just six days after the electrical conspirators had pleaded guilty in Philadelphia, the Tennessee Valley Authority opened supposedly competitive bids for lightning arresters—and found that GE and Westinghouse had submitted prices identical to the last penny. Both bid exactly $1680.12.

During the entire time that the price-rigging case was before the court, right down to a week before sentences were imposed, TVA continued to get an entire series of identical bids in a pattern so broad and so penny-exact it could hardly have been coincidence.

On January 5, 1961, TVA opened bids on instrument transformers. GE bid $2208, Westinghouse $2208.

On January 12, 1961, TVA opened bids on current transformers. GE bid $604.80, Westinghouse $604.80.

On January 30, 1961—just a week before the guilty price-rigging executives were to be sentenced in Philadelphia—TVA opened bids on bus-type insulators. GE and five other companies bid for this business—and all six bids were identical at $4274.50.

In a world in which, despite exposure, despite jail, despite anguish at the summit, identical bids and collusion still prevailed as a way of life, there was understandably some confusion about basic values. Only labor's view seems to have been forthright and unblinded by corporate pretense and mythology. James B. Carey, president of the IUE, pointed out that GE had paid Cordiner as board chairman $366,226 a year in salary and other remuneration and had granted Cordiner stock options on which he had a profit of $1,291,500; Carey stressed that Paxton had been paid $275,361 a year as GE's president and had stock options representing a $1,425,937 profit. "Thus," Carey wrote, "two GE presidents have been handed more than $3,912,000 in actual or potential compensation for not knowing a thing about their company's participation in the biggest criminal conspiracy in the history of the nation's antitrust laws!"

This, needless to say, was hardly the view that prevailed in the more gentlemanly purlieus of the corporate Establishment where it is considered crass to express truth in such crude terms. The Establishment, indeed, was so proud of everything in the best of all possible worlds—the world of big business—that it proclaimed

Ralph Cordiner the National Association of Manufacturers' Man of the Year. This honor that fell upon the Cordiner brow was most curiously and ironically timed. The announcement was made even as sentences were being passed on lesser GE executives in Philadelphia, and an ecstatic GE proclaimed the news in full-page advertisements in which its chairman was quoted on the virtues of free enterprise.

With deeds and the corporate image swearing at each other, evidence multiplied that a baffled public was finding it practically impossible to get any ethical meaning, any guidelines for personal conduct, out of the great electrical conspiracy. On the very day that Westinghouse's John Chiles was sentenced to a jail term, for example, he was also re-elected vice-president of the United Fund Organization in his hometown of Sharon, Pennsylvania. The Rev. Malcolm MacMillan, pastor of St. John's Episcopal Church, in which Chiles was the Senior Warden, explained emphatically: "The vestry still feels that Mr. Chiles is a man of high integrity and we have every confidence in him."

In Pittsfield, Massachusetts, virtually a one-industry city dominated by GE, bewilderment paralyzed those traditional guardians of the ethic, the churches. The Rev. Raymond E. Gibson described it this way:

"The sense of confusion was as marked in the churches and among the clergy as in the community at large. Throughout the whole turmoil the irrelevance of the churches to the stituation was evident. Pastors did not know what to say to the men in question. . . . On the moral issue the churches were mute. No statement of the affair came from the Council of Churches, which had been accustomed to take stands on issues of social concern. . . . To each other the ministers confessed the sense of confusion they felt in regard to the moral issues, their inability to grasp the complexity of corporate decisions, their feeling that many of the issues involved were beyond the reach of traditional standards of piety."

The result was that many of the executives caught and temporarily humiliated in the great electrical conspiracy were treated in the long run as if, indeed, they had committed no offense more serious than speeding at 35 miles an hour in a 30-mile zone. William Ginn, the GE executive who had been groomed to follow in the footsteps of Cordiner, survived his short jail term and stepped right into the job of president of the Baldin-Lima-Hamilton Corporation at a reported salary of $70,000 a year. A second of the imprisoned executives became president of a firm building earth-moving equipment; another became affiliated with a Massachusetts automobile business; still another was boosted into the presidency of ITT Europe, Inc., and made European general manager of the company. As Mary McGrory had written about the two petty bribe-takers in the Billie Sol Estes case, "pity not blame" was their lot, and the electrical conspirators went on to rewards that in popular mythology are reserved only for the deserving and the virtuous, their happy fates in sharp contrast to the almost universal scorn that had been Douglas Johnson's recompense for honesty.

6

Was the great electrical conspiracy, then, of no greater moment than a traffic ticket? Despite the conspiratorial trappings, the aliases, the camouflaged vouchers, the unsigned letters, the phonebooth telephone calls, was it really true that all that was involved here was a mere technicality of the law? Was it true that no really heinous offense had been committed?

To these questions there are definite answers—answers that show the electrical conspirators did far more than simply "stabilize" the market.

For example, there were repeated meetings and long discussions in 1957 about a low-priced Double O starter that Cutler-Hammer wanted to put upon the market. The other partners to the conspiracy were worried because this would undercut their existing products, and Cutler-Hammer was finally pressured into abandoning its plans and marketing a more expensive starter in line with those already being sold. This, certainly, represented the strangling of a new product to protect the old, existing order. It was the antithesis of free enterprise.

This repression of the new, this smothering of initiative, represented one of the inevitable evils of a secret and conspiratorial cartel. The gouging of the public in a greedy drive to obtain "optimum prices" for private profit was another.

General Electric tried desperately to convince its customers and the public that nobody, in Cordiner's words, had been "damaged." In a high-powered campaign, its publicity men ground out releases devoted to the Cordiner themes that "General Electric has given good value" and "General Electric's prices are helping to fight inflation." These pitches didn't convince anyone except their authors, if indeed they were convinced. Within a year, Cordiner had met not one but a whole flock of persons who complained loudly and in legal accents, "Cordiner, we've got a complaint, we've been damaged."

Suits flew against the electrical conspirators like snowflakes in a blizzard. More than 1500 were filed in the first year, and a shaken GE called Charles E. Wilson back into harness to try to arrange settlements. Quickly, the pretense that the electrical conspirators had been merely "stabilizing," not gouging, collapsed like all of the other corporate pretenses that had tried to hide the truth. On July 27, 1962, GE began the painful process of disgorging; it announced that it had agreed to pay the federal government $7,-470,000. Of this amount, $6,470,000, went to the Tennessee Valley Authority for overcharges on price-rigged bids in the years 1956 through 1959. In announcing the settlement with the government, Cordiner estimated that, if similar arrangements could be worked out with private utility companies and other claimants, the cost to GE "would be approximately $45 million to $50 million over the next few years."

Even this belated acknowledgment that quite a few persons must have been damaged proved utterly unrealistic. The suits piled up, and not all of them were so quickly and amicably settled. In Philadelphia, two utilities—the Philadelphia Electric Co. and the United Gas Improvement Co.—battled it out in the courts against six of the largest of the electrical conspirators, GE, Westinghouse, Allis-Chalmers, Moloney Electric Co., Wagner Electric Co., and

McGraw-Edison Co. A jury awarded the Philadelphia utilities $28 million.

And so it went. The courts ruled that the electrical manufacturers who had participated in the conspiracy were liable for triple damages; the U.S. Supreme Court held that they could be sued for the price-gouging that took place before 1956. The morass widened and deepened. After three years, various litigations were still under way, and the end was not yet clearly in sight. But some idea of how badly the utilities of the nation, their consumers, and the public at large had been gouged in the price-fixing cabal may be gleaned from the mounting costs to one company, the industry leader, mighty General Electric.

At GE's annual meeting on April 29, 1964, Gerald E. Phillippe, now its board chairman, told stockholders that agreement had been reached on about 90 per cent of the suits pending against it. The settlements, he said, would amount to about $160 million, more than three times Cordiner's optimum estimate two years earlier. GE had already paid out some $76 million in 1962 and 1963 operations, but in 1964 it was going to be really hit. It was going to have to cough up an additional $84 million in this year alone, a disbursement that would slice earnings by about 47 cents a share. Even this was not the end. Phillippe said it was "not yet possible to estimate the total over-all cost to dispose of these matters in their entirety."

Like all other reports emanating from the GE hierarchy, this forecast proved overly optimistic. When GE rendered its final 1964 accounting to its stockholders, the bite for the electrical price-rigging cut 1964's earnings not by 47 cents a share but by 82. GE in this one year had refunded $134,765,485.

The outcome establishes at least one clear point: when some of the most powerful corporations in the land, hiring the slickest lawyers, have to refund literally hundreds of millions of dollars in ill-gotten gains, there can be no question that the public and the economy of the nation have indeed been swindled on a colossal scale in the cause of private greed and profit. This was no traffic-ticket offense. This was no peccadillo of a crime.

7

The basis of the ethical dilemmas posed by the great electrical conspiracy may be glimpsed, ironically, in the government's almost instant and fearful reaction that, by prosecuting the conspiracy, it might break up the free-enterprise system. If there was to be no conspiracy to "stabilize" prices, a price war might be touched off that would leave the corpses of the weak strewn all over the corporate landscape and that would end with the enthronement of GE as a nationwide monopoly.

Catching sight of this specter, a shocked Justice Department virtually pleaded with GE to sign a consent decree not to cut prices to "unreasonably low" levels. In this action—and in this almost alone—there was some recognition of the realities of life in the mass industrialized society. For the simple truth was that GE was so enormously powerful that, in an unrestricted price war, it could kill off almost any rival at will. Suppose, for example, GE wanted to destroy a maker of industrial-control equipment. It could price the products of this GE division at such a ruinously low level the small competitor would be quickly driven into bankruptcy. GE would lose some money in the throat-cutting, of course; but its losses would hardly show on its corporate balance sheet when absorbed by the profits of other divisions. Unrestricted competition, the most precious myth of free enterprise, clearly places in the hands of the mighty the power to eliminate all competition.

General Electric, perhaps relishing a chance to play games with the government with justice on its side for a change, righteously refused to sign the much-desired consent decree; and, in a sequence that would have done Gilbert and Sullivan proud, the great utility and the government shadow-boxed with the basic issue until both wearied of the sport. In the meantime, the government's fears were gradually allayed by the very kind of evidence that had originally stimulated the electrical conspiracy probe—a wave of identical bids and sharply rising prices.

In early April 1961, the city of Cleveland asked for bids on eleven different types of watt-hour meters. Five electrical com-

panies bid, including GE and Westinghouse, and all submitted
bids identical to the penny. In early May, the federal government
rejected fifteen identical bids on more than $1,250,000 worth of
electrical equipment, and Secretary of Interior Stewart L. Udall
commented that "we were amazed at the fact that we continued
to receive bids offering identical prices." By late summer *The
Wall Street Journal* was reporting that federal fears that the convicted electrical price-fixers might "over-react" had been dissi-
pated by rising prices. Bids to utilities on steam-turbine generators
(identical bids, too) had risen 15 per cent in two months, the
Journal found. One could almost hear the boys getting together at
North Bay and warbling "Happy Days Are Here Again."

This, certainly, was fiasco. But it was fiasco with a very specific
meaning.

Recognition of the meaning wasn't general, but specialized
sources, some of them surprising, saw and made contact with the
truth. One such source was the *Value Line Investment Survey,*
devoted to analytical appraisal of the stock market and the condition of business. The survey, though it adopted in its entirety the
initial business thesis that nobody had been "damaged" by the
conspiracy, nevertheless recognized in blunt terms what was at
stake. In its issue of March 13, 1961, it wrote:

> The free enterprise system, in which prices are free to fluctuate
> without restraint, which is the system Judge Ganey says America
> professes to its people and the model it holds up as a free-world al-
> ternative to state control and tyranny, has not existed for a couple of
> hundred years. . . .
> The heart of the problem is that the anti-trust laws, if endorsed to
> the letter, would have the effect of destroying their own reason for
> being. General Electric and Westinghouse would, in a relatively short
> time, become the only competitors in their field. In the case of prac-
> tically all the major cyclical industries—steel, machinery and equip-
> ment, textiles—the entire market would soon be preempted by the
> strongest company if prices were allowed to fluctuate without control.

The survey pointed out that it is ridiculous to talk about free
enterprise in an economy in which the law establishes minimum
hours and wages; in which farmers and farm income are dependent

upon acreage controls and price supports; in which businesses rely upon tariffs to keep a platform under manufactured goods. "Today nobody really wants prices to fluctuate with perfect freedom," *Value Line* wrote, and concluded that American leadership had failed, but not just because it was "either hypocritical or ignorant."

Unfortunately, the far more terrifying truth of the matter is that the leadership is probably neither hypocritical nor ignorant, but schizophrenic—that is to say compulsively determined to believe in a fantasy at odds with reality. Naturally, it reacts with blind rage when its dream world is impugned.

In such terms *Value Line* delineated the issue, but in visualizing a solution, it demonstrated that it was itself a victim of business schizophrenia. It conceived of big business as altruistically holding an "umbrella" over the little fellow, protecting him by the price-setting conspiracy, and it suggested in effect that all that was needed was a change in the law to legalize the conspiracy—in other words, to let business set and administer prices at its own uninhibited will. This, of course, was nonsense.

It was a rare individual who saw the problem whole, both in terms of the fundamental issue and the inevitable solution. One such was T. K. Quinn, a former vice-president of GE and a severe critic of the price-rigging practices he had observed during his twenty-four years with the firm (from 1912 to 1936).

Adam Smith is outdated in this modern age largely because fixed overhead has become a principal factor in total cost, and because corporations have swollen so big as to make our whole society dependent upon them [Quinn wrote in *The New Republic*]. . . . So Big Business, preaching one thing and practicing its opposite, is obliged to pretend that it favors competition and the anti-trust laws while it secretly opposes them, establishes uniform and administered prices, sets up the barriers against the entry of new companies in its fields, stalls costly technological innovation and curtails production.

Thus otherwise respectable businessmen—the conforming bureaucrats in big corporations—become the carriers of misrepresentation and falsehoods and degrade themselves. They are victims of a dilemma most of them don't understand.

In about one-third of the national economy—an area that includes automobiles, steel, cigarettes, cement, oil products, chemicals, roofing materials, electric light bulbs and machinery—price competition has been eliminated by mutual understanding, legally or illegally, among the corporations represented. They have taken the position, in practice, that prices should be substantially uniform and profits so made secure.

Now if the American public is ready to accept this condition then the only remaining question is *who should fix the prices and what standards should be adopted.* Shall we permit these and other private collusive interests themselves to decide what their "take" is to be? If so, then the laboring man should also be permitted to set his own wages.

Quinn gave the obvious answer—"the public interest must come first" and, if prices are to be set, they must be set by government, acting on behalf of all the people. "The situation is not changed in the least by resorting to name-calling—e.g. 'socialism,' " he wrote. He would give business a choice: accept maximum prices fixed by government or rely on prices set by free competition without government regulation:

It becomes more apparent every day that powerful, giant, private corporations cannot safely continue to be treated as wholly private institutions. They have power over investment, output, employment, sales and wage policies that substantially affect the markets in which they deal, and therefore all of us whose lives are conditioned by those markets.

Moreover, they aspire to an ever-increasing role in our educational and political lives, as so much of the subsidized literature demonstrates. They have made a captive of competition in many industries and are more controlling than they are controlled.

Quinn's picture was not overdrawn. It is ironic but no accident that some of the most powerful corporations in the electrical conspiracy, at the same time they were price-gouging the American public, were bankrolling Radical Right doggerel. General Electric had close working ties and had given its emphatic endorsement to the program of Harding College in Searcy, Arkansas, the idea factory of the Radical Right, and Fred Loock's Allen-Bradley had spent a small fortune to make possible the nationwide dissemination of the views of Dr. Fred C. Schwarz, the rabble-rousing anti-Communist evangelist from Australia. Such subsidization of extremist views played a vital part in the campaign that led to the capture of the Republican Party in 1964—a development that enthroned an emotional faith in myths and slogans above intellect and reality. But then this was the way some of the gigantic electrical conspirators had planned it.

Their purpose clearly has been to dominate the entire life of the nation and to impose upon it their conception of the corporate ethic. This intention has been most clearly revealed in the conduct of GE. Ralph Cordiner, who by his own account lived in complete ignorance of the most momentous conspiracy in his own organization, has displayed a decided tendency toward omniscience in public affairs. Under his regime, a 1956 GE task force (its activities ironically coinciding neatly with the price-rigging) made a whole series of recommendations about reorganizing our lives in the corporate image. It suggested that business "might subsidize a 'brain trust' of competent writers (novelists, playwrights, etc.) to begin a popular campaign of turning public attention away from the left through the source of public attitude formation (television, movies, stage, radio, novels, magazine articles, etc.)." It was important, this GE task force said, "to pick out opinion molders in each community and 'work on them.' " Just what was implied by this indelicate *work on them* phrase was made clear a little later in this sentence: "For example, if the opinion molder to be influenced is a newspaper publisher, it might be best to have him approached by one of his biggest advertisers."

Such far-reaching proposals help to highlight the basic issue: Either our society must have for its purpose those ideals for the general welfare expressed in our Constitution or it must be dominated by the concept that business is holy and that the only viable ethic is the corporate ethic. The trouble with the second alternative is that there really is no such thing as a corporate ethic. Corporations exist to do business, to make the largest possible profit, and to expect them to have morals or ethics is much like endowing a robot with human emotions. To accept the standard—and we have largely accepted it—that what the corporation does must inevitably be right is to abandon to a huge and impersonal force all human responsibility, all human criteria for conduct.

8

Where then did the blame lie? Had the executives who were sent to prison committed a major crime? And had they had a personal responsibility for their actions?

The answers are paradoxical. Yes, certainly, in view of the hundreds of millions of dollars the electrical industry was forced to disgorge, in view of pricing policies that had priced American firms right out of some contracts—and workers out of work—these executives had committed a major crime. But the issue of their personal responsibility, in the context of an age of hypocrisy and schizophrenia, is by no means so clear. If they had balked, they could well have been fired from their jobs, but they could hardly have prevented what happened. Someone else would have rigged. Should they, nevertheless, have refused? Ideally, yes, but practically can we expect all such men—given the corporate climate of the times, the climate in which they lived and operated—to be such paragons of rectitude that they become martyrs?

A discussion that focused on this issue was conducted by *Playboy* magazine, which held a symposium on the moral problems implicit in the electrical conspiracy. Senator Jacob K. Javits (R., N.Y.) came perhaps closest to a recognition of what lay at the core of the case when he compared the dilemma of the price-rigging executives, caught in their corporate collectivism, with that of Eichmann, caught in his Nazi collectivism.

"What do you do if you are ordered to do something wrong and you might get shot if you don't?" Senator Javits asked. "Well, it seems to me that in international morality it is now held that, even if you're occupying the kind of a job in which you might get shot for not carrying out orders, you still don't do it. The individual is not covered by the fact that he's ordered to do it. The executive is not going to get shot, but the principle applies. You either resign and denounce them, or you denounce them then and there and fight them. Even when, as a practical matter, you may be fired for taking this position, your ethical responsibility is to run the risk."

There can be no question that Senator Javits correctly states the theoretical case. But, as the example of George Burens showed, the fight of the individual against the massed corporate hierarchy, when that hierarchy is supreme in its power and a law unto itself, is a doomed and futile one. When even so stout a man as Burens can be crushed and beaten and forced into actions against which his ethical sense rebelled, it is folly to suppose that the vast majority of weaker men, especially the conformist types favored in corporate structures, are going to marshal the Quixotic courage to attempt it. Fundamentally, then, what the great electrical conspiracy demonstrated above all else is the need of social restraint of overweening corporate power in the mass society. Otherwise, as Robert Lynd wrote, the corporate elephant is going to go trampling at will among the chickens.

In the mass society, power must be contained and put to work for the use of all or it will become, as it is today, a lawless force setting the standards for all—the standards that only power counts, that anything is all right if everybody is doing it and you can get away with it. Individual man, to have stature, to repossess himself and be able to battle for his own ethical standards, must achieve control over the brute, impersonal forces that now dominate his life. This can be done only through a democratic government capable of grappling with reality and establishing strong controls, *not over the individual but in defense of the individual*. Otherwise we are going to live in an age of mass hypocrisy—an age in which we will pledge perfervid allegiance to myths we disown in our daily actions. Chief Justice Warren's "sea of ethics" in which alone the law can flourish cannot flourish itself in a sea of hypocrisy—a truth we are daily demonstrating in many facets of our lives and conduct.

3

The Business Ethic:
Only Profit Counts

"POLYBIUS, THE GREEK historian, summarized a nation's decline in a single sentence: 'At Carthage, nothing which results in profit is regarded as disgraceful.'"

So wrote the Rev. Raymond C. Baumhart, S.J., in a probing article in the *Harvard Business Review* in which he sought to determine whether the curse of ancient Carthage is being repeated in twentieth-century America.

In 1961, the *Business Review* sent out detailed, carefully prepared questionnaires to a broad cross section of American businessmen. Some 1700 executives, about 45 per cent of them from top-level management, responded to the questions in what is probably the most authoritative and probing analysis of the business psyche that has been made in recent years.

Significantly, in view of the comprehensive nature of the study, it reflected in striking fashion the split personality of American business—its pretense, in many instances its sincere conviction, that it stands for principles the facts show it disowns in conduct. When asked, for example, if profit is business' only motive and justification, a thumping 94 per cent of the questioned executives emphatically disagreed. Some of them wrote eloquently about the social obligations of business, its responsibility to the community at large. But once the survey got down to specifics, the real face began to show through the façade of pretense and self-delusion.

The first peep at the hidden features behind the mask came in response to the question whether businessmen would agree that "whatever is good business is good ethics." Fifteen per cent could see nothing wrong with this proposition—a discrepancy that, as Father Baumhart wrote, "prompts us to exercise caution in praising our panel's posture of so-called awareness." If a business transaction's success is the sole determination of whether it is right or wrong, this is "pretty much like that Carthaginian creed that nothing resulting in profit is disgraceful."

As Father Baumhart pointed out, there is often a wide gap between what a person says he thinks or does and what he actually thinks or does, and this gap often is exposed if the questioning is turned around, if the emphasis is put not on what an individual says *he* would do, but on what he thinks his counterparts would do. Once the *Harvard Business Review*'s questions took this complexion, it became apparent that executives who insisted on their own personal high standards didn't believe that such standards were typical of industry as a whole. Father Baumhart wrote:

The possibility that general business behavior is quite different from the personal ethical attitudes reported by our respondents is increased by their cynicism about typical executive behavior. This cynicism is illustrated by our panel's reaction to this observation by a friendly critic of business, who said:

"The American business executive tends to ignore the great ethical laws as they apply immediately to his work. He is preoccupied chiefly with gain."

Almost half of our panel agree. The same cynicism is underscored in replies to a later question about adoption of industry-wide ethical practices codes. *Four of every seven* executives believe that businessmen "would violate a code of ethics whenever they thought they could avoid detection. . . ." [Italics added]

Every industry develops its own way of doing things, its generally accepted practices. Since industry climate is an important influence on unethical behavior, how does this influence manifest itself in specific practices that are generally accepted in the industry?

To find out, we asked:

"In every industry, there are some generally accepted business practices. In your industry are there any such practices which you regard as unethical?"

Taking away those who "don't know," we have the startling finding that *four out of five executives* giving an opinion affirm the presence in their industry of *practices which are generally accepted and are also unethical!*

More than 50 per cent of the executives participating in the survey described the "one practice in their industry they would most like to see eliminated." Here, condensed, are some of the answers:

An insurance executive decried "seeking preferential treatment through lavish entertaining." The manager of a consumer-services company struck at "kickbacks to purchasing department employees." The personnel director of a Western manufacturing firm: "The idea that industry should have a few women employees on the payroll for the entertainment of prospective customers." A financial counsel: "Payoffs to government officials." The secretary of a construction firm: "Price-rigging between supplier and contractor." The vice-president of a company making industrial products: "The payment of large gifts to employees of other companies, customers, or competitors for 'favors' or information." Many struck at misleading advertising claims, and the top executive of a mass-communications firm decried "Deliberate distortion of facts."

Overtones of a society adrift in a sea of unethical practices may be sensed in these replies. The picture grew even darker when the *Harvard Business Review,* probing more deeply, asked the executives in the survey to report on situations in which their own moral codes had been brought into conflict with business practices. Here is Father Baumhart's summary of some of them:

• A controller resented "repeatedly having to act contrary to my sense of justice in order to 'please.' In upper middle management, apparently, one's own ethical will must be subordinated to that of interests 'at the top'—not only to advance, but even to be retained."

• The sales manager of a very large corporation decried "the constant every-day pressure from top management to obtain profitable business; unwritten, but well understood, is the phrase 'at any cost.' To do this requires every conceivable dirty trick."

· A high-salaried assistant manager was worried because "my management has, in effect, required that I go along with certain anti-trust violations involving restraint of trade."

· Another executive wrote: "As controller, I prepared a P & L statement which showed a loss. An executive vice-president tried to force me to falsify the statement to show a profit in order to present it to a bank for a line of credit. I refused, and was fired on the spot."

· A young engineer declared that he was "asked to present 'edited' results of a reliability study; I refused, and nearly got fired. I refused to defraud the customer, so they had others do it."

Self-revealed in such voluntary answers is the portrait of a business society that has turned its back, to a great degree at least, on all principles of moral conduct. The Harvard survey did turn up instances of completely ethical firms, of businessmen who refused to hire call girls for customers and balked at the bribe and the kickback; but the prevailing climate of American business seems to have been expressed in the cynicism exhibited by the majority of the 1700 executives surveyed about their own business world. When four out of every seven executives believe businessmen would violate a code of ethics whenever they thought they could escape detection, when an overwhelming four out of five affirm the existence in their industries of "practices which are generally accepted and are also unethical," there can be little question that a nation so swayed by business as ours faces a grave moral crisis.

I

In a world dominated by the corporate balance sheet and dedicated to the proposition that sales and profits must grow even mightier, there is no lure like the oldest lure known to humankind —sex. Sex sells everything from multimillion-dollar defense contracts in the climate of the warfare state to the latest products of the garment center and kitchen appliances and magazine advertising. Repeated scandals during the past decade have temporarily shocked and titillated the public with their disclosures that, on many levels of business, prostitution has become almost a way of life.

One of the best-detailed of these exposés came in the mid-1950s when federal agencies cast a dubious eye on the activities of a buxom, stylish, Polish import by the name of Nella Bogart. Curvaceous Nella, it turned out, was a high-level call girl for big business; she was so expert at entertaining her customers that, in bursts of gratitude, they sometimes doubled and trebled their orders for electrical appliances. Nella herself testified with considerable pride how she became so adept at working visiting salesmen up to larger orders that she really considered herself not a prostitute but an executive-suite saleslady.

The firm in whose cause she labored so lustily was the General Electric Supply Co., of Newark, New Jersey. As mighty GE hastened to point out, this was an entirely separate corporate entity of whose bedroom activities in pursuit of the fatter contract the GE hierarchy could have had no possible knowledge. There was, however, no such ignorance on the customer-man's level, where so much of the buying and distribution is done, for court testimony showed that quite a number of gentlemen somehow got the idea that Nella went with the purchase of a suitable quantity of refrigerators. It was well established that Nella had put her charms at the service of GE Supply in apartments in New York; and on at least one unfortunate occasion (the event that led to her downfall, since it involved interstate trafficking in sex) she and a couple of other girls similarly endowed and similarly available had traveled to Newark to perform at an electrical dealers' convention, an affair that turned out to be such a Bacchanalia that fastidious Nella, according to her own account, quit the premises in disgust and fled by taxi back to the purer air of Manhattan.

The sexy sales techniques of Nella Bogart attracted some bold headlines in the press at the time but left unanswered the key questions: Was Nella Bogart an exception to the rule or the example that illustrates the rule?

In January 1959, Edward R. Murrow attempted to give the answer in a sensational CBS radio documentary on the state of the world's oldest profession. The program turned a searching spotlight on the call-girls-for-big-business routine. Several of the girls who had given their all in the cause of free enterprise told their first-person stories in taped interviews, and across the nation the Murrow radio exposé raised a great if temporary furor.

To hear the shocked masters of the executive suite and to read the earnest moralists of the press, one might have gathered the erroneous impression that Murrow had traduced motherhood by indulging in a bit of sensationalism about practices that could not possibly exist in the dimensions in which he pictured them. One might have thought, listening to the clamor, that Murrow had all by himself raised the issue for the first time, but actually every "disclosure" on the program had been a matter of fairly common knowledge. What was new was that it had been said bluntly on a nationwide radio hookup.

The entire flap encouraged *Advertising Age* to look at the record, and it recalled that, five years earlier, Vincent F. Sullivan, national advertising manager of the New York *Daily News,* had published a book, *How To Sell Your Way into the Big Money*. Sullivan had devoted an entire chapter to a description of how the call girl aids the big sell. Sullivan decried the practice and advised his readers to abjure it, but he left no doubt that some mighty important persons indeed were being catered to in very exclusive fashion. He described one well-appointed, twelve-room duplex apartment on "New York's snooty Central Park West" where a motor magnate from Detroit, a visiting nabob from Hollywood or any comparable emperor of business might present himself for an evening's erotic entertainment.

"It is known on Ad Row," Sullivan wrote, "that complete satisfaction is to be found from the moment the finger touches the doorbell chimes."

He explained that there were no single-admission tickets to this emporium of pleasure. There were only season passes, and a season's pass came high, being price-tagged at about $250,000 worth of advertising.

"This gilded palace of pleasure is maintained by the sales organization handling the advertising of a group of magazines that you probably read in your own living room weekly or monthly. As a salesman for this organization, the whorehouse is the final sales weapon. And it invariably produces the contract, too! . . .

"This type of selling is known in the sales profession as whore-house selling, and it is not at all uncommon. There are several apartments around New York City devoted exclusively to just one type of client—your client! Further, the entire picture of selling is complicated by a number of immoral and unethical practices where large orders are involved."

When *Advertising Age* took Sullivan to task editorially for writing such nasty things about the profession, the author fired back with a letter in which he offered a free demonstration.

"It is inconceivable to me," Sullivan said, "that your editorial writer is so naïve as to think that there are no heavy expense accounts, and sex, and bribes in the selling profession. Are we to keep such subjects hidden and buried? . . .

"It would be my suggestion that when your editorial writer is next in New York he telephone my offices. . . . I will take him to two 'gilded palaces of pleasure' on Central Park West, one, more elaborate, on Central Park South and three in the Sutton Place area of New York City. In these places, I am quite certain he will meet a number of his friends in the advertising and selling business."

And that, so far as the record goes, seems to have ended *that*.

Even more explicit were some of the details provided by sociologist Sara Harris in an article on "big-time procurers in gray flannel suits" in *Cavalier*. So-called "public relations executives," she found, were drawing fat salaries to pander to the sadistic tastes of certain buyers and to keep a fresh supply of young, teen-age girls flowing to the prostitution marts. Police vice squads' efforts to halt this traffic, she wrote, were half-hearted and inept.

". . . some big people might just be caught and that would not be good for our national morale," she jibed. "So police vice squads, instead of going after big business, lay their nets for poor unattached prostitutes, as easy to catch as fish in a stocked pool. They fill the jails with these derelicts and give the public the impression that they are controlling prostitution.

"In the meantime, big business protects its rich, successful prostitutes and goes blatantly on recruiting new ones."

Miss Harris gave this description of the typical big-business procurer—"a man in his 30s or early 40s, wholesome-seeming, good-looking, well-educated. He is substantial and respected in his community," married to a nice wife and with children of his own. His salary ranges between $10,000 and $20,000 a year, and the very nature of his calling makes him "a man who has his bosses' constant ear." And because he has, there are "ample opportunities for promotion."

Miss Harris quoted some of these procurers directly. One, a public relations expert for a New York textile house, told her: "I maintain a long list of call girls—white, Negro, Chinese." After he had fixed up a big buyer with one of these, the "public relations" man said, the buyer was so grateful he "placed a bigger order than the boss expected, much bigger. So . . . I got a beauty of a bonus."

Another executive of a big business firm told Miss Harris he got $500 and continued to receive expensive presents from "a sadist" who "almost killed one girl on my list." This particular procurer bragged: "And you know, he wouldn't buy from any firm but mine. He's not the only one I've got where I want him."

Miss Harris' researches turned up all kinds of specialists in the art of procuring. One described the technique of furnishing high-school girls for middle-aged buyers. Another told of staging obscene parties. A third mentioned importing movie starlets from Hollywood to New York for a night of prostitution.

"Of course, our clients have to be mighty big fish for us to go to such trouble for them," he added, "but it's always paid us off when we have."

Summarizing her impressions, Miss Harris wrote that such procurers were not unusual in big business, and she added:

"Here is the fact—like it or not: Big business and prostitution are intertwined."

The spicy Murrow–Harris charges led labor leaders to needle Washington officialdom about such unethical goings-on. After the Murrow broadcast, A. J. Hayes, chairman of the AFL–CIO ethical practices committee, urged the Senate rackets committee to investigate this morass of corruption. Committee spokesmen, giving the stock answer of officials whose souls are not inspired with crusading fervor, said the matter would be "studied."

It was still being "studied" some months later when Miss Harris added her firsthand observations. The publication *Labor* checked with the committee again to see what was happening. The spokesman acknowledged he had read Miss Harris' article, said the "study" was continuing, confessed nothing much was likely to be done.

"This is a purely management situation," he said. "Everybody knows it's being done, and on a big scale, and there's no excuse in the world for it."

But, he explained, call-girl hiring was a bit outside the purview of the labor-management relations problems with which the committee had been appointed to deal. Perhaps Internal Revenue could tackle the issue since it would be clearly illegal for big corporations to claim call girls' fees as legitimate business expenses. So *Labor* queried Internal Revenue. Would any great moral crackdown be launched?

"We would love to," an IRS spokesman replied, "but we don't have the staff. We cannot specialize in one area."

So prostitution gets the green light rather than the red in the upper strata of the corrupt society.

2

In a corporate world that on many fronts seems to be living up to the Carthaginian adage that "nothing which results in profit is regarded as disgraceful," the knifing and in-fighting among Organization Men—and between organizations for one another's secrets—achieves a venomous subtlety that would have done credit to conspirators at the court of Caligula. A business magazine, *Modern Office Procedures,* conducted a survey that reflected the ethics of life in the executive suite. It asked its readers: "Is it possible for a man to move up through the ranks of management solely by honest, decent methods?" An overwhelming majority answered "No!"

The internecine warfare to cut the throats of potential rivals utilizes sex, liquor, sabotage, espionage. No method is too low, no stratagem too devious. Norman Jaspan, a New York management consultant who has built a multimillion-dollar business largely on his skill in ferreting out embezzlers, has pointed out time and again that the atmosphere in the executive suite inevitably seeps down and affects all the lower levels of business. No single facet of top-level conduct registers with greater impact than the spectacle of bosses stabbing each other in the back with gangland professionalism. Yet, as Jaspan has noted, such back-stabbing and throat-cutting comprise "a rite being practiced by thousands of executives in hundreds of businesses."

So prevalent is the rite that *The Wall Street Journal* on one occasion became concerned and conducted a survey among businessmen on this ungentlemanly mayhem. In interviews with fifty executives in twelve cities, it discovered some startling examples of the ruses that have been used to kick scrambling rivals off the promotional ladder. The trickery ranged from spiking a rival's drink just before an important meeting (thus guaranteeing that he would disgrace himself before his bosses) to more complicated and really Machiavellian plotting.

The vice-president of one eastern corporation, sensing a rival for power in a rising new executive, went to the trouble of plugging the carburetor of his rival's automobile. This made the new man embarrassingly late for his first executive meeting and started him off under the most unfavorable auspices. In another instance, an elevator-company executive waited for a colleague's pet project to flop; then he submitted to his boss a file of memos—all carefully back-dated, of course—to indicate that he, in his wisdom, had been opposed to the venture from the outset. Almost as telling as these examples was the unconsciously revealing remark of the executive of a southwestern oil company. This man, upholding the corporate image, denied stanchly that there was any throat-cutting in his business; then, having put the dutiful disclaimer in the record, he turned around and commented ruefully, "Of course, some people in this company will do just anything to get ahead."

This attitude that a man is justified in doing "just anything to get ahead" spells, of course, the death knell of ethics. Such an atmosphere, as Jaspan has noted, "forms a natural breeding ground for white-collar crime. Its chief elements consist of trickery, a venomous subtlety and a complete lack of ethics."

All three elements were illustrated by a case that tied together back-stabbing in the executive suite and industrial espionage—a new, multimillion-dollar postwar industry. In this case, three partners were sharing in the profits of a multimillion-dollar business. One was a fine business executive, well liked and capable, a credit to the firm. The other two partners had no reason to be dissatisfied with him except one: if he could be in some way eliminated, the profits could be split two ways instead of three.

This was sufficient motivation. The two conspiring partners adopted a tactic in common use today; they hired detectives to "get" something on the good friend and colleague whose head they were seeking. The plotters had no idea what they might get, and frankly they didn't care: almost anything that they could use for leverage would suit their unscrupulous purposes. The hired investigators, of course, had no scruples either. They were simply doing a job that they were being paid to do, weren't they? And in a world in which only cash talks, what could be wrong with that?

With clear consciences, then, the hired detectives promptly wiretapped the unsuspecting victim's home and office phones. The result was a great disappointment. No nefarious and usable tidbit of information came over the wires. The conspirators were confronted with the horrible possibility that their partner might indeed be so clean they could get nothing on him; and, in desperation, they instructed the detectives to take the final step—to bug their pal's own private office.

Nothing in this age of electronic gadgetry could be easier. A minute wall-socket microphone was quickly installed, and this faithfully monitored every conversation held in the supposed privacy of the office. So, to the listening ears of the detectives, there came a volume of chitchat between the executive and his private secretary. The pair, the wall microphone revealed, were in the habit of staying late at the office several nights a week—and it wasn't just business that detained them.

Tape recorders kept a permanent record of the details of this executive-suite dalliance as revealed by the wall microphone, and with this kind of evidence in their possession the conspiratorial partners moved in for the kill. In a direct confrontation, they dropped the mask of friendship and gave their old buddy a fateful choice.

"Resign at once," they told him in effect, "or we'll play these records for your wife and children."

He resigned.

The downfall of the amorous executive, accomplished by the unscrupulous use of sophisticated modern detective devices, was typical in purpose and method of two worlds of business chicanery —the inner world of executive-suite treachery and the outer world in which the corporate gods recognize no scruple in the pursuit of profit. The extent of the shady dealings in this modern business jungle is demonstrated by the fantastic growth of a new postwar industry; industrial espionage—IE, as business calls it. IE today furnishes a fine livelihood to literally thousands of detectives bent on filching industrial secrets at any cost—an activity that has led inevitably to the formation of an opposing army of counterespionage specialists intent on thwarting their designs. So important has this new undercover activity in the world of business become that the counteragents have formed an organization, the American Society for Industrial Security, and when it held a convention late in 1962, it boasted some 2490 members from chapters in 58 cities.

In this new warfare between the forces of IE and counter-IE, no trick is considered too low; nothing that succeeds is beyond the pale of ethics. Seductive Mata Haris are employed to lure key executives into indiscretions—and indiscreet confidences. Knowledgeable engineers and office personnel are bribed. Even police and inspectors are corrupted to help IE operatives penetrate plant security screens. The only standard that has validity is: Does the method employed succeed? If it does, the wholesale corruption to which it contributes does not matter.

One New York agent who has been touted as the nation's No. 1 industrial spy justifies his activities in these words: "Espionage is a part of every big business, everybody does it. I just do it better than anyone else."

This operative brags that he never uses disguises—and that he can get into virtually any industrial plant in the nation on which he wishes to spy. His most successful tactic is a gem of simplicity. He finds a susceptible policeman or inspector, slips him a bribe, and then, escorted by this guardian of authority, he walks through plant gates on phony, trumped-up investigative tours.

There was the case of a midwest factory that had placed a new productive device in operation. The detective's big-business client wanted to learn the secret. Though the midwest plant had set up a security screen to protect its device, this was no proof against the IE operative's favorite tactic. He simply made contact with an obliging police officer, who informed plant guards that the law was searching for a robbery suspect believed to be employed inside the plant. The policeman, naturally, had to make a search, and he had to take with him the one man alive who could identify the suspect—the IE operative, of course. This masterful bit of deception worked like a charm. When the search for the non-existent "robbery suspect" ended, the private eye for big business had all the information he needed to know about the midwest plant's secret device.

On another occasion, posing as the plainclothes partner of a Long Island detective, the IE undercover agent searched a closely guarded plant for "a prowler." Chuckling about it afterwards, he commented: "There was no prowler in there, but plenty of information."

In a society in which the profit motive reigns supreme, no ethical scruples count when weighed in the scales against the potential profits from industrial theft. Some $20 billion annually is being spent on research, and the new drugs, the new products created by that research are worth literally millions of dollars to their discoverers. No pirate of old looting a Spanish galleon ever had such fortune at his fingertips, and so big-business piracy roars ahead unchecked, a relatively new and corruptive force in American life. With rewards so enormous for the complaisant conscience, the means that are employed to achieve the end of profit frequently approach the fantastic.

There was, for example, the multimillion-dollar eastern corporation that held a vital board of directors' meeting in the security of the conference room in its new, ultramodern office building. The chairman of the board outlined top-secret plans for the firm's future. So sensitive were the programs discussed that, after the meeting, the chairman personally walked around the conference table, picking up the descriptive papers that had been placed before each director, confiscating even the penciled notes each had made during the discussion.

"Everything we have spoken about here today must be carried in our heads," the chairman said. "All your papers, reports, and personal notes will be locked in the safe."

Nothing, it would seem, could be more secret, more secure; yet every word the board chairman had spoken had already taken wing to a rival.

On the roof of an apartment building half a block away stood a chunky man surrounded by a most intriguing collection of paraphernalia. He had a pair of binoculars mounted on a tripod, and the binoculars were trained on the broad glass expanse of the conference room in which the big corporation's directors were meeting. At the solitary observer's feet the spools of a tape recorder whirred away, and about his neck was draped a microphone. The chunky rooftop spy was totally deaf, but on this day, for his purposes, this handicap was a positive advantage. Because of it, he had become an expert lip-reader; and so, all the time the board chairman had been discussing his firm's most secret plans, the rooftop watcher had been reading his lips and dictating every word onto the slowly revolving tape of the recorder.

The prevalence of such fantastic long-range spying is perhaps best illustrated by the experience of Detroit, the Motor City. New-model designs have long been one of the most closely guarded automotive secrets, and the great auto firms have indulged for decades in the game of spying on each other. Traditionally, every scrap of leaked market news has been analyzed for the clues it might furnish as to what is in the mind of the opposition, and it has been standard practice to photograph any suspicious-looking new cars that might be spotted on the road in the hope of catching the prototype of some new model on a test cruise. These, however, were relatively Victorian methods compared to the kind of espionage that became the custom during the 1950s.

One manufacturer discovered that a rival had installed long-range telescopes and cameras on a hill overlooking its test site. Another lost all its secrets when a low-flying airplane photographed its new models on its testing grounds. So sensitive did the Motor City become to the stepped-up tempo of espionage that General Motors, in constructing its new multimillion-dollar technical center at Warren, Michigan, equipped it with devices that automatically draw curtains over the windows of its planning room when an airplane approaches. At the same time an alarm warns outdoor workers to get any exposed new models under cover.

Sometimes the effects of rampant industrial espionage are utterly calamitous for the victim. Typical was the experience of a chemical concern on the verge of a new and exciting discovery. The president discussed the progress of the research with his two vice-presidents only in the security of his own office. He refused to talk about the new development on the telephone, and he repeatedly warned his assistants not to let a word leak out until the research had been completed and a patent obtained. Everyone with intimate knowledge of the new process was so careful and so circumspect that it seemed impossible vital details could be leaked; yet, a few months later, when the firm's program had achieved final success and it applied for a patent, it discovered that it was faced with disaster. A large competitor had already patented the process.

What had happened was this: the huge competitor had hired an IE operative who had discovered that the president of the chemical concern was getting some new office furniture. Making a deal with the deliverymen, he managed to insert into the well-padded bottom of the executive's desk chair a tiny portable transmitter, no larger than a pack of cigarettes; and this transmitter, with its long-life batteries, had relayed every conversation held in the office to a hotel room a block away, where it had all been taken down on tape.

This bit of electronic thievery destroyed the smaller concern. It had invested so much in its key bit of research, it had depended so heavily upon it, that when it was beaten to the patent, its financial outlook became dreary, and within six months it was swallowed by the firm that had filched its secrets and its president was out of a job. Only the successful corporate thief and its IE operative could afford to chuckle.

"I had counted that transmitter lost," the IE man later recalled in recounting his coup, "and I had charged it to my client. But when he took over the other company, he got the furnishings, too, and I got it back."

In a business world in which the mightiest forces indulge in this kind of chicanery, it is inevitable that employees at the bottom and all along the middle rungs of the ladder will reach the conclusion that they are committing no truly heinous offense if they emulate the practitioners at the top. Virtually every IE operative in the business in his more candid moments will confide that it's a cinch to bribe the telephone operator, a file clerk, a chemist, or an engineer. For the right kind of cash, or sometimes the promise of a lush job, the kind of detailed information that can flit right out of a research file is amazing. And the rewards for such thievery run high into the millions.

Illustrative of the size of the stakes was the secret-stealing career of Dr. Robert S. Aries, a brilliant man in his midforties whom a federal court judged in late November 1964 to have been responsible for the theft of $21,275,499 worth of industrial secrets. The decision that placed this price tag on Dr. Aries' formula-filching came after a three-year court battle that left the scientist himself relatively unscathed. He had skipped off to Paris and the

French Riviera, where, by all accounts, he was believed to be living extremely well and suffering no special pangs of remorse.

Chemical engineer, economist, scholar, author, and teacher, Dr. Aries' achievements filled a solid five inches of type in *Who's Who* before the storm about his activities as a patent-snatcher broke in the press in November 1961. Until that time, he had been known as the head of R. S. Aries & Associates, Inc., of Stamford, Connecticut; as the author of several books; as a one-time teacher at Brooklyn Polytechnic Institute and a lecturer at the University of Geneva; as a consultant to major banks and corporations, to the U.S. Army and Navy and, indeed, to virtually the entire federal government.

Yet, all the time, behind this distinguished front, Dr. Aries, with the obliging help of corrupted office workers, had been looting the files of major corporations of the details of some of their most rewarding new research. Or so at least a flock of criminal and civil actions were to allege and a federal court ultimately to maintain.

One of the loudest howls of anguish went up from Merck & Co., Inc., the huge Rahway, New Jersey, pharmaceutical manufacturer. Merck had sunk some $1.5 million into research for a new compound that would eliminate coccidiosis, a poultry disease. Merck estimated that its new drug would enable it to tap a $25-million market; but, before it could get around to the tapping, it received a rude shock. Merck had been negotiating to buy a French chemical company, and it discovered that one of the prize patents of this company was a formula for a drug to fight coccidiosis.

Discovery led to discovery, and soon Merck learned not only that the French drug matched its own in all specific details, but also that the research and formula had been purchased from Dr. Aries. The French firm supplied Merck with the basic research papers Dr. Aries had furnished, and Merck later charged these papers matched word for word, comma for comma, paragraph for paragraph the research material in its own files. Convinced of the theft, Merck turned its eyes inward and searched its own organization for the employee who had supplied Dr. Aries the vital data.

It discovered him, it says, but it kept him under wraps as a "sympathetic witness" in the event Dr. Aries should ultimately be extradited and brought to trial.

The Merck experience matched in sad particulars the misfortunes that overtook two other American companies. Rohm & Haas, a major chemical concern, charged that Dr. Aries had "prevailed upon" one of its chemical engineers to rifle technical files and pass along to him vital information on "unique products," specifically new additives to improve the action of lubricating oils. In similar fashion, according to the Sprague Electric Co. of North Adams, Massachusetts, Dr. Aries had obtained the details of an electric device it had made from the rare metal tantalum for use in computers.

Before action could be taken on these revelations, Dr. Aries forsook America for France, leaving his wife and two daughters behind him. Two federal grand juries indicted him for his various piracies; and, though he was arrested in Switzerland, he was quickly released on bail and extradition proceedings hit one snag after another. More productive was a civil action brought by the victimized companies both to establish damages and to get injunctions to keep Dr. Aries' patents from being used on the American market. In deciding this suit, Federal Judge M. Joseph Blumenfeld in New Haven, Connecticut, ruled that Dr. Aries' depredations had cost Sprague Electric $8,600,000, Merck $6,-637,499, and Rohm & Haas $6,038,000.

Such were the financial ruins left by the trail of just one industrial pirate. For industry as a whole, such individual disasters, huge though they may be, do little more than hint at the magnitude of the evil.

"Industrial spying and preoccupation with moves and countermoves against a single large competitor is debilitating the creative research originality of many business firms," Harvey Smith, market research manager for the Vulcan Materials Company, warned the twelfth annual marketing conference of the National Industrial Conference Board in late 1964. ". . . Funds normally devoted to creative marketing and product research are diverting to the expensive hire of underground agents. . . ."

The scope of the practice was reflected in the tools of the industrial spy, he said, citing helicopters, matchbox cameras, long-range telescopes, small transmitters, duct-hidden TV cameras, parabolic microphones, contact bugs, duplicated office keys, wastebasket-refuse purchase, bribery, blackmail, theft. Smith urged business to recognize the Golden Rule and to discontinue rewarding employees for achievements based on unethical approaches.

Such a change in attitude would almost automatically abolish the flourishing world of IE, and there are, of course, few signs that this will happen. IE continues to prosper; its very health is indicative of the steady erosion of human values it fosters.

The depths to which the human species will stoop in this anything-goes world of IE are perhaps best illustrated by some of the cases in the files of Harvey G. Wolfe, a Los Angeles investigator. Wolfe, a wartime agent in the Army's Counter-Intelligence Corps, belongs to the school of ethical private eyes. He will not undertake industrial espionage, but confines himself to the role of protecting businesses from those trying to filch their secrets. In this capacity, he has become familiar with every scurvy trick to which the ingenious IE agent resorts.

In planning a *coup,* IE agents study the dossier of their target minutely. If he's an executive, Wolfe says, "They find out whether he likes blondes or brunettes. What kind of liquor the man drinks. And the agent—blonde or brunette—is told to be sure she has plenty of it when she entertains him. She's told to be friendly—make herself attractive, and develop this man."

One oil-company executive, subjected to thorough advance scouting in this fashion, fell unsuspecting into a carefully stage-managed trap. The setting was a lonely road; the props a racy sports car, a flat tire—and a beautiful girl, fashioned and tailored to the executive's taste, standing helplessly beside it. Before the executive had stopped playing the gallant gentleman to a damsel in distress, he was hooked—and his company's secrets were ready to take wing into the ears of a competitor.

Of all Wolfe's cases, one stands out unforgettably in his mind. The head of a large construction firm was being constantly underbid by a competitor. If he bid $300,000 on a project, his rival bid $285,000; if his figure was $100,000, his rival's would be $95,000. This happened so often and the construction firm lost so much business that the executive became certain the close bidding pattern could not be a coincidence; there had to be a leak.

Wolfe was called in, and he assigned one of his best agents to the case. The investigator worked diligently for weeks. Every suspect person and situation in the construction firm's setup was checked out thoroughly—and cleared. There was no leak, yet there had to be a leak. Baffled, the investigator reported to Wolfe: "We've investigated everybody but our client."

Reluctant though he was, Wolfe decided they had no choice; they would have to bug the home of the man who had hired him.

"The client had a beautiful two-story Tudor-type home," Wolfe later recalled. "We managed to get four of our miniature broadcasting stations into the house. We found what we wanted."

The electronic eavesdroppers revealed that, before every job on which he bid, the construction man discussed his problem with his wife. She would ask him, casually of course, what his bid was going to be. Naturally he told her.

"We had recordings of five such instances, but we wanted more before going to the client," Wolfe said. "We put a tail on the wife —twenty-four hours a day."

It wasn't long before the husband left town on a business trip. The wife dutifully drove him to the airport, kissed him good-by. Then she drove to a hotel and met a man—her husband's competitor. Watching the pair, Wolfe's detectives established that every time the husband left home his wife and his competitor spent the time playing house together.

Wolfe hesitated to tell the husband of his sordid discovery, but of course he had to.

"We showed him the movies and played the recordings," Wolfe said.

He was prepared, he acknowledged, for almost any kind of violent reaction—any kind of reaction except the one he got. The cuckolded husband watched the movies, listened to the sound effects, grunted, and said "Well, I guess we plugged that leak, didn't we?"

Then he wrote out a check for Wolfe—and included in it a fat bonus.

3

"The goal of a business corporation is to make a profit. . . .

". . . *the only goal* of a business corporation is to make a profit. . . .

". . . *more fully,* the only goal of a business corporation is to make *the maximum possible profit.* . . .

"*Completely,* the only goal of a business corporation is to make the maximum possible profit *over a long period.*" (Italics added)

Gaylord A. Freeman, Jr., vice-president of the First National Bank of Chicago, stated the business ethic in these blunt terms in a speech before the Installment Lending Conference of the Illinois Bankers Association in October 1958. In so doing, he said scornfully that bankers and businessmen had been so "buffeted" by the New Deal and its offshoot philosophies that they had been "timorous" about speaking the truth. But the time for such timidity was past. Profit was the truth, and it should be bluntly acknowledged.

In drawing the issue in these terms, banker Freeman put in clear perspective the choice that, in truth, confronts the mass industrial society of the twentieth century. It is a choice of goals, of purposes and, because it is, it is inevitably also a choice of methods. Shall the goal, the only recognized and valid goal, be the private profit of the huge organizations that almost alone have captured and arrogated to themselves the means and the power to produce and compete? Or must the private profit of such industrial satrapies be subordinated to social goals in the mass society—to the actual needs of that society and the benefit of the vast majority of its members?

There can be no question that Freeman correctly stated the cardinal tenets, whether openly acknowledged or not, that today form the basis of business philosophy, and few would argue against the proposition that it is this business ethic, if it can be called that, which dominates American life. Profit—"the maximum possible profit," "over a long period"—was the underlying motivation of the great electrical conspiracy. The electrical conspirators were by no means alone. When morals and ethics become related to this supreme motif, any deed becomes possible, and virtually no deed becomes repugnant. Prostitution labors for the bigger sell. The individual throat-cutting on the executive ladder is exculpated (for who can blame any man, in this ethic, for trying to get ahead?), and the dirtiest cloak-and-dagger tricks of industrial espionage are sanctioned in the holy cause of the greater profit to which virtually everyone has pledged allegiance with heart and mind. The inevitable result is the shoddy society—a society of falsely stimulated consumption, of planned obsolescence, of high debt and wanton waste.

Business Week in two articles in 1956 branded our society with the slogans that are its trademark. This magazine, one of the bibles of the business world, proclaimed that "it looks as though all of our business forces are bent on getting everyone" to participate in an endless tail-chasing carnival to "Borrow. Spend. Buy. Waste. Want."

The Ben Franklin-like precepts, those pithy sayings that expressed the moral outlook and tone of American society for two centuries, no longer have validity. "Neither a borrower nor a lender be. . . . Waste not, want not. . . . A penny saved is a penny earned. . . . A fool and his money are soon parted." To mouth such philosophy today is to cause laughter. A government economist, accurately appraising our times, startled the *Christian Science Monitor* with the frank acknowledgment: "If everybody in this country started to save, America would go broke."

It would go broke because the only way the present system of ever-greater production for ever-greater maximum profit can be maintained forever (if it can) is to stretch all the sinews of the country in a rat race of spending and consumption that has little relation to actual needs and wants. This means that to buy in copious quantities we must ever borrow; it means, too, that products must be made not the best way they can be made, not to last, because if they lasted, we would not want, we would not borrow, we would not buy, we would not spend.

Business Week, faithful to the business philosophy it represents, could see nothing reprehensible in these developments. On the contrary, with the kind of financial nearsightedness that afflicts the business community, it held up, to what it obviously believed would be the admiring gaze of all, those positive beauties it had discovered in the meretricious society.

General Motors, *Business Week* wrote admiringly, had "adopted the annual model change, helping to establish the auto industry's renowned principle of 'planned obsolescence.'" Renowned principle, yet! Henry Ford, according to *Business Week,* had not been with it. He had been "the archetype of the production man," and he had believed in his simplicity that it was his job to make a better car at progressively lower prices as sales increased—a car that the buyer might use for years and years until it wore out and needed replacement. This antiquated philosophy of Henry Ford would make the man a positive national menace today; for the essence of the struggle now is not to acquire the industrial capacity and the skills to meet the needs of a growing population and country, but to dispose of the virtually limitless production the technological revolution of the twentieth century makes possible. Under the compulsion of the ever-greater profit motive, this boundless productivity can be consumed in only one way—by making not the better product that will last but the shoddy product that will quickly wear out and have to be replaced. So not Henry Ford, with a production man's simple faith in creating and achieving, becomes the prototype of our age, but General Motors, which ingeniously invented the "planned obsolescence" that keeps us coming back into the market for a new car every two or three years.

The merry-go-round is financed by ever-mounting debt. Paradoxically, the business community, which becomes almost paranoid at the thought of governmental debt, exercises all its ingenuity to pile up the load of individual debt, to make credit for the consumer easier, longer-termed and more alluring. This double standard most probably has a very simple explanation. A larger and more powerful government might come in time to regulate, to temper the excesses of business, and so any governmental spending outside of the colossal billions poured into the arms race (a delightful stimulant to the economy in a society of waste because military weapons become so quickly obsolescent and must be perpetually renewed) is *per se* bad. But consumer spending, even though it represents on many occasions crushing individual debt and tragedy, must be stimulated at all costs because otherwise, in this world of the new technology, the ever-greater profit motive would collapse and cease to be a generating force in our economy.

All recent assessments of the American scene agree that we have cut loose from the Puritanical, thrift-and-hard-work morality of our ancestors and that we are now embarked on a carnival of "borrow, spend, buy, waste, want" whose end no man can foresee. "Time has wiped away the Puritan connotations of immorality in debt and godliness in thrift," *Newsweek* proclaimed in January 1962. It found that, at the end of 1961, U.S. consumers were in debt some $290 billion. This included $175 billion in home-mortgage debt, some $43.5 billion due on installment purchases and loans (about $18 billion on automobiles alone), and some $13.5 billion for charge accounts, medical bills, and single-payment loans. "Debt . . . ," *Newsweek* found, "has been transformed from stigma to status symbol, from a last resort of people in need to an entrée to the good, material things of life." Today, *Newsweek* declared, the once-suspect " 'debtor class' has become the Great American Debtor, the very bulwark of the economy and the creator of the U.S. standard of living."

But "credit gone wild," *Newsweek* added, "can breed immorality and harm." It cited some examples.

An Indianapolis aeronautical engineer tried to keep a wife and three children, maintain a home in the suburbs and enjoy all the delights of modern technology on a salary of $7500 a year. He took out twelve consecutive loans to pay for a variety of merchandise and gadgets, including five new cars. He owed money on cars he no longer owned and interest on money borrowed to pay interest on other borrowings. He wound up $80,000 in debt, with cash assets of just 22 cents—and then was packed off to a state mental hospital. "Whether his mental troubles were the cause or the effect of his money troubles is not known—least of all by the merchants who kept extending him credit," *Newsweek* concluded.

In Atlanta, a $100-a-week store clerk became saddled with monthly payments of $78 for a car, $44 for a color TV set, $50 for furniture, $93 for his house, $12 for a watch, and $11 for toys. He had left only $28 a week on which actually he could live. "He finally just walked off one day and left the whole damned shooting match," his employer told *Newsweek*. "He was just an old country boy who came up here and everybody told him he could buy anything on credit, so he bought."

Such individual tragedies have become commonplace in American society. They represent, of course, the wild excesses, not the norm. But they typify the atmosphere in a nation torn loose from old moorings and careening on a reckless course, trying to shore up its god of maximum private profit in a technological world whose excess capacity makes profit not a generating virtue but a vice. To reconcile the irreconcilable, worth must be sacrificed. Only built-in obsolescence can keep all the wheels furiously spinning on maximum-profit terms.

The automobile industry, one of the bellwethers of the American economy, is a prize example. What American manufacturer could advertise, as does Volkswagen, that it has kept the same body design for some twenty years—that all its improvements have been made under the hood? Or like Volvo that its cars are built to last an average of ten to fourteen years? No American manufacturer, even with the leeway allowed by advertising's notorious flexibility with truth, could make such claims, and the reason they cannot is notorious. They are not building for wear and worth.

In Detroit a couple of years ago, I was talking to an executive of Walter Reuther's United Automobile Workers Union. I was inveighing against the $3000-and-up price tag on most new cars and said I couldn't understand how the industry could find enough suckers to market cars by the millions when, almost as soon as one was paid for on thirty-six-month credit terms, it was generally so worn out another had to be purchased in an endless round of perpetual buying and perpetual debt. My companion shook his head and acknowledged that the worst thing about the whole unending sequence was that cars "aren't made to wear; they're made for obsolescence."

James Carey, head of the International Union of Electrical Workers, has charged repeatedly that the electrical cartel has downgraded the electric-light bulb in its manufacturing process to insure that it will expire after relatively limited use and will need regular, periodic replacement. Similarly, the industry has built obsolescence into other products. Talk to repairmen and they will shake their heads and tell you that, while obsolescence has been enshrined in American business philosophy for years, it really came into its own as an all-pervasive way of life about 1954–1955. Products built after that are far less substantial in construction, many repairmen insist. "There's no metal in them," they will say.

On one occasion, I became personally incensed because an electric dishwasher, a product of one of the most famous appliance manufacturers, collapsed and needed repairs after two years of use. Among other items, it needed an entire new pump, without which a dishwasher is not much good, and by the time I finished paying for repairs, I had put out about one-third as much as I had paid for the new machine just two years previously. The appliance firm's own repair specialist listened to my gripe, then tried to reassure me.

"Oh, this is nothing," he said. "You're really lucky. We get a lot of machines worse than this."

"When they've been used only two years?" I asked.

"Oh, sure," he said. "You should see what some of the other big firms put out. Our stuff is good by comparison."

He explained that there was a certain fraternity in the repair business. He and some of the boys working for other big appliance firms sometimes got together. "We swap shop talk," my cheerful repairman said, "and you should hear some of the tales the other fellows tell. They have a lot more trouble than we do." So I was supposed to feel fortunate that I had his firm's two-year-old champ in my kitchen—but I didn't.

Evidently, I have a lot of company in my reaction, for Sylvia Porter, whose specialty is writing about the economic scene, reported in one of her syndicated columns:

"Planned obsolescence is coming in for increasingly tough, rough criticism, open disdain. *A practice which is an integral part of the American economy* is being condemned as manipulated waste by a majority even of its leading practitioners." (Italics added)

She reported that *Printers Ink,* an advertising trade journal, had made a survey of marketing leaders in the nation. Sixty per cent believed planned obsolescence wasteful and contrary to the consumer's and the nation's interest, and 65 per cent saw it as "somewhat harmful" or "very harmful." On the other hand, one-third of those interviewed still defended planned obsolescence as vital to the nation's economic health. Even these diehards, however, condemned "built-in" obsolescence through deliberate under-engineering.

As in the case of the *Harvard Business Review* survey, there appeared to be a clash between fine attitudes and practicing reality. Deliberate underengineering to insure obsolescence is equivalent to "fraud," these business experts agreed, but then they proceeded to make specific accusations that, coming as they did from marketing leaders themselves, were graphic evidence of the extent of the practice.

A full 39 per cent of those questioned accused auto and auto-accessory manufacturers of being guilty of deliberate under-engineering of products. An even one-third accused appliance makers of the same practice. Others denounced the makers of light bulbs, clothing, toys, nylon stockings, razor blades.

What emerged, in essence, was the picture of a society that, however much its leading practitioners may disapprove, is based on built-in obsolescence and deliberate, wholesale fraud. Under the matchless slogan of "borrow, spend, buy, waste, want," we have abandoned all criteria of worth in favor of quantity; all criteria of need in favor of consumption. Professor Hans J. Morgenthau, in an article entitled "The Social Crisis in America: Hedonism of the Status Quo," summed it up this way:

The unrestrained and self-sufficient hedonism of contemporary society has brought in its wake what must be called a society of waste. For where the productivity of the nation feeds, as it were, upon itself and does not serve as a means to transcendent ends which select and assign the goods to be produced, waste necessarily ensues. Production, engendered first by the needs of life and carried forward by the desire to make life easier, more attractive and more complete, becomes like a cancerous growth, multiplying wildly and creating with elaborate and costly artificiality demands which can be called rational only in view of the goal to produce more and more goods. This system of production is irrational because it replaces human needs and genuine human desires as the determining factors with the quantity of production for its own sake. . . .

This is our time, this our society. Founded on myths, in conflict with reality, hypocritically pledging itself to standards its actions disavow, it plunges madly on, with business biting the public in the sacred name of maximum profits—and the public, dimly appreciating it is all a racket, biting back.

≈ *4* ≈

Business Bites the Public

IN A SOCIETY whose guidon is maximum profit for the longest possible period, in a society of "borrow, spend, buy, waste, want," in a society in which the planned obsolescence of a deliberately shoddy product has become a "renowned principle," the gates are wide open to chicanery, and it astonishes virtually no one that a business community ethically so oriented misses no opportunity to filch nickels and dimes—and dollars in copious bundles—from the pockets of the American consumer and taxpayer.

The filching is done in Union League style, of course; no weapon so crude as a gun is used and in most instances no laws are fractured—they are only circumvented. Often even this is not necessary. Such is the ingenuity of the manipulators who have taken over from old-line production geniuses like Henry Ford that vast new areas are discovered in which the law, trailing the times as it invariably does, has taken no formal stance. Into such shadow areas of the complex American economy, the hand of greed dips deep, without, of course, any regard for that "sea of ethics" Chief Justice Warren prescribed as an environment essential to the preservation of law.

Take a simple illustration, one that affects virtually every family in America—the shelves of the supermarket. Just go on a stroll down the aisles. "Six cents off" cries your favorite toothpaste, begging for purchase. "Ten cents off on this package" screams a widely advertised laundry detergent. "Five bars for the price of four" is the lure held out by a package of hand soap. Actually, as you find when you pay your bill at the checkout counter, you have saved little or nothing on these gaudy promises; you may even have paid more than you would have for competing brands that did not flaunt giveaways—and for the simple reason that the manufacturers, who made the promises, do not control the retailers, who must keep them.

This is just one simple example of the widespread and daily fraud practiced on the American housewife by some of the largest food-packaging and processing concerns in the nation. A U.S. Senate subcommittee headed by Senator Philip A. Hart (D., Mich.) has held extensive hearings, focusing a national spotlight on what might well be labeled "The Swindle of the Supermarket Shelves."

Senator Hart himself recalls another time and another ethic. He was reared in those long-gone days of the corner grocer, whose business and prosperity depended on the quality of his goods, the willingness of his service, the honesty of his dealings. In one nostalgic flashback to this period, Senator Hart recalled "the grocery store only a block from the house where I grew up. The owner's name—Mr. Edie—I remember quite clearly, though his face has been refracted by time and glimmers only dimly from the depth of thirty-five years. My mother chose Mr. Edie only after several weeks of tentative dealing, during which she carefully took the temperature of his integrity and price policy. That having been established, even I could be trusted to make the store trips.

"Besides cash, all that was necessary to the purchase was a brown paper bag and the assurance that Mr. Edie would be there the next day in case an orange was missing or a clay bean turned up in the soup. The relationship, in short, was a very personal one. Mr. Edie provided both sales and service. Most of the packages you took home were ones that Mr. Edie filled himself out of his bins of sugar, beans and cookies. There was no nonsense about weight or volume, either. Products came in pints, pounds or pecks. There were no fractional ounces, no 'giant half-quarts,' and you could tell at a glance how prices compared with those in the store down the street."

The days of the corner grocer, of course, are gone forever; the supermarket is here to stay. It offers an enormous selection of goods far beyond the capacity of Mr. Edie's corner store. It relies on volume of sales and fast turnover and self-service, all practices that have gone hand-in-hand with factory prepackaging—a system that permits mass distribution at lowered cost. These, certainly, are all advantages to the shopper. But there are disadvantages, too, many of them associated with this very system of prepackaging that makes the supermarket possible. Senator Hart has listed these disadvantages in this order:

"1. It [prepackaging] deprives the consumer of an opportunity to examine the product.

"2. It makes price and product comparisons difficult.

"3. It makes it virtually impossible for the retailer to guarantee the product on any personal basis.

"4. It tends to conceal price increases by encouraging manufacturers to 'cut weight' instead of 'hiking price' and invites competitive use of non-standard and sometimes deceptive package shapes.

"5. It encourages the 'cents-off' deals that are often fictitious."

The typical supermarket scene is tailored to trap the unwary or the harassed purchaser. The shopping housewife, wheeling her basket, a child sitting in the carriage, another trotting at her heels, faces a mountain of between 6000 and 7000 items from which she must choose the thirty or forty needed to run her household for the week. There is no Mr. Edie to advise her. The "salesmen" in today's supermarkets are the packages themselves, and each tries to outsell its competitor by looking bigger and more imposing or by screaming in large-type labels that it offers a better bargain. The housewife is on her own, half-distracted as she searches the shelves, trying to make certain that Junior doesn't knock down a whole row of cookies or smash a soft-drink bottle; and, if she tarries, comparing price and quantity among the different brands, other mothers and their children come treading on her heels as she blocks the aisle. So, almost inevitably, she grabs the package that looks as if it promised the most. It is a promise often un-fulfilled, for the cluttered supermarket aisle, with its crowded shelves, offers an open invitation to deception and high-level cor-porate larceny, and great food corporations have been taking full advantage of the opportunity.

Colston E. Warne, professor of economics and president of Consumers Union, told the Hart committee that, in the twenty-five years of CU's existence, no issue had so aroused the public as the deliberate fraud practiced in packaging. In one year, he said, Con-sumers Union had received some 500 complaining, it-happened-to-me letters, with many correspondents enclosing comparative box labels as evidence. "The actual number of different commodities mentioned is over 100," Warne testified, "and runs the gamut from baby food to liquor."

Most of us probably know, if we have not forgotten, that a pound contains sixteen ounces; that a quart has thirty-two liquid ounces. But not today on the supermarket shelves.

J. Lyle Littlefield, chief of the Foods and Standards Division of the Michigan Department of Agriculture, cited to the Hart com-mittee numerous examples of tampering with weight and size. He exhibited a container of chocolate-covered cherries. In one corner the label read "one pound net," but this had been partly obliterated and the true figure printed in smaller, almost illegible type: "12 ounces net"—a full 25 per cent gyp.

The standard quart has become a joke. A quart is a quart, one would think. But the Hart committee found it wasn't in the super-markets. There the shelves were loaded with objects blatantly pro-claiming themselves "a full quart," or a "jumbo quart," or even a "giant imperial quart." Now what is a "giant imperial quart?" It is the same old quart, but producers contended to the Hart com-mittee that they had to scream this news to customers in the high-flown imagery of the Madison Avenue advertising man because unscrupulous competitors were using bottles that looked like "full quarts" but actually contained twenty-eight instead of thirty-two liquid ounces.

The same deception is practiced in luncheon meats. What looks like the old standard pound package often contains only fourteen ounces, sometimes only twelve. In an effort to counteract such 25 per cent chisels, some packers have taken to proclaiming loudly on their labels that they are giving "a full pound."

It is in package goods, however, that the corporate deceiver has a field day. The shelves reek with bright-colored labels proclaiming that bulky-looking boxes are "king-size" or "economy-size" or "large family-size." Actually the "king" may be a cleverly disguised gnat. Take dry cereals, for instance. Littlefield compared several kinds, all labeled "large size." Two of the "large sizes" actually did contain a pound. But of the others one contained only twelve ounces, another ten and a half, still another only nine and a half—about as close to a 50 per cent deception as one can get. The big, imposing-looking boxes were what the trade calls "slack-filled," and the customer could never possibly know unless he took the time to hunt the obscure, telltale weight label, often printed on the back of the box and hardly legible.

Testimony before the Hart committee showed that, as a result of phony labeling and packaging, the consumer who thinks he is economizing by buying the largest-size box actually is paying more per ounce of product. He is buying an illusion.

One telling study of a wide variety of products was made by Dr. Ruby Turner Morris, professor of economics and chairman of the economics department of Connecticut College in New London. Dr. Morris demonstrated that, all too often, the consumer who is impressed by a package's size is buying a lot of packaged air. She produced containers with the top portions painted white to represent the amount of air that had been found inside. The white bands illustrated the sizable air chambers that had been found in a box of bran flakes, a box of crackers, a box of baking powder, a can of salted mixed nuts. The mixed-nuts can was especially interesting. It had contained just fourteen ounces of nuts, but it was so large that a demonstration showed it could comfortably harbor the contents of three efficiently packed seven-ounce cans. What had happened here was that any consumer, deceived by the size of the can into thinking he was getting a bargain, was buying two-thirds nuts and one-third air.

It was in the field of detergents, however, that Dr. Morris' study showed the most uniform exercise of packaging ingenuity and deception. Just six large companies dominate this field, with the result that price competition, as in the electrical industry, as in many other lines, has been all but eliminated. Since it has, packaging becomes an especially important key to selling, and no device is overlooked in the campaign to convince the purchaser he is getting a bargain. Sizes range upward from "regular" to "giant" to "king" to "home laundry." This last is the true jumbo job, equipped with a carrying handle, that looks as if it must be the best bulk buy of all. But it isn't. What the customer is really purchasing is a larger percentage of air.

Dr. Morris made a detailed analysis of the contents of the packages produced by all six detergent makers. She discovered that, in four out of the six lines, the second most costly buy was the huge "home laundry" size and the best buy was the "giant" size that really is the second smallest package. One brand outsold all others in the New London stores. Yet this brand's "home laundry" size package contained 16.8 per cent of air, almost 5 per cent more air than the best buy in the line, the "giant" package, which was only 11.9 per cent air.

"The bigger the box, the bigger the hoax," Dr. Morris told the committee. ". . . There is a principle of economics for you."

The cost of the hoax is spread through many facets of the economy. Dr. Morris emphasized that such packaging deceit brings in its train a whole host of collateral evils. To make the larger box to contain more air involves "a waste of container material." To put the bigger, air-padded box into the larger shipping carton necessary to contain it involves additional waste and expense. To store the larger shipping carton in a warehouse, more storage space must be provided, and to transport it, to put the final product on display on supermarket shelves, to package it at the checkout counter—all of this adds to the costliness of handling and marketing a bloated product. "Obviously," Dr. Morris told the committee, ". . . it should cost the country a great deal of money moving boxed air around in boxcars and trucks though the air inside the package is absolutely free. Boxed air is anything but free."

Yet boxed air continues to be bought by the deceived consumer.

Educated to believe there is economy in large sizes, deceived by the impressive bulk of the packages, he buys the product that *looks* as if it gives him more for his money—and so helps to keep the fraud going in an endless cycle. Could the customer, if he shopped with maximum wisdom, force a change in such deceitful practices? Theoretically, yes; practically, no. To be sure of what he is doing, the shopper would have to stop, read the fine print detailing the actual content, and calculate every purchase. And specialists have made certain his calculations won't be very productive unless he has brought his slide rule and his MIT-graduate son along with him. Mr. Edie's easily reckoned and understood pints and quarts, ounces and pounds have vanished along with his corner grocery. Modern packaging resorts to odd ounces of content, odd half and quarter ounces even, producing a weight-price maze that keeps all but the higher mathematicians from understanding how badly they are being rooked.

There can be little question about the thieving calculation that gears the fraud. Thomas P. Wharton, president of Packaging Consultants, Inc., of Washington, D.C., described in detail for the committee the extreme effort one manufacturer of chocolate mints had made to insure the cheating of his clientele. The cheater's carton was the same it had always been—the same size as the cartons of competing candy manufacturers. But their cartons contained sixteen full ounces of mints, his only ten. The deception, said Wharton, had been practiced this way:

"In the inner package, the ends have been recessed a full half-inch. Two hollow partitions have been provided, each of which occupies another half-inch of space. This deception isn't even subtle. A full two inches of length had been faked within the package."

The result was that this firm's customers were being short-changed 40 per cent on their candy mints, but the customers, deceived by the box, apparently didn't realize it. And so, Wharton said, two competing brands had begun to resort to recessed ends, hollow partitions—and fewer mints.

Frequently, the Hart committee discovered, the processor, having accustomed his clientele to one standard-sized box with a full-legitimate pound of content, will begin to chisel and deceive in a deft and calculated way. The size of the box will remain the same; a glaring blurb may even proclaim that it contains a "new," or an "improved," or even a "super" product; the price will be the same. But inside the package, slack-filling techniques will have taken over. Sometimes such frauds are practiced gradually, with two or three unobtrusive reductions in the ounce content before the irreducible minimum is reached. All the time, of course, the price remains the same, and the consumer, who may have bought this brand for years, remains for a long time unaware that he is being gouged when he pays the same old price for less and less product. Obviously, such frauds cannot just accidentally happen; they have to be calculated and planned. As Professor Warne told the Hart committee, "the redesigning of packaging is a very costly process. This isn't something that is done very quickly, and where it is undertaken by a great many of these concerns, it does seem as if the purpose falls short of being aboveboard."

Marya Mannes, of New York, a well-known writer and social critic, herself one of the victimized housewives, did not put it so mildly. She pointed out that major corporations have spent "millions of dollars studying us—the consumer." She added:

They know what colors and what sizes and what shapes and what words we go for. Compared to them the Big Brother in George Orwell's *1984,* who knows all and sees all, is a piker. The big brothers in our society today are not government dictators—they are the sellers and their handmaidens, the behavioral scientists.

Together, and under the banner of "free choice" and "open competition," they have made us believe that we are getting what we pay for. Their purpose is that innocent goal of free enterprise—to make an extra buck. But when their profit becomes our loss, how innocent is that goal?

. . . Little deceptions of single consumers can add up to a mighty deception of the whole people. You may only lose a penny here and there, but the loss in dollars sustained daily by American consumers who pay for more than they get is estimated to be greater than the staggering amount we forfeit to crime and corruption. But it's not sensational. It doesn't hit the headlines. And who is going to bring it to your attention? The press which depends on advertising? Television which owes its existence to products? The makers of the products? As Eliza Doolittle said in *My Fair Lady,* "Not bloody likely."

Contrasted with the honest indignation of Marya Mannes were the self-serving rationalizations of industry. Business spokesmen were shocked at Senator Hart's suggestion that a new "Truth in Packaging" bill was called for. Not necessary, they said; not necessary at all. Why not? The American housewife, said industry piously, is a smart customer, "too savvy to get fooled more than once"; she will shun those fraudulent packers and take care of everything. And besides, all that was involved here were "nickel and dime" amounts, too picayune to merit the serious attention of a distinguished Congressional committee.

The sleazy rationalizations stirred Senator Hart to wrath. He pointed out that "no one has denied there is a problem," a fact that in itself demonstrates responsibility cannot be shuttled onto the shoulders of the mythical astute housewife conjured up by industry. As for the "nickels and dimes" argument, the purchases involved added up to 30 per cent of the family budget and nourished industries doing $100 billion annually in sales. Not just "nickels and dimes" were being filched, but literally millions upon millions of dollars. Even this was not the total cost. There was another and a greater cost—a moral one.

Dr. Carroll Quigley, Georgetown professor of history and an expert on the causes of the decline of civilizations, assessed the moral implications and their importance in these terms:

". . . every society is safe, every society is in a healthful condition of vim and vigor, capable of defending itself against the dangers which face all societies, only to the extent to which that society can distinguish between reality and fable.

"If misleading labels, if changes in meaning of words, if reversal of the content of terms, continues in any society, it reduces the ability of the members of that society to make this basic distinction between reality and fable. And no society can survive which isn't firmly anchored in reality."

Senator Hart agreed.

"Some witnesses have said the housewife is smart enough to know that 'serves eight' on the label really means 'serves four,' " he said. "That is a sign of moral deterioration, and if it is true, it shouldn't be.

"You wouldn't want your children to adopt a philosophy like that. There's nothing good about this attitude."

I

The greatest highway robbery of all time was not the work of professional highwaymen. It was—and is, for it hasn't all ended yet—the distinctive achievement of a business ethic that finds nothing that results in profit repugnant to the soul.

No Jesse James of the past ever envisioned such loot. Instead of the limited contents of a cash box hauled by stage or rail, here is a boundless cornucopia, overflowing with literally billions of dollars—the funds supplied by Uncle Sam and all of us taxpayers for a nationwide superhighway program designed to link every major city in the nation, coast to coast. The conception is one to make the American motorist salivate. There will be a 41,000-mile chain of expressways with no intersections, no traffic lights, wonderful ribbons of concrete on which by the mid-1970s the tourist can bat along at 60 to 70 miles an hour all the way from the Atlantic to the Pacific. The cost has been estimated at $41 billion—and that is the kind of money that makes a lot of people salivate.

The result has been a scandal, nationwide in its proportions, virtually unmarked by a single island of rectitude—a development that is perhaps one of the most graphic demonstrations in our time of the prevalence of the corrupt society.

It is a corruption that has historic antecedents and deep roots, but that only now, watered by such copious billions, has blossomed into full flower. If the definitive saga of corruption in the twentieth century could ever be written, one of its most gaudy chapters would almost certainly be provided by the highway-construction industry. At the beginning of the century, the relatively few roads that existed were little more than rutted dirt tracks. Then came the automobile, the phenomenon of a nation on wheels, and the al-

most frenzied proliferation of roads, tunnels, bridges. In the space
of less than fifty years, the nation was transformed from the
agrarian world of Senator Norris' boyhood and all its past centuries
into the mass, industrialized society of today and tomorrow. The
transformation was not accomplished without gluttony.

It happens that I have a personal peephole into the beginnings.
In 1933, as a cub reporter still wet behind the ears, I had the good
fortune to come under the tutelage of William H. Fischer, a crusading country editor, one of the last of the upright men. Fischer,
a small, bouncy man with a plume of flowing white hair, had edited
a weekly newspaper in Toms River, New Jersey, for more than
forty years; he had twice headed runaway grand juries that kicked
the prosecutor out of the jury room and proceeded to indict
county officials. One of these indictments (it has an archaic ring
to it now) was against the entire Board of Freeholders, the govern-
ing body of the county, for an offense that today would not cause
even a lifted eyebrow—spending so much that they regularly exceeded their appropriations. Anyway, Fischer had been in a position to see it all from the beginning; and though neither he nor I
could envision at the time the society into which we were headed,
he had a clear perception of the change that was taking place—of
the ethical differences in the society we were forging and the societies of our yesterdays from which we had sprung.

"You'll laugh at this," he told me once, "but graft first came
into rural communities in a small way when a law was passed providing for free textbooks in the public schools.

"At the time, one book company had a virtual monopoly on the
printing of textbooks. There was another firm, however, that was
also in the business, and they sent men into New Jersey. There was
a bitter rivalry between the two concerns, and it eventually came
to the point where it meant that book agents had to go into the
field and buy up the members of the local school boards in order
to sell their books."

Bookselling was a penny-ante racket, however, beside the kind
of corruption that came along when the rural road systems started
to expand and steel bridges began to be flung across the streams.
Fischer used to tell the story of how one bridge concern took the

entire Board of Freeholders to its plant in Ohio and then on a junket up into Canada.

"I had a very good friend of mine on the board at the time," he told me once, "and I argued and argued with him, but I could not make him see that his first duty was to the people, to vote for the firm that he thought would build the best bridge.

"He told me, 'Bill, after all these people have done for us, I simply can't go back on them now.' And he was a man, too, whom I never knew to do a thing in his life that he thought was dishonest."

Such were the simple beginnings; such the ethical dilemma of an honest man feted on the expense account and unable to distinguish between the claims of gratitude and those of duty. The surrender of Bill Fischer's officeholding friend to the temptations of corporate largesse had had about it a naïveté, an innocence, that inevitably, as "a way of life" developed, would be supplanted by the coldness of calculation.

Typical of what goes on today in the highway-construction field, a mere preface to the bolder chapters of corruption, was the case of Southern Equipment Sales, Inc., a machinery-sales company of Jackson, Mississippi. When the firm collapsed into bankruptcy in 1961, attorneys for the creditors began to trace mysterious entries in its books. It developed that these entries represented kickbacks to county officials. Southern Equipment had been kicking back a fixed percentage on every piece of highway-building equipment it sold. Traceable payoffs came to $125,000. In addition, Southern Equipment had paid thirteen of its own salesmen $32,161 to compensate them for the income taxes they had had to pay on the kickback money passed along to county officials. Representatives of Southern Equipment told a referee in bankruptcy that they had been paying off county officials for nineteen years; such kickbacks, they said, had become a way of life that amounted to policy "throughout the industry."

When the foundation stone of an industry is the payoff, it does not take much imagination to visualize what was fated to happen when construction giants rolled themselves up to the $41-billion smorgasbord of the federal superhighway program. Details of the gluttony performed at public expense have been unfolded by a House of Representatives subcommittee headed by Representative John A. Blatnik (D., Minn.).

In May 1960, the Blatnik subcommittee disclosed that the $6-million, thirteen-mile Skelly Bypass in Tulsa, Oklahoma, was already beginning to crack. The reason? The contractor had billed the state (the individual states have supervision over their sections of the program, though nine-tenths of the funds are supplied by the federal government) for some $524,689 worth of materials that had never been put into the road.

In December 1960, the Blatnik committee turned its searchlight on Florida. It established that six contractors handling $70 million in road work had distributed gifts ranging from $54,000 to $75,000 a firm to thirty-three Florida state highway engineers. The figures covered a four-year period, and the favors had taken the form of cash payments, liquor, lumber, hunting licenses, unrepaid loans, and bonuses for extra services. William L. Cobb, head of a large construction company, admitted he had also made such gifts to state road officials in Georgia, Mississippi, Alabama, and North and South Carolina.

Cobb had the decency to deplore the practice, said he ordered it ended; but other contractors professed to see nothing really wrong with a little gift-giving. Charles E. Bailes, Jr., general superintendent of Cone Brothers Contracting Company, said his firm had mailed state engineers secret payments of $25 a week to get "that little effort" the company needed to help it complete jobs. "And I believe the payments helped," Bailes said. "I am obligated to my company to do the best job I possibly can. . . . As long as I didn't engage in anything that I thought was faulty, I would employ many different things to get this accomplished." Once again, he was expressing the all-too-prevalent business ethic: What is good for business is proper.

But what happens to the public interest? Doesn't that get fractured? Oh, no, said the kept men, the engineers of the state highway department. They had not shaded the public interest in the slightest in return for that bounty of $25 a week apiece. Much evidence to the contrary seems to dispute them. H. C. Weathers,

Florida's chief testing engineer, testified he found substandard material, poor workmanship, and faulty construction on a $2.5-million strip of highway near Tampa. The road had been built by Bailes' Cone Brothers outfit. Some of the deficiencies, Weathers testified, were serious.

More blatant were some of the other goings-on in Florida. David Brinkley, in one of his most scathing telecasts, publicized several of them on NBC's *David Brinkley's Journal*. For example, said Brinkley, there is a broad highway near Kissimmee that was built on the orders of J. Rolfe Davis, a member of the Florida State Highway Board. Brinkley noted:

"It starts out and goes twelve miles to absolutely nowhere. It just stops, in the middle of a pasture. The county commissioners protested . . . the Attorney General said this too was illegal . . . but they built it. And there it lies, empty of traffic . . . used occasionally by a crop duster's airplane, the only 12-mile airstrip in the world. It cost $220,000."

Then there was the Howard Franklin Bridge over Tampa Bay. The bridge was built under the supervision of Joseph R. Maseda, Jr., a state engineer who in four years had received $4700 from several contractors, including the Hardaway Construction Company, builders of the bridge. The bridge cost $6,250,000. When its forty spans were tested, thirty-nine of them failed to meet specifications. Within two years, the surface began to heave and break up. The reason? The contractor, to save money, used salt water right out of the Bay for mixing concrete.

One of Brinkley's investigators questioned Manuel Hodges, a construction worker who helped build the bridge. It went like this:

Q. Mr. Hodges, do you think that bridge is going to stand up? Is it well built?

A. No, sir. I would stake everything I have on it, it won't.

Q. Why would you make a statement like this?

A. Well, because for one thing it's put up with salt water—

Q. Why did you use salt water?

A. Well, I had to have a job. I was working, and you have to do what your boss says to do.

Q. What effect would this have on the bridge?

A. Well, your cement will not hold up like it would be with fresh water. And also your steel where it's in it, your rods, will be eaten up by the salt atmosphere from the cement, and also your cement will crumble and break.

Further along in the program, Brinkley pointed out that William H. McLeod was the state highway engineer in charge of all highway building in the Tampa area, including the Howard Franklin Bridge. McLeod, an investigation had disclosed, had received more than $10,000 in cash from contractors, plus some $7500 in building materials for his new home. "We find him now to regard all this with an easy, comfortable philosophy," Brinkley told his television audience. Then he put McLeod on camera.

"I never owned a home of my own, and I had always called Tampa my home," McLeod said. "And I bought me a home and the contractors over the area that were on my jobs, they did furnish some materials possibly to put in my house. They would send out whiskey, cases of whiskey. They would send out hams, they would send out turkeys, and they would send out cash— envelopes with cash money in it.

"It's statewide. It's been that way for years. I was never asked by any contractor to do—let them get by with anything. I have never asked an inspector, I have never asked an engineer who worked under me, to let a contractor get by with anything. The jobs that I have always worked on have been built in accordance with the plans and specifications of the State Road Department."

Yet, somehow, salt water had gotten into the concrete.

After studying a number of such cases, Representative Blatnik, in a commonsense summing-up, said that he found "it difficult in the light of all the testimony to believe that the conditions prevailed without involvement of a *quid pro quo,* whatever its nature may have been."

Florida was by no means alone. At Lordsburg, New Mexico, a $500,000 section in the new superhighway program began to collapse even as state officials were approving it. And just nine miles east of Lordsburg there was, said Brinkley, "a real marvel of highway building—a $300,000 overpass . . . with signs pointing to the turnoff to Gary. Well, here's how it goes. You drive along the highway to the overpass . . . turn right where the sign says . . . drive up the ramp toward the road to Gary . . . whereupon you will find there is no such place as Gary and never was. The road goes a few feet into the desert and just stops. If anyone should care to start a town and name it Gary, here's a nice place to put it . . . because the $300,000 entrance to it is already there."

Such scandals, Brinkley emphasized, were not a "minor problem confined to a few places." They occurred *everywhere* a road was built. Representative Jim Wright, a member of Blatnik's committee, summed up the score sheet of corruption in late November 1963. He reported that various investigations by different agencies had uncovered "fraud or carelessness involving right-of-way acquisition in 24 states, shoddy or deliberately dishonest construction practices in 21 states, payola accepted by highway department employees in seven states." Of the 284 witnesses who had appeared before Blatnik's committee, he wrote, 101 admitted "irregularities."

What is the cost of such chicanery on a nationwide scale? Federal investigators put it at 10 per cent of the over-all program. At the time they made the estimate, some $16 billion had already been spent—and that meant that the loot had already totaled some *$1.6 billion*. If the swindling should continue on the same scale for the entire $41-billion program, it would mean that *$4.1 billion* would be filched out of the pockets of the American taxpayers. As Brinkley said: "Nobody ever stole that much before."

The thievery encompassed all phases of the program, not just the actual highway construction. It began at the very beginning, with the acquisition of the land needed to build the new expressways. Originally, Congress had estimated that land acquisition would cost $5 billion. The figure later was boosted to $7 billion, and no one seemed quite certain whether even that would be enough. In any event, most of that extra $2 billion could be carried on a ledger sheet under one word: *swindle*. For insiders with advance knowledge of where the new through routes would go, the opportunity to loot and to gouge proved irresistible. In one Florida case, testimony showed, insiders acquired a tract of predestined right-of-way land in 1956 for $165,000 and sold it to the state a year later for $240,000—a neat profit of $75,000, almost 50 per cent on the original investment. Some deals of this kind fell into the category of sharp practice, but others involved conspiracy and collusion.

In Massachusetts, the systematic kiting of land values and the looting of the public till achieved such status as the regular way of life that the federal government, at one point, froze some $12 million in funds that had been allocated to the state for land acquisitions. Though virtually every state participating in the program suffered from scandals to some degree, greed reached its apex in Massachusetts. There the trebling and quadrupling of land values became common practice.

Just what this meant in dollars and cents to the American taxpayer who had to foot the bill may be illustrated by some specific cases. One right-of-way appraiser in Massachusetts was named William M. Jacobs. His division chief had given him an unsatisfactory rating, but this in no way adversely affected his career. Between 1956 and 1961, indeed, Jacobs handled more assignments than any other appraiser in the state, and he earned $150,587 in fees. In one case, he helped persuade the state to pay Ernest Reiss, an officer of the Joada Realty Company, $120,000 for a parcel of land subsequently valued at $31,000. In another appraisal, Jacobs put a $427,526.35 price tag on a stretch of property on Interstate 290 near Worcester; an independent firm later estimated it was really worth just $27,800.

Such cases, however, seemed to lack the poetic finesse involved in the disposal of a South Attleboro lumberyard belonging to a businessman by the name of Walter Webb. Webb had decided to sell his yard in 1958, strictly as a business proposition, and his initial asking price was $27,000. He later modified his aspirations to $23,000—and couldn't get that. The best price he was offered was $12,000, but Webb and the broker to whom he had gone, Felix Myette, were determined to hold out for $20,000.

It was at this point, sometime in May 1959, that Francis L. Harney, Jr., a low-salaried "interviewer" in the right-of-way division of the state highway department, heard of Webb's plight.

Harney was a name-dropping former football player who liked to sport around in a new white Cadillac and pose as an operator with all the contacts. The event would seem to show that he really had them. Harney, realizing that the Webb lumberyard was strategically located, right where the state would have to acquire it for the new interstate route, went to real estate broker Myette and Myette's boss, C. H. Lawton, Jr., the head of the realty firm. He advised them to have Webb see James S. O'Connell, a lawyer who "had a brother in the governor's office."

Webb, as he testified later, didn't see at first what good this would do. He knew that the state was going to acquire his lumberyard for the new interstate route and that an appraisal had already been made, fixing its value at $20,000. The state wouldn't pay any more than that, would it? Harney assured him it would.

It took a few months, but then, out of the blue, Webb got a notification of the state's decision—and almost dropped from the shock. The state had agreed to pay him $60,000 for his $20,000 lumberyard. Webb hurried over to collect from O'Connell and Harney—and got another shock. The lawyer handed him a check for $17,383.37. He explained that the remainder of Webb's share had been used to pay off the mortgage and back taxes. This had left $30,000 in the kitty—and that was O'Connell's fee.

"I suppose a lot of this money has to be passed around," Webb said.

"Of course," Harney replied.

How had the state been induced to pay $60,000 for a $20,000 property? It hadn't been too difficult. True, the state review board had spotted the discrepancy between the kited $60,000 price tag and the earlier $20,000 estimate, and it had called for a new, "independent" appraisal. Harney had taken care of that. He had arranged to have this "independent" evaluation made by C. H. Lawton, Jr.—the man whose real estate firm had been trying to sell Webb's lumberyard in the first place. Not too surprisingly, in the circumstances, Lawton's "independent" judgment confirmed the $60,000 price, and the state review board, unaware of the hanky-panky, promptly authorized the payment.

For anyone interested in the ethics of our times and the stature of man, it is illuminating to read the testimony that Walter Webb subsequently gave the Blatnik committee in Washington. Representative Jim Wright of Texas did the questioning, and this was the way it went:

WRIGHT: Mr. Webb, at what point in this transaction did you realize that you were engaged in a conspiracy with Mr. Harney and Mr. O'Connell?

WEBB: I would say probably in December of 1959.

WRIGHT: At the time you realized it was a conspiracy, why did you finally go through with it?

WEBB: I have asked myself that question innumerable times. I haven't yet found the right answer to that.

WRIGHT: Is this a part of what goes on in the mind of the individual? Does a person think at some point, it isn't as though we're cheating somebody [because] it's only the government?

WEBB: It's like a trough. I mean, when you have a bunch of animals that go to the trough . . . the ones that are there first, they are going to get fat and healthy and the rest go by the wayside.

There may be those who rebel at the idea of casting man in a piglet's image, but the evidence would seem to indicate that such rebels are in the minority and that the power structures of our time, comprised of many of our most eminent citizens, aren't rebelling very hard. Walter Webb's intriguing lumberyard deal in 1959 was little more than a drop in the ocean of corruption brought to light by the case of the Worcester Bounty in January 1961. This was a shocker that touched off a series of investigations and a flood of indictments and convictions—a flood that rolls on and on and is not ended at this writing. For the case of the Worcester Bounty peeled away layers of pretense and hypocrisy and exposed in rare detail the mechanics of a system under which virtually no public business in Massachusetts was done without its meed of bribery.

Thomas Worcester was an engineering contractor. In three years, he did $2,750,000 worth of business with the state. He kicked back 10 per cent, an even $275,000. Worcester concealed the bribe money in various ways in his firm's accounts and charged it off on his income-tax returns as necessary business expense. An Internal Revenue investigation exposed the dodge, and Worcester was indicted for income-tax evasion. Though the indictment was returned in 1957, it hung fire for three years before being brought to trial before Federal District Court Judge Charles E. Wyzanski, Jr. Worcester was convicted, and then Judge Wyzanski, in an unusual step, offered him a choice: eighteen months in prison or full revelation of the kickback-corruption story before federal and state grand juries. Worcester chose to talk.

Subsequently Judge Wyzanski spread on the record the details of Worcester's testimony and then held public hearings to determine whether the contractor had told the full truth as he knew it. By this deed, the judge thrust aside the veil of secrecy and exposed to public view an incredible succession of troughs at which the human animals were industriously swilling.

Worcester's story, briefly, was that during World War II he had done more than $100 million worth of work for the Army and Navy. His firm's performance was high, its reputation one of the best in the business. Then, in 1948, Worcester struck up an acquaintance with a man named Frank Norton, a mysterious figure who had some shadowy business ties in Canada and Mexico. A glib talker, Norton assured Worcester he was "certain he could get jobs for me" because he knew one of the most powerful and influential officials in Massachusetts, William F. Callahan, former State Public Works chairman, later head of the Massachusetts Turnpike Authority. In recompense, Norton wanted a job with Worcester's firm, and he would have to have a kickback of 10 per cent, no questions asked, on every contract he obtained.

Worcester bought the deal. Norton moved into his firm as assistant to the president. Contracts began to flow in. The 10 per cent cash kickback was siphoned off in various ways and given to Norton, who never told anyone what he did with it. But he indicated clearly that he didn't keep it; the money, he said, simply "went in and out."

Just what was involved in "out" Thomas Worcester didn't know, nor did he want to know. But eventually a certain degree of knowledge was forced upon him. In the fall of 1949, Norton was hospitalized with a heart attack, and Worcester himself had to take a package of cash to Norton's home. He testified that he delivered the package to Norton's wife; that she put it in the over-coat pocket of a man sitting in the next room; that she didn't let him see the man, but she told Worcester he was Callahan.

Long before the scandal finally erupted in Judge Wyzanski's court, Norton had died of his heart ailment. Mrs. Norton and Callahan did their best to avoid testifying. Callahan, indeed, was so reluctant that he fought the Wyzanski subpoena to the U.S. Court of Appeals on two separate occasions. By the time he had lost his last legal battle, Mrs. Norton had testified, swearing under oath that she could not remember any such episode as the shoving of a package of money into Callahan's coat pocket. Once this version was in the record, Callahan himself came charging into court, trumpeting "Never!"

Aside from the issue of Callahan's involvement, other aspects of the Worcester case rocked Massachusetts. Worcester testified that he had contributed heavily to the unsuccessful re-election campaign of Democratic Governor Paul A. Dever in 1952 because "we had received all his work and there was more in the offing." The Worcester payroll—the Worcester Bounty, Judge Wyzanski was to call it—had been loaded with political hacks, a form of payoff in which both parties participated happily. One lawyer was paid $11,000 in ten months for nonexistent "legal consultations"; ex-State Senator Edward M. Rowe was paid $20,000 because, as one witness put it, "The Democrats wanted Rowe to run [for Governor] in the [Republican] primary in order to create a division in the Republican Party." Vincent J. Shanely, then a Boston City Councilor, spent seventy-seven weeks on the Worcester payroll on the recommendation of Governor Dever. He was paid $50 a week, was listed as a "public relations man," did virtually nothing. John G. Curley, a Democratic state representative at the time, was paid $75 a week for six weeks, did nothing. The list went endlessly on—a morass of phony jobs and padded payrolls, of political con-niving and favoritism, all of which the public paid for in the inflated cost of the nearly $3 million worth of business the state did with the Worcester firm.

The breadth and scope and infinite variety of the corruption made it clear, however, that more than Worcester and his $3 million worth of business was involved. What disturbed Massachusetts was the disclosure of a well-established, entrenched, functioning system—"a way of life" by which, and by which alone, business was being done. Worcester's nearly $3 million looked big to Worcester, but it was only a tithe of the $243.5 million the state was receiving in federal highway aid, only a pittance of the more than $1 billion the state had spent on its road programs since 1948. In this perspective, the Worcester Bounty, great scandal that it was, did little more than hint at the magnitude of the scandals yet to be revealed.

In a final summation of the Worcester disclosures, Judge Wyzanski put the issues into focus in scornful, accusing words that rocked staid Back Bay. He called Worcester's testimony "candid, credible, complete." He accused Mrs. Norton of "direct falsehoods and inexplicable failures to remember." He dealt with Callahan in these terms: "No one who reads in full Callahan's testimony . . . would care to stake much on Callahan's oath." The judge denounced what he termed "the sordid racket of extortion, bribery and corruption," and he asked a number of questions that, in effect, suggested a widespread moral decay. He said:

Upon what basis was Worcester singled out for prosecution? Can it be true that of the successful bidders for contracts with the state, Worcester alone paid bribes and took them as deductions from federal income tax?

. . . What sort of responsibility have the press and other media of communication displayed in reporting this case? Can it truly be said that with a high standard of detachment they have told the public all the court evidence that was discreditable, no matter whose ox was gored?

. . . How far has the bar initiated reform based upon its daily experience with the suffering its clients have undergone at the hands of a network of corruption? Were sophisticated lawyers unaware, until this case began, that to secure certain types of public business a contractor had to get his performance bond, or his materialman's bond, or his bond for wages, or his trustees' bond from a relative of a judge, or of a public official, or of a legislator?

. . . Is the only method by which this venal system will be supplanted a public-insurance system modeled on other governmental insurance systems?

Have the private interests which professedly care about the capitalist system no awareness of what kind of free enterprise they have been fostering?

Do they not realize that the people will smite them when they see what this corruption costs in taxes, and, more important, in the trustworthiness of judges, legislators and executives?"

2

Judge Wyzanski's scathing questions led inexorably to consideration of a system that sanctifies in law all major elements of the corrupt society—the American income-tax system. When the judge asked "private interests" whether they did not realize that "the people will smite them when they see what this corruption costs in taxes" and the trustworthiness of officials, he broached a vital issue; for all the lesser corruptions of the corrupt society are enshrined and sanctified at the summit in a tax system that says, even to the most stupid, "anything goes *if* you can get away with it." It is a system, of course, that makes it difficult for Joe Average to get away with very much; he, poor devil, has all his earnings reported on a withholding-tax form, and even though he may recognize the delightful ethic of our times and even though he may try to face up to the challenge and show how smart he is by chiseling what he can, he really doesn't have the kind of opportunity that produces the real artiste. So the system bestows its most beneficent rewards on those who have the most, on the extremely rich and powerful and on that American "new class," the inner clique of management manipulators—groups that can and do get away with almost anything.

For these favored citizens of the Republic, all kinds of tax-escape hatches have been written into law and are maintained there as most precious American free-enterprise heritages. There is the 27½ per cent oil depletion allowance, a bounteous device that helps to keep many a millionaire from paying any taxes at all; there is the foundation tax dodge (and there's nothing like a good, family foundation to take care of one's old age or to send the son to college with tax-free dollars); there is the capital gains tax, which assures the man who makes a couple of million wheeling and dealing in the stock market that he won't have to pay more than 25 per cent on his windfall; there are the special stock options by which management rewards itself with a can't-lose, capital-gains proposition that mulcts both its own stockholders and the rest of the taxpaying public; and then, finally, gloriously, rapturously, there is the expense account, the corporate slush fund that enables the manipulators of the new breed to live high on the hog, with girls, parties, yachts, hunting safaris—all of it tax-free, all of it at the expense of the rest of us.

This is a profligate way of life, nurtured initially by wartime billions and now, in the postwar era, an established pattern accepted by a society that is lethargic, that has been brainwashed into the glorification of conformity and a concomitant distrust of criticism and rebellion. In the vacuum that has been created, this Roman-holiday high living by the favored and the privileged has come to epitomize our civilization and to set the standards for the less fortunate to ape. It goes on and on, sanctified in law, and there are no signs that the people, in Judge Wyzanski's word, are ever going to "smite" anybody, for we've all been taught that it isn't nice to "smite" nice people who are just enjoying the fruits of their own cleverness in cultivating their own special rackets. So, lacking in indignation, deprived of righteousness, barren of convictions, we can only imitate, we can only join them, we can only try (as Robert Lynd wrote) to get a piece of the racket for our very own.

A harsh verdict? Not at all. Proof may be found in an examination of what has happened whenever some misguided idealist has tried to change the system.

The major idealist to champion change in our time was President John F. Kennedy. Early in his administration, he realized that the banner of the corrupt society was hardly one under which America could march to the New Frontier, and so in May 1961 he proposed sweeping changes in the income-tax laws. He struck heavily at the expense-account profligacy of our times; and, in calling for a more Spartan code of conduct, he cited the kind of hi-jinks that had been ratified by the courts as perfectly legal under existing law. In so doing, he called prominently to public attention a whole broad category of gay excesses, the trappings of the expense-account way of life. Hunting trips to Africa, the maintenance of elaborate hunting lodges, expensive yachts, the purchase and upkeep of swank apartments in Miami, champagne parties, nightclubbing, football and fight and theater tickets—all were for free on the expense account, a tax-deductible way of life. As Robert J. Donovan wrote in the New York *Herald Tribune* after the disclosures, "among the deep social lessons" preached was this: "If you've been turning in low expense accounts these last few years, go shoot yourselves."

The Kennedy disclosures resulted from the minute analysis of just 38,000 business returns in 1960. A résumé showed the kind of claims made and the kind of money involved. The tabulation went like this:

1689 returns claimed deductions totaling $14.7 million for company-owned or leased airplanes.

2732 returns claimed deductions totaling $2 million for amusement tickets.

5384 returns claimed deductions totaling $5.7 million for club dues or initiation fees.

4188 claimed $12.9 million for convention costs.

179 claimed $599,000 for the expenses of hunting lodges.

61 claimed $1.1 million for entertaining on ranches or farms.

156 claimed $529,000 for fishing-camp expenses.

250 claimed $626,000 for maintaining resort properties.

881 claimed $2.6 million for the operation of yachts and boats.

309 claimed $1.2 million for the maintenance of suites and apartments.

6590 claimed $11.5 million in deductions for business gifts.

Some of the individual cases that had been fought through the tax courts—and upheld as perfectly proper under the laws and regulations of the corrupt society—were enough to increase that impulse to suicide Robert Donovan had mentioned. There was the case of the president and principal shareholder of Sanitary Farms Dairy, a milk-processing and distributing company. The boss man was an experienced hunter, and on one occasion in the early 1950s, he took off with his wife on a safari to Africa—a trip that lasted six months and included stays in London, Paris, and Rome, areas in which lions and leopards have long been extinct. Except for a few hundred dollars, the entire cost of $16,818 was allowed as a tax deduction because, the tax court ruled, Sanitary Farms Dairy got publicity every time the papers back home carried pictures of its president posing with his foot on the neck of a downed lion.

The yachting business supplied some titillating examples of all that is embraced in the tax-deductible way of life. One firm wrote off $16,943 to maintain a yacht "to demonstrate to customers value of sneakers with non-skid soles." Naturally, you can demonstrate this only on a yacht. The Cleveland-Sandusky Brewing Corporation wrote off $10,481 as the cost of maintaining a cabin cruiser for the years 1949 and 1950. The president of the corporation testified its headquarters were located in a slum area; you couldn't very well entertain customers in such surroundings—and so it was necessary to maintain the cabin cruiser for "sales meetings" and to take the boys "fishing down to the islands if the weather permitted."

Then there was the case of the jolly mortician. He too maintained a yacht. Since an undertaker's undertakings usually come his way in the natural course of events, it might seem at first glance that he would hardly need a yacht to drum up business. But this mortician explained that he "prepares and ships bodies to other areas for burial." To get this kind of business, you need the good will of other morticians and clergymen—and it's certainly a lot pleasanter entertaining on a yacht than in a mortuary. So the seagoing undertaker wrote off $35,000 worth of yachting as a business expense, and the government had to allow $25,000 worth of it.

There's nothing like the good life, lived to the hilt at the expense of Uncle Sam—and of all us little suckers who have to pay taxes on the money we spend for our homes and enjoyment. If you don't believe it, read on. There was the case of Doughboy Industries. It spent $10,000 redecorating the first floor of the home of its principal shareholder-officer, and it charged off the entire cost as a business expense because, it said, the home was used to entertain customers. Not content with this, the firm also passed along to Uncle Sam the $6600 tab for the installation of a lavish swimming pool so that the customers could dunk themselves after imbibing. The case was fought out in the courts, and 95 per cent of the over-all cost of the two projects was allowed as a tax-free business expense.

Some few persons who still retain a capacity for indignation might leap to the conclusion, from studying such examples, that it's time to go out and start the revolution; but they would be premature. All the cases we've cited so far are mere trifles—nothing really. Look at what happens when you get into the big money.

There was, for example, the case of the traveling insurance man. He was on the go practically every hour of the day and night keeping in contact with his clients; he must have been, for, in the single year of 1957, he claimed deductions of $138,500. His swindle sheet read like this: meals, $25,000; lodging, $20,000; transportation, $30,000; food and beverages for entertainment, $30,000; tickets, $2000; conventions, $2000; apartments, $6000; gifts, $10,500; autos, $10,000; other, $3000. The insurance man and the government wrangled a bit over some of these items—and the government lost more than it won. It wound up allowing $97,500.

In the corporate realm, the high living gets even fancier and more expensive. There was one tightly controlled manufacturing company that maintained a luxurious hunting lodge, with well-stocked streams, plenty of small game, and "a large deer population." The lodge was no primitive affair; it was valued, for taxing purposes at least, at some $230,000. And each year executives of the firm, their favored management people, and their best customers, some 500 to 600 in all, would get away from the old grind for a few days at a time, just to fish, shoot, drink, and commune with nature. The tax-deductible tab over a three-year period came to $187,000—and it was allowed.

Even this was almost chickenfeed compared to the adventures in tax-free expense accounting indulged in by a supply firm owned by just two persons. The two stockholders had also acquired such other appurtenances as night clubs and ranches, and the green paper that flew when they had their own supply firm patronize their own night clubs could have covered the walls of the government mint. Christmas parties in the night club ranged in cost from $8000 to $14,000. Executive hunting trips to Canada never cost less than $5000 for parties of eight to twelve. Then there was a yacht for which the firm was allowed to deduct $111,804. Ranch and hunting-lodge expenses came to $116,400. The night club expenses totaled $125,249, and even this wasn't enough—there was another $119,647 for "other entertainment." It all came to nearly half a million dollars, and it was all allowed. But the government did balk when one of the partners tried to charge off $20,000 in repairs to his home as a business expense and the other sought to charge off the entire $9000 cost of a trip he made with his family to Europe and Africa.

Such is life in the executive suites of the corrupt society. *The Wall Street Journal,* after making its own survey of the world of tax-free yachts and hunting lodges and "toothsome hostesses" hired to make customers forget the cares of the business world, concluded that top executives were "still enjoying the frills enjoyed by the Mellons, Morgans and Baruchs." And it is quite obvious, though the *Journal* didn't say so, that they are enjoying their potentates' dream worlds at the expense of the rest of us. First, of course, they are cavorting at the expense of their own stockholders, for the yachts and hunting lodges, the safaris and the parties and the "toothsome hostesses" don't come cheap; they come out of a firm's total cash flow and reduce its profits. Second, and on a broader scale, this carnival life is lived at the expense of every one of us, for every taxpayer who pays a reasonably honest bill is being gouged to make up for those bawdy-life millions of dollars that escape being taxed at all.

As an antidote to all this, the Kennedy administration, in all seriousness, proposed a code so Spartan that it can only be described as positively un-American. The program, as explained to Congress by Secretary of the Treasury Douglas Dillon, would have:

• Fixed a maximum $10 outlay annually for each recipient as a "business gift."

• Limited expenditure "somewhere" between $4 and $7 each for entertaining one individual daily for business purposes. (No "toothsome hostesses" on that amount.)

• Established a $30 daily ceiling on deductible expense per individual for business travel.

• Banned all tax deductions for expenses incurred for entertaining business guests "at such functions as parties, night clubs, theaters, country clubs and fishing trips. . . ."

• Forbidden any tax deductions "for luxury entertainment facilities such as country club dues."

These, said Dillon, were "realistic recommendations." They were indeed, but from the outcry that went up you might have thought that the Kennedy administration had just proposed selling the country lock, stock, and barrel to the Russians.

It would appear that, at the outset, the Kennedy administration had looked hopefully for the support of responsible businessmen —and that optimistically it had equated responsibility with true leadership in the business community. For, in sending the President's recommendations to Congress, it had cited some eminent supporting opinions. Foremost among these were the views of Clarence B. Randall, former head of Inland Steel, who had attacked "The Myth of the Magic Expense Account" in an article in *Dunn's Review* in August 1960.

Randall had pulled no punches. "Some companies are more widely known for their parties than they are for their products," he had written. ". . . Lights would go out along the Strip in Las Vegas and chorus girls would be unemployed from New York to Los Angeles if it were not for that great modern invention, the tax deduction. But who are the silent underwriters of this frenetic spending? You, and I, the general taxpayers. It is we who make up to the U.S. Treasury the revenue lost through expense-account deductions.

". . . It is disturbing that business does not put its own house in order while there is still time, that it does not speak out boldly against expense-account abuses. . . . If we cannot correct these things ourselves, we can hardly protest if Government steps in to do it for us."

Randall's vision was certainly 20–20 on the ethical issues, but as an eminent businessman himself, his judgment was optimistically biased toward the belief that business was better than it was— that it could and would take a stand on the basis of lofty principle. It quickly became apparent that if business could it wouldn't. All the power of the hotel, restaurant, night club, and entertainment industries was thrown into the battle to kill off the Kennedy–Dillon austerity program. The hullabaloo that was raised was tremendous. A parade of business spokesmen appeared before congressional committees and predicted that any clamp-down on expense-account phoniness would kill off whole industries and possibly precipitate a depression. Headlines exaggerated these prophecies of doom, and the vital issues to which Kennedy had called attention rapidly got lost.

The real showdown came before the Senate Finance Committee, headed by that veteran conservative and devotee of fiscal responsibility, Senator Harry Flood Byrd, the Virginia Democrat. In two beautifully complementary actions in the summer of 1962, Senator Byrd and his committee wrote a vivid chapter in the annals of the corrupt society.

Among the Kennedy tax-reform proposals had been one to withhold taxes in income received from dividends and interest. The Treasury had estimated that some $650–$800 million a year was escaping collection because such earnings went largely unreported. Business howled about the great added bookkeeping expense that would be imposed upon it if it had to withhold such taxes; some major business chains granted employees time off from their duties to sit down and compose indignant letters to their congressmen to be put in already-stamped and addressed envelopes; and Senator Byrd's committee, under his aegis always responsive to the outcries of business, dutifully wielded the hatchet. It killed the withholding proposal. Hardly had it done so before it turned around, like a boxer delivering a one-two punch, and knocked out Kennedy's proposed Spartan expense-account code. Not only did it kill expense-account reform; it actually opened the gates even wider to chicanery by coming up with the doctrine of "the Prudent Man."

Under this novel conception, anything—virtually anything at all —could be deducted from income taxes provided it was a business or entertainment expense that might be incurred by "a prudent man in the exercise of his sound judgment." This is a definition, of course, that means anything and everything to all types and classes of men. It moved James Reston, *The New York Times'* Washington correspondent, to muse satirically:

This obviously has possibilities. Suppose a citizen of the Great Republic absolutely has to go to Paris on business, or to New York, or anywhere else where the women are recklessly beautiful. In this situation a Prudent Man, in the exercise of his sound judgment, would obviously take along his wife and write her off as a prudent deduction. . . .

Consider the agony of living in the same world with both Nikita Khrushchev and Mortimer W. Caplin, the new Commissioner of Internal Revenue. No less an authority than President Kennedy has told us that this is a dangerous time. Khrushchev has said that he now has an intercontinental ballistic missile that can hit a "fly in the sky" and cannot be brought down by anything in the arsenal of democracy.

In such a world, equipped with such ghastly fly-swatters, a Prudent Man would surely provide some means of escape for his family—say a yacht well stocked and lubricated with provisions capable of maintaining life for a considerable period of time. Or a hide-away in the mountains equipped with a large, deep pool of water for protection against radiation. And these would, of course, have to be maintained and kept in running order by periodic use, say on weekends.

Undeterred by such journalistic ridicule, Senator Byrd's committee brought its new concept of expense-account ethics to the Senate floor. There the bill inspired Senators Paul Douglas (D., Ill.) and Albert Gore (D., Tenn.) to go into a satirical vaudeville routine, feeding each other questions and answers.

"I am sure," said Douglas, "the Senator has seen reports on domestic discord which has arisen when the husband rides the expense account and the wife sits home and eats hamburgers."

"I have heard neighborhood rumors," Gore conceded.

"Is it not to be expected," Douglas continued, "that if the husband is living at the Ritz-Carlton or in Miami and is cruising in a yacht and paying $10 for lunches, or is eating expensive dinners at Antoine's in New Orleans, and the poor wife is at home eating a humble sandwich, she becomes discontented and domestic discord increases—"

GORE: And she feels neglected.

DOUGLAS: She feels neglected. Therefore, in order that the business executive may function more efficiently he must take his wife along and dish out the gravy to her, also.

The buffoonery nettled a couple of other Senators, Russell Long, of Louisiana, in whose locale Antoine's is located, and George Smathers, of Florida, who took not kindly to those unkind cuts about yachting and Miami.

"I recognize," said Smathers haughtily, "that many musicians, restaurants and hotels make conventions their business and thereby contribute to the welfare of the economy of the States in which they are located. I do not wish to see them put out of business. . . ."

He wished, he said, that Senators would stop "ranting and raving about the safari, about taking wives on trips and all that sort of thing."

Nothing, however, could deter Douglas and Gore. They went into a staccato routine that Gilbert and Sullivan would have delighted to set to music.

DOUGLAS: Sixty-five-dollar tickets to see *My Fair Lady*.

GORE: Yes.

DOUGLAS: Expenses at the "21" Club.

GORE: If that is amusement.

DOUGLAS: It *is* amusement.

GORE: Or entertainment.

DOUGLAS: Or for good will.

GORE: Is that not wonderful?

Wonderful, indeed. Neither reason nor ridicule could stir the Senate to conscience. In late August 1962, by a vote of 58–39, that august body buried the Kennedy expense-account reform and placed its official imprimatur upon the prevalent American ethic—anything and everything is all right as long as you can get away with it. As Senator Douglas commented, the bill the Senate passed "would give legislative approval to hunting lodges, yachts, theater tickets, and the Lord knows what. The sky is the limit."

The event was to prove the accuracy of this denunciation. The new revenue bill, it was true, did put a veneer of respectability on the real deed that had been done. It provided with seeming sternness that entertainment to qualify must be tied to a bona-fide business discussion, and it left the interpretation of all this up to Internal Revenue.

So began the final act of the farce. Business yowled with unabated anguish lest Internal Revenue should go berserk and clamp down on its more licentious pleasures. And Internal Revenue, betrayed in Congress, bowed and scraped and assured business, before every periodic "interpretation" of the code, that this really wasn't going to hurt very much; it really wasn't going to change things drastically. The inevitable dead end of this campaign of retreat and obeisance came in late June 1963, when in a final "interpretation" Internal Revenue abjectly capitulated. As *The New York Times* commented editorially on June 26, 1963:

"The latest version of the Internal Revenue Service's regulations on expense-account deductions is a craven retreat in an obvious attempt to give offense to no one.

"Husbands will be able to claim a tax deduction for entertaining their own or their customers' wives in the pursuit of business; and owners of yachts and hunting lodges will be permitted to deduct their operating costs for business entertainment, provided that the facilities are used at least half the time for such purposes. . . ."

A Congress that couldn't find the heart to curb even the blatant excesses of the phony expense-account way of life naturally wasn't going to correct any of the other gross inequities of the tax system to which President Kennedy had directed its attention. It is a system so riddled with ratholes that, if you don't have to work for your money, if you just have enough of it piled up working for you, you can easily arrange matters so that you don't have to pay any taxes at all! "To the very rich, our tax system is just like passing around the hat," says Representative Wright Patman, the doughty Texas Democrat who has been warring on the foundation tax dodge. "If they want to put in, they can. If they don't want to, they don't have to."

Patman has demonstrated that foundations, ostensibly organized for charitable purposes, all too often adopt the rule that charity begins at home. They are used to pile up tax-free dollars and control vast businesses. (At the close of 1960, seven Rockefeller foundations held 7,891,567 shares of the common stock of Standard Oil of New Jersey.) They often serve as a tax-free shelter in which the donor can keep his funds and use them to bankroll his own businesses or to defray his own living expenses. (Frank Lloyd Wright, the noted architect, hadn't even filed an income tax return in the last twenty-five years before his death in 1959; all his earnings had gone into his private foundation, and his living expenses had been siphoned off from that.) Patman, in his diligent digging into what he calls "the foundation mess," even uncovered a gimmick that enables real wheeler-dealers to send their children to college with tax-free dollars. It works like this: You set up a foundation to grant college scholarships to worthy students; you bankroll it with, say, an initial donation of $25,000; by so doing, you whittle down your own taxes because, of course, you are rewarded with a tax exemption on the $25,000 you have bequeathed to "charity." Comes the time to award the "scholarships," and your "charity" comes home. Who gets the scholarships? Your own sons, of course. "There's one wealthy residential area outside Philadelphia where virtually every other house has a foundation set up to send its kids to college at the taxpayers' expense," Patman declares.

There is certainly nothing like sweet charity, or a few good oil wells, to keep the extremely wealthy from paying taxes. In the long 1963–1964 debates over the Kennedy tax-reform proposals (every one of which died ignominious deaths at the hands of Congress), Senator Douglas momentarily shocked the nation by revealing that twenty taxpayers, with *incomes* ranging from $500,000 into the millions, had paid "not one cent of taxes" in 1962. Five of Senator Douglas' nontaxpayers had had *incomes of more than $5 million; one had had an income, in this one year, of $28 million—and still had not paid a cent in taxes!*

The 27½ per cent oil depletion allowance, the no-limit rule on "charity" contributions, and a host of other loopholes, all sanctified in law, all retained by a Congress that resolutely turned its back on reform, permitted all of these multimillionaires to enjoy their tax immunity in perfect legality. As Wright Patman says, if they don't want to put into the hat, they don't have to—and, being human, they didn't want to, and they didn't.

But what can be said for a Congress and a society that sanction such perversions of equity and justice? Clearly, the system that has been underwritten in the highest legislative hall in the land is the racket system—the system that says if you're smart, you'll find a way to beat paying. It's a racket that can be used only by the wealthy who don't work for their money, who have oil wells and can take advantage of the 27½ per cent depletion allowance and other tax dodges. The working sucker, poor slob, hasn't any oil wells or the resources to set up a foundation, and so he can't participate. But, being human, he doubtless wishes that he could; he knows that this is the way his world is run and that his only real chance in life lies in being able, someday, some way, to grab himself a piece of the racket.

In the meantime, all he can do is watch from the sidelines and get a vicarious thrill when some superscoundrel occasionally comes along and plays the big boys for suckers. Ethics have long since gone out the window. Who is to say what is right and what is wrong in this society? Certainly not the average man who has been victimized by it. He feels no impulse to go out and expose the superscoundrel; instead he is more inclined to chuckle and to cheer. In this world, in this dearth of ethics, a Billy Sol Estes strides upon the scene, and to many he seems, for a time at least, more hero than thief.

5

Silent Partners of
Billie Sol Estes

BILLIE SOL ESTES, stocky, chubby-faced, weak eyes framed by large dark-rimmed glasses, was the perfect archetype of the age of manipulation. He scorned such moth-eaten old credos as Ben Franklin's "A penny saved is a penny earned" and adopted as his maxim the witty saying of a modern man—Texas multimillionaire Clint Murchison's only half-joking remark: "A man is worth twice what he owes."

A poor farm boy, Billie Sol Estes marched to meet his future under the guiding star of Murchison's philosophy. No matter how much money he amassed, it was never enough because success to him meant just one thing—the Murchisons—and he could never be content until he possessed as many millions as they did. Toward this eminence he struggled by trying to be worth not twice but several thousand times what he owed; and for a time he kept the illusion real with three Cadillacs, three private airplanes, and a $150,000 mansion with a fifty-foot living room, at one end of which a waterfall came cascading into a palm garden.

Such were the gaudy trappings of success that rewarded an empire founded on fraud—a fraud that was widely recognized and that was countenanced, if indeed it was not actually cheered on, by a vast cross section of American society. It could have happened only in the world of the manipulators, of the fast-buck artists, each trying to short-change the other and no one caring about the ethics of the game. In this kind of competition Estes excelled; he could even at times look almost like a hero, skinning cats more fat and powerful than he.

Billie Sol (it's pronounced "soul") was born in 1925 on a farm three miles northwest of Clyde, a dusty hamlet set in the wide, sandy, sunbaked, desolate plain of West Texas. The second child in a family of six, Billie Sol went to a nearby one-room school and got an early introduction, against which he appears to have rebelled, to the unceasing round of hard work involved in tending sheep, cattle, and pigs, and laboring in the cotton and wheat fields. His parents were honest, hard-working, devout, attending services of the Church of Christ every Sunday. Some of this early and strict religious training evidently left its mark on Billie Sol, for in maturity the unscrupulous manipulator was to parade a kind of fanatic religiosity. He became a Church of Christ lay preacher; he didn't drink or smoke, looked on dancing as sinful, and wouldn't let boys and girls go swimming together in the same swimming pool.

It seems to have escaped general notice, but Billie Sol Estes' character and career so paralleled those of P. T. Barnum, the nineteenth century's Prince of Humbug, that it's almost enough to make one believe in reincarnation. Both Barnum and Estes were born in small rural communities; both, in youth, knew poverty and hard work. In both there was a deeply religious strain that drove them to lay preaching and enabled them to pose as saints on Sundays and practice as pirates the other six days of the week. Both were country boys who derived an unholy glee from making yokels out of city slickers, and both operated on the theory that there's another sucker born every minute and the devil take the hindmost. There was between them this difference: Barnum devoted his talents to showmanship, to the field of entertainment, which has about it a great deal of make-believe in any event; Estes concentrated solely on his victims' wallets. Like Barnum, Estes was precocious; like Barnum, he showed quite early in life precisely what might be expected of him later.

In Estes' case, this boyhood demonstration centered about the story of the ewe lamb. When he was a mere ten years old, his parents gave him the beribboned ewe as a Christmas present. Billie Sol cared for her, reared her, and when she grew up, he sheared her, sold the wool, reared and bought more lambs—and soon had a flock of sheep. He then traded the sheep for hogs, the hogs for cattle, and by the time he was fourteen, he was the owner of a respectable herd. Possibly it was this experience in multiplying one ewe lamb into a herd of cattle that gave rise in later years to one of Estes' favorite sayings: "You can shear a sheep every year; you can't skin him but once."

Garnishing the tale with such reflections, Billie Sol Estes, during his career as a successful poseur to millions, never tired of orating before captive audiences about his boyhood experiences with the ewe lamb. He usually coupled this with a call upon his audience to exercise "vision"—the kind of vision, of course, that he had shown as a boy in making that ewe lamb grow into a whole herd of cattle. He became so repetitious and so righteously, insufferably boring on the subject that one leathery old West Texas rancher whose patience had been exhausted was overheard once to remark: "Wouldn't you think he'd give some credit to the ram?"

For the purposes of Estes' own industriously promoted legend, there was nothing like the story of the ewe lamb. Less well known but perhaps of greater significance as a portent of things to come were a couple of other events of this boyhood period.

There was, for example, the story of the "four-gallon" cow. Estes waxed so eloquent about the miraculous milk production of this remarkable animal that he talked a credulous neighboring farmer into paying him a fancy price for her. When the cow did not produce any more milk than any other cow, the angry farmer came storming to Estes' father, protesting that he had been bilked. Estes, only fourteen at the time, explained with the wiliness of a Barnum that he had never said how *long* it took that cow to deliver four gallons of milk.

Equally indicative of the future was the story of Estes' first manipulative ten-strike as a high school wheeler-dealer. Estes discovered (just how a high school boy should discover such things remains one of the mysteries of personality) that the Commodity Credit Corporation was selling wheat in bulk for less than the going market rate around Clyde. This meant that any dealer who could keep his distribution costs down could make a profit. Filled by this vision of dancing dollar signs, young Estes persuaded a friendly banker to lend him $3500 and bought a carload of government wheat. He then used the boxcar for both warehouse and store, advertising cheap wheat to be delivered at the railroad siding to all comers on a cash-and-carry basis. The West Texas farmers, smelling a bargain, came and carried. Estes recruited a crew of his fellow high school students, and they shoveled the grain into buckets, baskets, anything that would cart it away. Estes was sometimes a little slow at paying off his high school helpers, but this didn't seem to dim his popularity. He was elected "King" of his junior class, and he kept the wheat deal going into 1943, by which time he had disposed of fourteen carloads.

World War II was at its height, and Estes normally would have been draft bait. But he had physical handicaps—bad eyesight and one leg that was slightly shorter than the other. Rejected by the services, he finally got into the merchant marine in 1945, just as the war was building to its climax. He served as a wiper and mess attendant on ships plying the Atlantic, and naturally it didn't take Billie Sol's built-in radar long to detect opportunities for making money.

War-starved Europe was eager for all kinds of American goods, from cigarettes and candy bars to mink stoles, and Billie Sol, on his trips to New York, never failed to load up on wares that could be easily transported, smuggled into France, and sold at a handsome profit. American postage stamps were the going currency for much of this traffic in those days, and when Billie Sol finally left the merchant marine and returned to Clyde, his pockets were bulging with some $700 worth of stamps. Billie Sol was a big boy now. He had served his apprenticeship, and he was ready for the big time—ready for the first of those colossal manipulations that ultimately would make an entire nation gasp.

I

The alkali dust had hardly settled on his boots before Billie Sol, the farmer home from the sea, began to wheel and deal in housing. The construction-starved war years had resulted in great housing shortages for America's burgeoning population; at the same time, with the coming of peace, the government had on its hands a lot of surplus barracks for which the now-drying-up military camps had no use. Billie Sol quickly decided that there was a fortune to be made by putting need and surplus together. And so he began to bid on military barracks in West Texas, New Mexico, California, Washington, and Arkansas.

There are indications that, even this early, he had discovered the secret of how to win friends and influence officials, for competitors later recalled that it was "damned near impossible" to bid successfully on any barracks that Billie Sol wanted. He always seemed to win, even when his bid was as low as $35. Having obtained a barracks for such a pittance, Billie Sol would chain-saw it in half, board up the open ends, and dispose of it as two separate houses. Purchasers desperate for homes would sometimes pay as much as $3000 to $4000 for such shacklike accommodations, yielding Billie Sol a fantastic profit.

All the evidence seems to indicate that Billie plowed the money back into the land—and not too successfully. He went into cotton farming in the Texas Panhandle, developed a sideline selling feed grain, and put on as always a great front. After two years, however, the front began to wear thin. As a local banker in Earth, Texas, was later to tell the House Committee on Government Operations, Estes left the area "owing about everyone . . . from $9.50 to $750." From this the committee concluded that Estes, all the time he was living like a millionaire, actually never had been anything but insolvent.

The town of Pecos in West Texas about 220 miles from Clyde didn't have any suspicion of this, however, when Estes wandered upon the scene in early 1951, carrying a battered old brief case and wearing rumpled, dust-streaked, country-boy clothes. Estes loitered around the town for several days, like a man looking for something. He never told anyone just what it was he was seeking, but he chatted with gas-station attendants, waitresses, and truck drivers, getting the feel of the place. He evidently liked what he found, for he decided to settle down in Pecos. Soon he was asking for the name of "an honest real-estate broker," and soon he was purchasing from the honest broker "a section," 640 acres of land on which, he said, he was going to farm and raise cotton. On the tract that he purchased was a shacklike structure, flung together with wood from icebox crates coated with stucco and set above an abandoned Army swimming pool that served as a cellar. Into this home, Billie Sol Estes moved his wife—his former high school sweetheart, Patsy Howe—and the first two of the five children that were to be born to them.

Pecos had no intimation at the time that, within a few years, the shacklike home was to be transformed into a $150,000 mansion, complete with palm garden and waterfall in its living room, but it didn't take the town long to become amazed at how fast Billie Sol Estes could run from a seemingly standing start. For hardly had Billie Sol settled into residence above the old swimming pool before the manipulator in him began to manipulate.

He discovered that the Agriculture Department, to encourage the expansion of grain-storage facilities, was offering financing at 2 per cent for the erection of prefabricated buildings. Billie Sol, reading the fine print in the government regulations, found there was nothing that said specifically that the prefabs *had* to be used to store grain, and so he was soon wheeling and dealing in prefabricated structures, selling them for garages, airplane hangars, housing for Mexican laborers. His customers were farmers eager to do business with him after he had shown them just how they could take advantage of the government's 2 per cent money.

No one knows just how much Billie Sol amassed from this venture and from other deals with which he was incessantly occupied. *Fortune,* which did an extensive analysis of his rise and fall, estimated that he had probably accumulated about $28,000 when he first came to Pecos, but the House Government Operations Committee's report would indicate that, even then, he probably owed more than he had. Estes' own balance sheets, which in the light of events are subject to deep suspicion, put his net worth by December 1951 at $176,197.05. Estes arrived at this total by putting a value of $128,000 on his 640 acres of land; he also listed a tourist court valued at $37,000 and eleven tractors worth $20,000. Just two years later, in December 1953, he was listing his net worth at $743,679.76, including among the assets 150 apartments in Port Neches, a half-interest in sixty apartments in Frederick, Oklahoma, 1440 acres of farmland in Reeves County, and (most suspect of all his items) $271,500 worth of cotton on hand.

Not many men can increase their net worth by more than $500,-000 in two years. Decidedly, Billie Sol Estes was making a tremendous splash in Pecos, but even at this early date there were some disquieting ripples on the water. For a man of such supposed affluence, he had the unenviable reputation around Pecos of never paying even the smallest bill if he could get out of it. Perhaps it was this trait that made the Pecos Junior Chamber of Commerce balk in 1953 at the suggestion it submit Billie Sol's name to the state organization as one of the five outstanding young men of Texas. Despite this flat rejection by the selection committee, Billie Sol triumphed. One of his partisans on the board sent in Estes' name anyway. The result: he was picked as Texas' most outstanding young businessman, and just a few months later he was named, along with Governor Frank Clement of Tennessee, one of the ten outstanding young men in the nation.

One Pecos resident, later recalling the episode, remarked: "Billie Sol bragged to everybody that he was one of America's outstanding young men. But not many know he never was voted one of the outstanding young men of Pecos."

The designation, like so much about Billie Sol Estes, rested on a strictly phony base. It was significant—a point to be emphasized time and again in his later career—that he impressed most the people who knew him least, not those who knew him best.

The years immediately following his designation as one of the outstanding young businessmen of America were years of frantic Estes activity. He built himself to millionaire's status, and though he always owed far more millions than he possessed, this was not immediately apparent to the general public. Estes' enterprises expanded all over the Texas landscape, and many persons along the way, as the House committee later pointed out, must have had cause to suspect that they had reached the sleight-of-hand stage where Estes used the resources and borrowing capacity of one enterprise to offset the losses of others.

When the Estes bubble finally burst in the spring of 1962, it became almost a journalistic cliché to dub the wheeler-dealer from the Pecos "a welfare-state Ponzi" because two phases of his operations involved the storing of government grain and the rigging of cotton allotments. The phrase had a delightful ring to a business and journalistic world in which the concept of the welfare state is anathema, but its glibness hid, if it did not deliberately ignore, the deeper implications of the Estes scandal.

No doubt about it, Estes was a Ponzi, but he was a Ponzi who had flourished because, at no level of American life that he had touched—and he had touched them all—was there any valid, operative ethical concept. Chief Justice Warren's point that a "sea of ethics" is vital to the survival of law was never better illustrated than in the career of Billie Sol; the plain truth is that Estes pyramided his swindles into a multimillion dollar debacle only by (1) taking advantage of the cupidity of millionaire businessmen out to amass more millions and not possessed of too many scruples about how they did it; (2) buying, bribing, and wangling political and bureaucratic influence; and (3) taking virtually an entire countryside, possessed of the same cupidity as the businessmen, into his larcenous confidence.

The House Government Operations Committee put it this way:

Although one man was responsible, it took more than one person to build the Estes empire. Billie Sol Estes received assistance from employees who did what they were told without asking questions. He was helped by local bankers who gave him consistently favorable recommendations. Estes benefitted from poor procedures and poor judgment involving Government agencies and private firms with which he had dealings. . . .

Billie Sol Estes' fraudulent operations were disclosed not once but several times, beginning years before his arrest. Many people knew he was engaging in unethical business practices. A substantial number of firms or individuals knew—or had reason to believe—that Estes was engaging in fraudulent transactions long before he was arrested. A few of them even knew—or should have suspected—that he was insolvent. . . .

Some of the firms or individuals who knew—or had reason to believe—that Billie Sol Estes was engaging in fraudulent transactions were owed substantial sums of money by Estes. When they discovered

possible or probable fraud, they had two choices. They
the evidence of Estes' fraud to the proper authorities,
risk of throwing him into both jail and bankruptcy. On the
they could remain silent and continue to receive full or
ments of Estes' indebtedness. The subcommittee is not
y instance in which a creditor of Estes who had reason to
susp─ honesty reported such suspicions to appropriate authorities
for the purpose of having him prosecuted. . . .

2

Business had the first and best chance to put an end to the
depredations of Billie Sol Estes before he became virtually a national menace. It also had the opportunity, by acting ethically,
to save itself millions in future losses and untold grief. But business
wasn't interested in the ethics of the case; it was concerned only
with money; and so, in the end, it became its own victim.

The golden lost opportunity (there had been lesser exposures
dating back to 1953) came in 1959 and involved the matter of
the nonexistent irrigation pumps. The West Texas prairie that
stretches far and wide on every side of Pecos looks like one of the
most godforsaken areas in the universe. It is a wasteland of
parched sand, scrawny mesquite, and coarse buffalo grass, a desert-
like wilderness where even a jack rabbit has to keep on the hop for
survival. But the roll of the land to the far horizon is vast and awe-
compelling like the roll of the sea; the sky above is limitless in the
blue immensity of space; and at night the moon turns the prairie
into one tremendous, mellow ocean of silver. It is the kind of
country that breeds grandiose dreams in the minds of men. What is
more, it is a deceptive country, not half so barren as it seems, for
the *caliche* soil, if it can be irrigated and fertilized, becomes lush
with cotton. And, fortunately for Pecos, there is plenty of water
deep down under the prairie once wells have been sunk and pumps
installed to tap the supply.

There is some reason to suspect that Billie Sol Estes, with his
knowledge of cotton, sensed this hidden bounty under the prairie
when he first came to Pecos, that it was the thing that lured him—
this knowledge that prairie land worth $40 an acre could be turned

into cotton land worth $300 an acre with the aid of irrigation. In any event, he quickly organized affairs so that he could take his profit from every step in the transformation process. He was one of the founders of the Pecos Growers Gas Co. in which, in 1958, he owned 1600 shares worth about $5 a share. The gas company furnished the fuel to the farmers to drive the irrigation pumps that brought up the water. The pumps themselves offered another opportunity of profit for Estes. He organized the Equipment Supply Co., which sold and serviced the pumps the farmers used. In August 1958, Estes, needing cash to keep some of his various enterprises afloat, sold a lot of mortgages on the pumps to a finance company, Associates Investment, Inc.

So far, so good. On the surface it all seemed like a perfectly legitimate business transaction, the work of a smart operator with the vision to see his opportunities and profit from them. But in early 1959, Associates Investment discovered that farmers were falling into default on their mortgage payments. And almost before the finance company knew what was happening, it found it had on its hands some $600,000 worth of mortgage paper that was seriously in arrears. Investigating to determine why so many farmers had defaulted at the same time, Associates Investment uncovered a real shocker—a huge number of irrigation pumps on which it held mortgage paper simply did not exist.

Billie Sol's contract with Associates Investment made him personally responsible for the payment of any mortgage in default; but once he was faced with a $600,000 tab, he balked at honoring it. However, Associates' discovery that mortgage paper had been written on nonexistent pumps evidently put pressure on Estes, for he finally agreed to make good the losses, given time. Here, of course, the first great ethical question arose, the first great ethical decision had to be made. Associates Investment had caught a daring swindler red-handed. Should it protect him in the hope of getting its money back—and so leave him free to swindle others? As the House committee later reported, there is no record that Associates Investment waged any life-and-death struggle with its conscience. It wanted its money back above all else. And so it resolved, for its own protection, not to accept any more Estes paper—and not to take any action against him.

This decision left Billie Sol free to wheel and deal, and it is almost axiomatic that a swindler, protected and successful in his first swindle, will swindle more. In Billie Sol's case, as he afterward acknowledged, he had been taught a lesson, but it wasn't quite the kind of a lesson that might have been expected to register with a lay preacher of the Church of Christ. All Billie Sol had learned was that he would have to be more careful. He realized, as he later explained it, that he had made just two mistakes: he had operated under his own name, and the bulk of his mortgage paper had been concentrated with one finance company. The way to work the deal was to keep himself well hidden behind corporate fronts and to spread the paper around to avoid such quick suspicion. All that was needed was a new field in which to operate.

It did not take Billie Sol Estes long to find the opportunity. In addition to water, the West Texas prairie needs just one major ingredient to make it bloom with cotton—anhydrous ammonia. This liquid fertilizer is essential, and Billie Sol, early appreciating this, had formed the Farmers Co. and had begun, as early as 1956, to sell ammonia and insecticides. Before long, he had run up a bill of more than $500,000 with Agricultural Chemicals Inc., a Murchison enterprise.

Billie Sol was, of course, unable to pay, and here once again vigorous action by a firm which he had bilked out of half a million dollars might have put an end to his career. But Agricultural Chemicals, like Associates Investment, was not at all interested in the ethics of the case or the general well-being of the business community; all it wanted was its money. And so it permitted Billie Sol to work out a repayment schedule, postponing the evil day of reckoning into the future—a procedure that left Agricultural Chemicals still holding the bag for some $350,000 when Billie Sol's house of cards finally collapsed.

In hock to Associates Investment for $600,000, in hock to the Murchison interests for another $500,000, Billie Sol needed a new angel, especially one who would supply him with anhydrous ammonia for his fertilizer business. So he quickly switched his affections from the Murchisons to Commercial Solvents, a New York firm; and with this change in business allegiance he began a caper so wild and so desperate that it was later to become a matter of dispute just who led whom along the daisy trail of corporate dalliance. Only one thing seems clear: in 1958, just about the time his irrigation-pump fraud was reaching the point of exposure, Billie Sol decided to wheel and deal in anhydrous ammonia in a fashion to beat anything West Texas had ever seen.

Lloyd Stone, who became a manager in Estes' expanding ammonia-fertilizer business, later testified in a Texas inquiry about the precise manner in which Billie Sol explained to him his plans:

"To use his term, we'd just surround them and then hit them. We can go in here and work real hard for fifteen years and build a business. But these people have all this business just in their hot little hands. If we try to get it this way, we're not going to be able to get it. If we hit them, it will all fly up in the air and when it falls down, then we'll grab our part of it."

Did Billie Sol "hit them"? Stone was asked. "Yes, sir," he said. "And it flew."

The conversation, Estes' one-time manager made clear, took place in connection with the first cutthroat price-slashing that Estes introduced with the intention of driving all competitors to the wall. Ammonia ferilizer was then selling in West Texas for $120 a ton. The wholesale price to distributors was $90 a ton. Billie Sol began selling retail to farmers at $80 a ton, taking a $10 loss on every ton he sold. Obviously this was a madly ruinous way to do business; but Billie Sol's object, as he had told Stone, was to "hit them" so hard smaller competitors would be driven right over the brink of bankruptcy. By such tactics he hoped to corner the entire ammonia fertilizer market in all West Texas, and once he had the corner, he would be able, of course, to establish his own prices. If it worked, the future held millions; but, in the meantime, the present represented only additional millions of debt.

By the end of 1958, Estes was in debt to Commercial Solvents to the tune of another $500,000, and Commercial Solvents didn't seem to be able to get any money out of him. Understandably, the big New York firm began to feel some twinges of concern, and it suggested to Estes that he come to Manhattan for a discussion of their mutual problem. Not at all loath, worried not in the slightest by that mere bagatelle of another half-million dollars' worth of debt, Estes hopped into his private plane and arrived bubbling with plans that included a major role for Commercial Solvents. "If you get into anybody far enough," he often said, "you've got yourself a partner." What he wanted now was to get into Commercial Solvents so far that Commerical Solvents would be committed forever to Billie Sol Estes.

His pitch to Commerical Solvents went, in essence, something like this: "Let's not worry about that mere $500,000 I owe you. There's a fortune to be made, and I'm the man who can show you how. All I need is a little *further* backing."

This "further backing" involved Commerical Solvents' willingness to loan him another $900,000. Some $550,000 would be applied to the liquidation of Estes' old debt. Another $125,000 would be used to buy more ammonia. And some $225,000 would be spent for the purchase of a grain-storage elevator in Plainview, Texas. Estes would pay off the entire debt over a five-year period. As security, he offered Commercial Solvents a lien on the receipts of the grain elevator that he was to purchase with its money. And, a point not to be overlooked, Estes, having re-established his credit with Commerical Solvents with Commerical Solvents' own funds, would be permitted to buy more anhydrous ammonia from the company on credit.

Obviously, the legendary character who sold refrigerators to Eskimos had nothing on Billie Sol Estes—yet Commercial Solvents, a multimillion-dollar concern whose worldly wise officers must have realized they were dealing with a slippery customer, showed no repugnance. Instead, they bought the deal. Why? The answer tells a lot about the ethics of big business.

Fortune, in its subsequent analysis of this complicated transaction, wrote that "Solvents seems to have known what it was doing." *Fortune*'s breakdown of the figures showed that, though Billie Sol Estes ultimately left the big fertilizer firm holding the bag for an ostensible $5.7 million, actually Solvents came out $620,000 ahead on the deal. If this sounds insane, follow *Fortune* step-by-step through the labyrinth of high finance. It worked like this:

A key figure to keep in mind is the cost of ammonia fertilizer to Commercial Solvents. The firm's production and shipping costs came to only $40 a ton, but the wholesale price in the industry (and no one yet seems to have wondered how this figure was arrived at by all of the supposedly competing fertilizer companies) was $90 a ton. This markup of more than 100 per cent above cost gave Solvents enormous leverage. What it meant was that Estes could run up quite a sizable debt with Solvents before Solvents even began to be really hurt. The guarantee of grain-elevator receipts from the federal government promised to cover the base cost figure, and Estes, in his price-slashing war, would be carrying the ball for Solvents in West Texas; he, regardless of what happened to him, would be opening up a vast new market for the big New York firm.

This, of course, was precisely what happened. When the Estes bubble burst, Commercial Solvents came out smelling like a rose. It could claim a tax writeoff of some $2.6 million on the bad Estes debt; it had received the heavy cash flow from the grain elevators, guaranteeing its basic costs; and so, cashwise, though it showed a huge loss, the loss was mainly on paper—actually, it was far ahead of the game. And this wasn't all. It took over the huge distributor-dealer network Estes had built up in his effort to corner the West Texas market, and so it had established itself in a strong position in a profitable territory. *Fortune* predicted that Commercial Solvents, instead of being Billie Sol Estes' major victim, would turn out to be the major beneficiary of his operations. It was a perceptive forecast. In 1963, Commercial Solvents showed a profit of $2 a share, and in 1964, its earnings continued to zoom. It raised its quarterly dividend from 25 cents a share to 27.5 cents—*the sixth such dividend increase since the third quarter of 1959.*

This prosperity of Commercial Solvents was not achieved without cost. Those who paid were a lot of honest fertilizer dealers who were ground to bits by the Estes steamroller that Commercial Solvents had made possible. The testimony of what happened to mere average people when they got in the way of Billie Sol (and the

Commercial Solvents shadow behind him) was developed in il-luminating detail at the subsequent Texas inquiry.

Typical was the testimony of James L. Winders, a former fer-tilizer dealer in Earth, Texas. He said he had been selling an-hydrous ammonia for about three years when he got a telephone call from Billie Sol himself.

"I heard that Mr. Estes was moving his anhydrous ammonia organization into the South Plains area," he testified. "And in the conversation he told me if I did not buy anhydrous ammonia from him the next year he would put me out of business."

Q. What did you respond to that?

A. Well, I asked him if he didn't think he should come up and talk with me about it. At that time, I didn't have a large business, but I didn't owe anything, and I thought the man ought to come and talk with me before he just took over my business. He said, "There's nothing to talk about. That's just the way it is."

Winders discovered that this was indeed "just the way" it was. He held out for several months, but Estes cut costs so far below the established wholesale price he couldn't compete. By the time he sold out his business to Estes in 1961, he was some $30,000 in debt.

Fred Simms was another dealer who was told to "line up" with Estes if he wanted to stay in business. He heeded the advice and was told to sell fertilizer at below cost; Estes, he was promised, would guarantee him a margin of $10 a ton for his own profit. Simms joined the Estes group, and soon he had farmers lining up at his office signing contracts for the cheap fertilizer he offered. This went on for three weeks, and then suddenly, without explana-tion, Simms was cut off from his source of less-than-cost fertilizer.

"What happened?" he was asked.

"Well, I still don't know what happened," he said.

His pleas to Estes to be reinstated in the Estes cartel were ignored. He couldn't fulfill the contracts he had signed with the farmers; he lost "between $15,000 or $20,000" on the deal; his business was ruined.

Even larger and well-established firms couldn't buck the ruth-less Estes drive. One of Estes' first victims was the West Texas distributorship of Lester–Stone. In 1959, early in his price-cutting war, Estes bought out one of the partners, the Lloyd Stone who later became one of his fertilizer managers. Glenn R. Lester, the other partner, watched unhappily as Estes' price-slashing piled up a $300,000 loss for the concern. When Estes, still not satisfied that he had driven the price low enough to ruin all competitors in the area, decided on still one more cheap ammonia sale, Lester protested.

"I said, 'No, I believe we have sold enough of that,' " he testified. "He said, 'Whether you like it or not, we're going to sell it.' "

Lester said Estes threatened to foreclose the partnership, a threat he could well carry out since Lester–Stone was now so completely in hock to the Estes enterprises for its fertilizer losses. But Estes gave Lester a choice. He would, he said, buy out Lester's share of the business for $25,000, about a third of what he had paid for Stone's share a year earlier. When Estes made the offer, Lester testified, he said: "Well, we'll just temper the rod with a little mercy here." Lester, helpless, had to accept the "mercy" deal.

By such tactics, Billie Sol Estes expanded his chain of distributors and dealers from ten in 1959 to seventy-eight in early 1962. Such rapid expansion may have had the look of phenomenal success to an outsider, but to an insider the cost, by any reasonable standards, had to be judged prohibitive. Estes had run some $1,750,000 in the red, and the end was not in sight. To keep plunging at this pace and to maintain at the same time the public posture of a millionaire rolling in ever greater millions, Billie Sol Estes had to generate an enormous amount of cash; and he could do this only by a new swindle—one that would soar high into the millions.

3

At the heart of the machinations in which Estes now became involved lay the dilemma of superabundance in the mass and largely affluent society. Though the farm population had been drastically reduced, use of new fertilizers and new, mechanized techniques had resulted in the production of a flood of foodstuffs beyond the capacity of the American public to consume. In this context, free enterprise in the world of agriculture would have been both ridiculous and an insurance of national disaster. Without some kind of control, the market would be glutted, prices would plummet to ruinous levels, and a disaster of the magnitude of 1929–1932 might well confront the nation. To avert such calamity, the federal government embarked on a variety of programs. It tried to hold down production by imposing limits on the acreage that could be tilled and paying farmers for taking land out of cultivation. This program was largely self-defeating, for the farmer who was being paid not to plant some of his acres quickly found that, by putting the rows a little closer together and fertilizing more heavily, he could bring in almost as large a crop as before. Such bumper production threatened ruin, and the federal government adopted a price-support program based upon buying up and storing the unusable surplus. Soon the government was spending close to one billion dollars a year just to buy up food surpluses—and another billion to store the ever-growing hoard. By 1962, a total of some $9 billion in surplus foods had been piled up in government warehouses. The individual figures were astronomical, incredible. There were more than one billion bushels of wheat, enough to meet the needs of the entire world for a year; about 1.2 billion bushels of corn; 1.5 million bales of cotton; 240,000 pounds of butter; 400,000 pounds of dried milk; and tons upon tons of other commodities.

The handling and storage of such foodstuffs was a remunerative business for the warehouse owners who engaged in it. For Billie Sol Estes, it represented opportunity—the chance to keep his fertilizer war going, the chance to keep his financial arrangements with Commercial Solvents afloat.

From Estes' standpoint, there were two wings to his endeavor. First, to maintain his credit with Solvents, he had to expand his grain-elevator operation so that ever-increasing government fees for storing surplus grain would underwrite his ever-increasing fertilizer deficits. But to build more elevators to store more grain took ever more millions. The money had to come from somewhere, and

Estes, who had dabbled in fraud in the irrigation-pump deal, now refined the technique and began to float clouds of spurious mortgages on ammonia fertilizer tanks.

Let's consider separately for a minute the two halves of this enterprise. The storage of government grain inevitably involved Estes with the U.S. Department of Agriculture, gave him a more intimate personal interest in politics, and led to the purchasing or wangling of influence. Estes, from his earliest days as a purchaser of government barracks, had operated on the theory that he could grease his way by handing out presents—a car, expensive clothes, a thousand dollars in cash. Such bounties placed recipients under obligation to return the favors. It was a technique of grass-roots, bureaucratic bribery; and, with it, Estes combined wheeling and dealing in the higher echelons, where the dropping of an important name is often a passport to all kinds of good will.

A Democrat, Estes prated a liberal Democratic line, and on the wall of his $75,000 office building in Pecos, a huge panel displayed portraits of party leaders, many of them affectionately autographed. This gallery was dominated by a huge, autographed portrait of President Kennedy, and it included the smiling faces of such Democratic eminents as the then Vice-President Lyndon B. Johnson, former President Harry S. Truman, Adlai Stevenson, Senator John McClellan, and Texas' own Senator Ralph Yarborough. It was not by accident that Estes came to possess such seeming evidence of high-level good will; he had worked for it, had been a lavish contributor to the party war chest.

In the 1956 campaign, for instance, he became so carried away by Democratic enthusiasm that he made a complete fool of himself. He tried to persuade the president of a Pecos bank to finance a wacky scheme that, Estes was convinced, would help Adlai Stevenson win the election. Estes planned to train large flocks of parakeets to chirp "I like Adlai." The parakeets would be released to fly over the nation's largest cities, chirping in unison. When the unenthusiastic banker tried to point out to Estes that it would be virtually impossible to teach large numbers of parakeets to chirp for Adlai, much less to chirp in unison, Estes became purple with rage and stormed out, accusing the banker of being anti-Stevenson.

On more practical levels, Estes made his influence felt. He threw a huge barbecue for Senator Yarborough, and he contributed some $7500 to Yarborough's campaign. For Estes this was little more than chickenfeed. After the 1960 Presidential election, in which he worked energetically for Kennedy and Johnson, he liked to flash a gold-laminated card that attested he had contributed $100,000 to the Democratic Party treasury.

Just how much actual influence Estes managed to cultivate—and just how much good it did him—still remains a matter of considerable dispute. Common sense says that, one way or another, he must have amassed an unholy lot. Though he was a Democrat, he swung a lot of weight with Republicans, too. His grain-storage operations began under the Eisenhower administration and carried over into the Kennedy administration. Under Eisenhower, he was able to get government grain for storage in his first Plainview elevator, and under Kennedy his operations expanded fantastically. In 1961, some 5.2 million bushels of grain were moved from Kansas into his Texas grain elevators; in this year and in early 1962, he more than doubled his storage capacity and (a major point) kept his warehouses 58.3 per cent full. At the end, he was being paid as the caretaker of some $50 million worth of government grain. In all, $6,959,000 in federal grain-storage payments found their way through his bank accounts and into the account of Commercial Solvents.

This tremendous flow of cash kept Estes' credit with Commercial Solvents healthy, but to get it, to get the millions necessary to buy more grain elevators, he had to perpetrate a colossal fraud. The scheme he devised was so complicated it bears the stamp of crooked genius. Estes had learned from his past unfortunate experience with Associates Investment never to expose himself by using his own name. So now he decided to use the names and credit of all the farmers in the West Texas area whose acquaintance he had cultivated. His lure was what seemed like a foolproof, something-for-nothing proposition.

Billie Sol explained to the farmers that he needed to buy more fertilizer tanks for his expanding business and he would like to make the purchases in their names and use their credit—for a handsome fee, of course. The deal, as Billie Sol outlined it, would work this way: the farmer would buy a fertilizer tank in his own name, assuming the heavy mortgage on it. But the farmer needn't worry about that. Billie Sol would provide the farmer with the down payment. And from that point on, the farmer was protected, said Billie Sol. He would "lease" the fertilizer tank from the farmer for an amount that would exactly match the mortgage payments. The farmer didn't have to bother even looking at the tank; all he had to do was sign a delivery slip showing that he had received it. For this, for use of his credit, Billie Sol would pay the farmer a fee of 10 per cent. Why was Billie Sol doing all this? Well, he explained, a multimillionaire like himself, a man in his ruinously high tax bracket, could save a lot of money in income taxes by "leasing" the tanks because he could charge off the rental at a faster pace than he could depreciation if he owned them. The West Texas farmers, not dwelling in Billie Sol's rarefied stratum of high finance and having no way of knowing that Billie Sol's income-tax returns for 1959, 1960, and 1961 had showed only multimillion dollar losses, reckoned that this just possibly might be so, and hardly anybody, of course, has any scruples about gyping the federal government on taxes, especially if it can be done legally and safely. Besides, how could the farmers lose? If Billie Sol bought $100,000 worth of tanks in a man's name, he paid the man $10,000 clear for the privilege. And $10,000 is a lot of barking cash in any man's country.

What the farmers didn't know, at first at any rate, was that Billie Sol Estes wasn't actually buying fertilizer tanks; he was kiting paper mortgages. The tanks ostensibly were purchased from the Superior Manufacturing Co. of Amarillo, which had indeed manufactured the original tanks owned by Estes, and from the Lubbock Machine and Supply Co. of Lubbock, Texas. Superior Manufacturing, the major supplier, was run by Estes' own associates, and Lubbock was subsequently to be identified in court as a "broker" for Estes' enterprises. Thus, though Estes' name and hand appeared nowhere in the deal, they were present at every stage of it. Even the down payment made to Superior wasn't legitimate, for Superior refunded this money to Estes by checks made out to the Texas Steel Co., a dummy corporation that Estes set up with an account in the First National Bank of Pecos.

Estes cleaned up, of course, through the final stage of the process—the disposition of the mortgages to the finance companies. There was nothing on the paper surface of things to make the finance companies suspect a wrong deal. Superior could show photostats of the farmers' down-payment checks, photostats of delivery receipts the farmers had signed, indicating the tanks had been delivered. Convinced by such "factual" evidence, the finance companies would accept mortgages for 80 per cent of the tanks' presumed value and then they would discount this paper by 6 per cent. In other words, Superior would receive about 75 per cent of the tanks' listed value; it would deduct a 10 per cent fee for its cooperation; and it would pass the remaining 65 per cent along to Estes through checks made out to his dummy, Texas Steel.

Clearly, Estes was paying an extortionist's rate on every dollar he swindled by such means, but he was raking in millions in the process and evidently he wasn't worrying about full, final repayment. He was being impartial, too; he was spreading his mortgage business around among a dozen finance companies. One of these (and here a touch of decidedly poetic justice creeps into the tale) was Associates Investment, which had blinked at Estes' first $600,000 irrigation-pump swindle in the hope of getting its money back. Not only did Associates not get its money back on that deal, but now, all unknowing, it poured another $1,168,006.22 down the new and neatly camouflaged Estes rathole. Even so, Associates Investment was a relative piker. The firms Estes really hooked were Walter E. Heller, $6,243,588.86; CIT, $5,240,318.27; and Pacific Finance, $3,264,859.16. In all, from a dozen finance companies, Estes obtained the grandiose, incredible total of $21,845,-730.72.

Here it seems appropriate to pause and ask some questions. This was certainly one of the least-secret swindles of the century. Hundreds of farmers and scores of other persons, bankers, businessmen, citizens in all walks of life, certainly knew about Estes' peculiar wheeling and dealing in fertilizer-tank mortgages. Some of them may have been deceived at the outset into believing the deal was legitimate as Estes pictured it, but West Texas is not country inhabited entirely by drooling innocents. Many must have suspected from the outset that Estes was pulling a fast one, and there is absolutely no question that scores of men had positive knowledge long before retribution finally caught up with him. The reason that this knowledge became so widespread was that it was impossible for Estes to keep all his maneuvers secret; to keep the fraud going, he had to practice fraud openly, practically in public view.

This public exercise in deviousness developed the instant the finance companies began checking up. Finding themselves holding millions of dollars worth of fertilizer-tank mortgages, they sent investigators into West Texas to make certain the tanks existed. This led Estes into his final, frantic caper—an act in the play that might be entitled Publicly Pulling the Wool over Snooping Eyes. Estes himself, when he was finally caught, candidly explained everything to an attorney for one of the victimized finance companies.

"Imagine those sons of bitches," he said, referring to the finance companies that had supplied him with so many millions. "I don't have much respect for them. They'd come down here, send two or three men. They'd first go to the farmer, and the farmer would say, 'I don't have the tanks. I rented them. You go up to Estes Enterprises.' When they'd get here, I'd say, 'Just what tanks do you want to look at?' They would give the serial numbers. I'd say, 'It's going to take some time to find out where they are; they're hauled around from farm to farm, you know.' Then I'd just go back here to this room where the serial numbers were. I'd get the numbers we needed, get them flown to my ammonia dealer in the area, and tell him to put those numbers on the tanks right away."

Estes actually owned some 1800 tanks (though he had sold mortgages on 30,000), and the actual tanks were strategically placed so that a number of them would always be on hand in any given area. On some tanks the serial numbers could be screwed on; on others they had to be spot-welded. Then they would be painted with a special white-lead paint that was quick-drying.

ad been done, Estes' workmen would wet the number
hrow some dust on it to give it a properly scrubby
in two or three hours from the time Estes got the first
tanks were ready for inspection.

couldn't do it that fast," Estes subsequently explained,
them that some of the tanks they wanted to see were
in the county farthest away; that would give us some extra time.
Then when they got there, we might tell them some other tanks
they were looking for were maybe twenty-five miles from where
they'd started out in the first place. Can you imagine those guys
driving all over West Texas? They'd have tanks coming out of
their ears! One CIT fellow inspected the same tank three different
times, with three different serial numbers on it, and identified it as
three separate tanks."

A fraud practiced so brazenly, on such a scale, could not be a
secret fraud. Estes' dealers, his airplane pilots, his workmen, his
office help—all knew what was going on, and all, being human,
must have talked to their wives and friends about it at one time
or another. As one of Estes' dealers, G. S. "Mutt" Wheeler, later
testified at the Texas inquiry, Estes himself made no secret about
what he was doing; on the contrary, he even bragged openly about
it. The question-and-answer sequence with Wheeler went like this:

Q. Did Estes tell you to change the tank numbers?

A. Yes, sir.

Q. When was that, and tell us the circumstances of it.

A. Well, he laughingly told this joke—he says, "Oh, they will
never catch up with you," he says. "These people are stupid. I
know a man who borrowed a lot of money one time from a
Kansas City bank on cattle, and they came down and checked the
cattle, and he took those city boys out to a water hole where they
drove up what cattle they had, and counted them.

"And then they took the fellow to another water hole and drove
up the same cattle to this water hole, until they came up with the
correct tally on cattle of what this mortgage consisted of." And he
says: "We can do the same thing with the tanks."

One of the more shocking features of the entire Billie Sol Estes
case is that this unabashed acknowledgment of fraud by Estes

does not seem to have shocked or disgusted anybody. We live in an age in which individual man is becoming increasingly alienated from his society. At war with the power structures that dwarf him and rob him of his individuality, he relishes those rare opportunities that come his way to get even. To cheat on income taxes, to loot the corporate till, to hornswoggle an insurance company, become in this society tactics that enable man to reclaim a bit of his own. In addition, in the Great Southwest, these tendencies of our time were reinforced by powerful strains of bucolic prejudice. It was the country boy versus the city slicker, the hometown sharpie against those Wall Street moguls; and there was a decided tendency in the prairie country to root for its own, regardless of the ethics of the situation.

The attitude of Pecos was captured best perhaps by Fletcher Knebel in an article in *Look*. Pointing out that the very name *Pecos* originally meant "crooked" in Indian language, Knebel wrote:

For almost two years, Billie Sol's scheme of getting rich by borrowing on anhydrous-ammonia fertilizer tanks was the talk of Pecos. Hundreds of people thought the scheme was fishy, and their doubts became the town's gossip. Everybody talked about it, but nobody did anything about it. Why?

Some felt a natural reluctance to be a busybody. Mrs. Estelle Clinton, Reeves County clerk, saw hundreds of chattel mortgages on fertilizer tanks being recorded in her office, but figured "it was none of my business." The Rev. W. S. Boyett, the Church of Christ evangelist whom Estes furnished with a Cadillac (later bought from Estes by him), says he had no suspicions of Estes: "I don't consider it my function to dig into the business of members of the congregation." Although stung once himself by Estes and highly dubious of some of his deals, Walter H. Holcombe, president of the Security State Bank, did nothing, because, he says, "It was none of my business." Estes, who was into everybody's business, was nobody's business.

There was also a secret admiration for Billie Sol, which persists in many parts of Pecos today. Fenton Alley, a gnarled, 79-year-old justice of the peace and former cowpuncher, put it thus: "I admire Estes in a way. He's a damn thief, but he's no petty thief. If you're gonna get caught stealing, don't go to stealin' chickens."

With all the gossip, with all the aerial ferrying of serial numbers to distant points, with all the hasty spot-welding and painting to camouflage the fertilizer tanks, it strains credulity to believe that none of the investigators sent into Pecos by the finance companies should have picked up the first faint whiff of suspicion. The evidence, as it was later educed, indicates indeed that some of them knew very well what was going on; but, in the corrupt society, they too had their price. As the House committee later reported: "Some employees of private firms who suspected Estes' activities were placed on his payroll." These payoffs seem especially to have involved CIT, bitten by Estes for more than $5 million. It seems evident from the sequence of the action that CIT developed some strong suspicions, for, almost a year before Estes' final exposure, it refused to finance any more fertilizer tanks. But it let the matter rest there. Like Associates Investment, like the Murchison interests, like Commercial Solvents, it took no action to put an end to the fraud. Perhaps one of the reasons it did not was that Estes, the veteran favor-giver, had cultivated good will on several echelons of CIT. Testimony in the Texas inquiry showed that one CIT credit man had accepted two $115 suits from an Estes associate; a vice-president of CIT had received a Chevrolet from Billie Sol; and a CIT field representative was being paid a $500-a-month "consulting fee" by Superior Manufacturing. After Billie Sol's exposure, the vice-president and field representative resigned their positions with CIT; but it seems significant that, virtually up to the moment of exposure, the mere mention of Billie Sol's name was enough to take all the eagerness out of any eager-beaver CIT investigator.

Typical was an incident that occurred in the spring of 1961, when the finance company sent sixteen investigators into West Texas to try to locate the fertilizer tanks on which it held mortgages. Thomas Bell, a Pecos-area farmer, testified under questioning by Assistant Attorney General Jack Price of Texas how an investigator came to his farm looking for tanks registered in his name.

Q. And you confirmed [to the CIT investigator] that you did have a leasing arrangement with Billie Sol?

A. Yes, sir.

Q. And that you had never seen the equipment?

A. Yes.

Q. Did he appear satisfied? Did he go off then?

A. Yes, sir, I told him that I had the equipment leased to Mr. Estes. So he left very nice; and I haven't seen him since.

It is possible that investigators might still be walking away and being "very nice" if it hadn't been for Billie Sol Estes himself. It took Billie Sol to expose Billie Sol.

4

Like a lot of men who have made fortunes in shady enterprises, Billie Sol wanted not only the money; he wanted status too. He wanted to be respected; he wanted to be loved.

In 1960 this urge for respectability and public applause led him to seek election as an elder of the Church of Christ. A strong faction among the 345 church members balked. They wrote letters saying that in their opinion Brother Estes was "not of good report" in the community. The resultant battle tore the church apart and became the talk of most of Pecos' 12,800 residents.

Billie Sol fought the way he always fought—dirty. For example, he telephoned his lawyer and demanded that the lawyer fire his secretary because she was one of the church dissidents. The lawyer obeyed; the secretary was fired. By such bludgeoning tactics, Billie Sol won his way to status as a church elder, but he had not endeared himself to the sturdy faction that had held he was "not of good report." This group walked out and formed a new congregation.

The bitter residue of this religious war was still frothing under the surface in Pecos when Billie Sol, his drive for status still not appeased, decided in 1961 to run for election to the local school board. He was unopposed on the printed ballot, but at the last moment a write-in candidate entered the lists against him. Write-in candidates are usually hopelessly doomed, and so it was perhaps an indication of Billie Sol's true lack of status in Pecos that, on this occasion, he was soundly trounced.

Billie Sol was not the man to take kindly to such rejection. In this instance, he blamed his misfortune on the Pecos *Independent and Enterprise,* a semiweekly newspaper founded in 1887. The *Independent* had ridiculed his anti-dancing and anti-mixed-swimming stands. Billie Sol, who prided himself on being a liberal, charged that he had been subjected to this journalistic attack because the paper's owners (two doctors, a dentist and a C.P.A.) were John Birchers. One of the owners, Dr. John Dunn, actually was a member of the Birch Society, but his partners were simply conservatives who did not happen to trust Billie Sol Estes. It did not matter. Estes, seeking revenge, set up his own newspaper, the Pecos *Daily News,* and he put the heat on his 400 employees not to buy goods from stores that advertised in the *Independent.*

This turned out to be the crowning error of Estes' career. A man needs a clean conscience and a spotless past before he indulges in all-out war with a local newspaper, for it is a safe bet the newspaper knows more about him than he suspects. In Estes' case, Dr. John Dunn and the *Independent* knew a lot. One of Dunn's patients, a Pecos farmer, had given the doctor a full description of Estes' fertilizer-tank deals and their peculiar aspects. "Listen," the farmer had said, "you don't get something for nothing, and that's just what Billie Sol is offering."

Dr. Dunn and his medical partner on the controlling board of the *Independent,* Dr. Harlow Avery, were also proprietors of a semimonthly credit sheet published by the Retail Merchants Association. From this vantage point, they began to notice and keep track of dozens of chattel mortgages on fertilizer tanks being filed at the Reeves County Courthouse. Publication of these figures evidently disturbed Estes, for in early 1961 he contacted Mrs. Sue Hodges, manager of the retail association, and asked her to discontinue printing information on the chattel mortgages in her bulletin. Mrs. Hodges reported to Dunn and Avery. They decided to pretend to let Estes have his way by granting his request—but to keep a careful eye on all fertilizer-tank transactions in the future.

As the chattel mortgages mounted high into the millions, the determined Dr. Dunn compiled a Billie Sol Estes dossier and set out to try to get someone to take action on it. Through Dan Smoot, the extreme-right-wing radio and television commentator, he brought the case to the attention of the FBI. What happened next was recounted subsequently by the House Government Operations committee in these words:

> The information was presented by the FBI to an assistant U.S. attorney in El Paso, who decided that there was no apparent violation of the federal banking laws. Although FBI agents from the El Paso office discussed the case with the assistant U.S. attorney on three separate occasions, the subcommittee found no indication that they disagreed with his decision. The arrest of Estes in March, 1962, after a further FBI investigation, was based on confirmation of essentially the same information that had been submitted in 1961.

Unsuccessful in his attempt to enlist the aid of the FBI and the Justice Department, the persistent Dr. Dunn turned to Congress. He sent his dossier on Billie Sol to Senator John G. Tower, the hard-right Republican from Texas. In a lengthy letter, bolstered by documentary evidence, Dr. Dunn urged a Senatorial investigation of Estes, but Tower did nothing. It almost seemed for a time as if Estes, despite the blatant fraud he had practiced, despite a multimillion-dollar swindle that was the talk of Pecos, would defy all the odds on exposure and go on wheeling and dealing to the end of his allotted days. But it was not to be. He was under pressure now from still another direction, and all it needed was one tiny break in the dike to produce the overwhelming flood.

5

If there was a way to make money by fraud, by a fast shuffle of the deck, Billie Sol Estes was almost certain to find it. It was not enough for him that he was kiting fertilizer-tank mortgages to pyramid his grain-elevator business so that he could still further pyramid his ruinous fertilizer purchases from Commercial Solvents. In addition to all of this, he had to finagle in still another area—this time in cotton-acreage allotments.

The federal government, as a part of its price-support program, had put a limit on the cotton acreage a farmer might till. Acreage allotments, issued to individual farmers, were not transferable, but Billie Sol had found a way around the prohibition. Federal regulations provided that, if a farmer's land were condemned to build a new highway or a water reservoir, for example, he might transfer his allotment to any other new farm he purchased. Taking advantage of this special dispensation, Billie Sol had his agents hunt out dispossessed farmers in Texas, Oklahoma, and Georgia. The farmers would enter into a phony contract with Billie Sol to "buy" acreage from him in Texas; he would promptly "lease" back from them the land they had just "bought"; and he would pay $50 an acre for the transfer of the farmer's cotton allotment to these "bought-leased" acres. In this manner, Billie Sol began to accumulate cotton allotments in early 1960, during the Eisenhower administration, and he stepped up his acquisitions in 1961 until he had acquired cotton-planting rights on 3100 additional acres. Incidentally, a point to which virtually no attention has been paid, he was not alone. Other bigtime operators were doing exactly the same thing, and ironically the first suspect contracts that came to the government's attention—documents that matched Billie Sol's in vital particulars—were *not* Billie Sol contracts.

The McClellan committee in the Senate later examined with great care the incredible laxity and red tape in the Agriculture Department that kept any action from being taken for more than a year. Its investigation showed that a blank contract, identical with the Estes contracts, had been obtained by Texas staff workers in 1960. On December 20, 1960, H. L. Manwaring, then Deputy Administrator for Production Adjustment, issued a strongly worded memorandum in which he warned local administrators that the contract appeared to be nothing more than a device for the sale of cotton allotments. Through some still unexplained bureaucratic bungling, Manwaring's memorandum never was transmitted to the Texas branch offices, but its substance was included in a memorandum to field men on January 12, 1961. It was this subsidiary memorandum that seemingly precipitated one of the most sinister developments of the entire Billie Sol Estes case.

A regional meeting of Agriculture Department officials was

held in Dallas on January 16, 1961, and this was followed by a meeting of field men the next day in College Station, Texas. A leading participant in both meetings was Henry Harvey Marshall, chief of production adjustment for the Agricultural and Conservation Office in Texas and so a key man in the handling of cotton-acreage allotments in the state. At both of these meetings, the contents of the Manwaring memorandum were discussed, and there was to be later much confusion about what had been decided, if anything. The best witness, Henry Marshall, the man who might have set everything straight, never got to testify because, long before the McClellan committee studied the case, he had become violently and mysteriously dead.

Several witnesses maintained, however, that Marshall was convinced the Estes-type contracts represented a clever fraud and that he had been determined to investigate thoroughly every one that came up in his territory. There was agreement, too, that on the day of the second meeting at College Station, January 17, 1961, Marshall met with two of Estes' attorneys, John Dennison and Richard Naylor. But there was almost complete disagreement about the trend of the discussion that then took place.

Both Dennison and Naylor testified, in effect, that Marshall told them he could see nothing illegal in the Estes contracts. Another participant in the meeting, J. Taylor Allen, who had accompanied Marshall, gave a diametrically opposite version. He testified that Marshall had told Dennison that the contracts did represent an illegal scheme. Allen was asked to summarize the conclusions reached at this conference with Estes' attorneys, and the testimony went like this:

ALLEN: Well, the net result of that meeting was that Mr. Dennison, as I recall, was quite unsatisfied with the outcome of that meeting. . . .

SENATOR KARL MUNDT: Does that mean that, when Mr. Dennison left, when the meeting broke up, it was Mr. Dennison's understanding that his contracts were not going to be approved, because they were considered to be illegal or improper?

ALLEN: Well, he was given that understanding; yes, sir.

SENATOR MUNDT: There was no question about that?

ALLEN: No question about that.

Though there were conflicting versions of Marshall's subsequent actions and his intentions, the preponderant weight of the testimony seemed to show: (1) that he was fully aware of the details of Estes' scheme and considered it illegal; (2) that he had it in his power to disallow the cotton-acreage transfers and ruin Estes' scheme; and (3) that Estes was aware of all this. Such was the background situation when, on June 3, 1961, the bullet-riddled body of Henry Harvey Marshall was found sprawled in the dirt beside his station wagon in a pasture on his own ranch eight miles outside Franklin, Texas.

The investigation of Marshall's violent demise was strictly limited. A coroner certified that Marshall had committed suicide; the sheriff closed out the probe. And that was that.

Not until the Estes empire had collapsed in scandal did officials take a long and sober second look. What they then discovered made Henry Harvey Marshall a definite candidate for the title of the hardest-working and most unusual suicide in history.

Item 1: Marshall had been killed with a .22-caliber, bolt-action rifle. He had been shot five times in the chest and abdomen. To accomplish the feat himself, he would have had to lever the gun five times and shoot himself five times—a deed of truly superhuman determination.

Item 2: Marshall could never have done this because three of the five wounds were "incapacitating," and in the words of Col. Homer Garrison, Jr., chief of the Texas Rangers, to fire more shots after being so repeatedly incapacitated "would have been impossible."

Item 3: Marshall had been banged up in a manner suggesting that, if he had committed suicide, he must have given himself an unholy beating first. He had a cut over his left eye, severe bruises on his hands, and a serious brain injury.

Colonel Garrison concluded that Marshall undoubtedly had been murdered. But by whom? For what purpose? These questions have never been answered.

The fact that they were ever even asked was attributable almost solely to the Pecos *Independent*. When no government agency would interest itself in the investigation of Billie Sol Estes, Drs. Dunn and Avery decided to try the power of the press. They hired an investigator to check the records in a number of nearby county courthouses. And they discovered that, on the same days, mortgages had been filed in different courthouses on fertilizer tanks bearing the same serial numbers. Clearly, either the same tanks were being mortgaged more than once, or they simply didn't exist.

Oscar Griffin, Jr., who had been hired to edit the *Independent*, now carried the investigation one vital step further. He interviewed a farmer who, ironically, was named L. B. Johnson. Courthouse records showed that Johnson had taken out $93,600 in mortgages on 131 fertilizer tanks. When informed of this, Johnson was amazed. Billie Sol, he said, had propositioned him, but he had rejected the deal. He had had no idea his name and credit had been used. Subsequently, in the Texas inquiry, Farmer Johnson testified about the manner in which Estes had practiced fraud and deceit, not on just the finance companies, but on *him*.

When Estes originally explained the scheme to him, Johnson said, he had thought he might go along, and so he had signed the necessary papers in Estes' office. But—

"I had a verbal agreement with him [Estes] which to me was just as good as a written agreement."

Q. I see. He called you down to the office and he had you sign a bunch of papers?

A. Well, I signed them at 11 A.M. and I had a verbal agreement with him that I would call him back by 1 P.M. and let him know whether I wanted to go or not.

Q. Is that when you told him that you wanted to talk to your wife about it first?

A. That's right. I went home and discussed it with my wife a little bit. And then I called him back and told him I didn't want to go, that I didn't want any part of it—just count me out.

Johnson went back to Estes' office that afternoon and collected, so he thought, all of the papers he had signed. But Estes, unknown to him, evidently had squirreled away one of the signed documents and later used this to file nearly $100,000 worth of fertilizer-tank mortgages in the name of the unsuspecting Farmer Johnson. And Farmer Johnson, not knowing, hadn't even collected his 10 per cent.

With Johnson's story in hand, with the detail on the doubling up in tank mortgages established from the courthouse records, the *Independent* broke a series of articles on the wheeling and dealing of Billie Sol Estes. For Estes, this public exposure spelled doom.

Some of the largest finance companies in the nation had been stupid enough to let the Pecos manipulator play them for suckers, but they weren't so stupid that they couldn't read. And, reading, they began to wonder.

The first to become alarmed was Pacific Finance in Los Angeles, a firm that had bequeathed Estes more than $3 million. On the night of February 23, 1962, Pacific Finance called the Dallas law firm of Irion, Cain, Cooke & Magee. What about those articles in the *Independent*? Was Pacific Finance really holding worthless paper? Frank Cain and M. R. Irion discussed the problem with two officials of Pacific Finance. Cain advised: "You'd better send out every available man and hit the farmers all at the same time."

Pacific followed his advice. It set up headquarters in Amarillo and dispatched eighteen investigators to talk to farmers and find tanks. Within six hours, the investigating team reported that it had not been able to find any tanks with Pacific Finance serial numbers on them. And it was becoming hard to find farmers to question, too.

Estes, of course, quickly realized that he was in deep trouble, and he engaged Hobert and Bert Nelson of Lubbock as his counsel. Irion and Cain arranged a conference with Estes and the Nelsons in Lubbock on February 28. On the way, Cain stopped off in Amarillo and made some inquiries at the Superior Manufacturing plant. He discovered that Superior, even working around the clock on a three-shift basis, could produce only 800 tanks in a month. Yet the tank mortgages filed on its product in Reeves County alone during January 1962 had run to 3376 tanks. Any way you looked at it, the colossal fraud that had been practiced by Billie Sol Estes was beyond doubt and beyond contest.

But were the finance-company representatives who had uncovered this state of affairs so outraged that they ran at once to the law to jail Billie Sol Estes as a thief? They were not. They were still interested in just one thing, their money, and it is significant—a point that cannot be too strongly stressed—that, had Billie Sol had any possible way of repaying them, he might have remained still free to wheel and deal, to defraud and finagle, to bluster and intimidate and get law secretaries fired for not relishing him as a church elder.

Cain put the finance-company ethics of the case in plain language to Billie Sol in that February 28 conference in Lubbock.

"I want you to know our main interest is in getting paid out," he said. "I want to know where the tanks are."

Estes smiled broadly, like a kid who has just euchred his best friend. "There aren't any tanks," he said.

Irion, shocked, grew red in the face and almost shouted: "Do you mean to tell me there are no tanks?"

Estes smiled more broadly still. "No," he said, "there are no tanks."

Cain then wanted to know how many finance companies were involved in the swindle. Estes calmly handed him a detailed list, which later proved to be quite accurate. The list named the dozen finance companies he had bilked and showed he was making monthly payments of $527,751.09 to keep afloat the incredible swindle of nearly $22 million.

"You sure have made a damn fool out of some of the most brilliant financial men in the country," Cain told Estes, trying a little flattery. "What have you done with the money?"

Estes ducked the question.

In a long discussion (and what, one wonders, would there have been to discuss in the truly ethical society?), Cain invited Estes to cooperate and "see if we can work this out." Estes agreed. He invited Cain to come out to Pecos and visit him. Then, as the meeting was breaking up, Estes dropped a remark that showed how his mind was working.

"I've got two and a half million worth of contracts that I haven't been able to peddle yet," he said. "I can peddle it pretty fast."

Irion, aghast, exploded in angry and significant terms.

"Don't you tell me anything about that!" he shouted.

There could have been no question about the character of
Billie Sol Estes, about the enormity of the fraud he had practiced,
but still nobody rushed to the law to see justice done. Almost
two weeks passed before, on March 13, Cain went to Pecos and
spent three days visiting with Billie Sol in the mansion with the
living-room palm garden and waterfall. Cain was a bit startled to
encounter, in the palm garden, a monkey in a cage. What, he
asked Estes, was the monkey doing there?

"You know why I have that monkey there?" Estes replied,
laughing. "I want to keep reminding myself how goddam dumb
those finance companies are."

Such was the beginning of what, for Cain, was an incredible
experience. Estes, in his office with the autographed photographs
of Presidents and high politicians, bragged hugely of his great
influence. He was a member of the Department of Agriculture's
Cotton Advisory Committee, he said; he had made nearly half a
million dollars in 1961 from his cotton-growing scheme; he had
money rolling in from grain storage. Sure, he could repay the
finance companies. Cain noted that the grain-storage cash was
pledged to Commercial Solvents, but Estes' familiarity with the
mighty and the highly placed impressed him so much that he was
startled when Estes, answering a phone call, said: "Hello, Mr.
President."

For one horrified moment, Cain thought Estes actually was in
touch with the White House, but when Billie Sol finished and
hung up, he explained:

"That was Maynard Wheeler; he and his wife are coming down
to spend the week end with me."

Cain knew that Maynard Wheeler was the president of Commercial Solvents, and though this wasn't quite like being in the
White House, he was still impressed.

The lawyer, half-convinced that Estes might find some way to
pay his debts after all (and this was really all that mattered,
wasn't it?), flew to Los Angeles and reported to Pacific Finance's
president, Maxwell King. King decided it was "an industry prob-

lem" and asked Cain to call a meeting of all finance-company creditors. In discussing Estes' relations with Commercial Solvents, Cain mentioned that Maynard Wheeler was visiting Estes in Pecos that week end—and King was incredulous. To prove the point, Cain telephoned Estes and confirmed the information. Then he asked whether he could be present because, he said, "I need the cooperation of Solvents." Estes agreed, and so there took place what remains one of the most disputed confrontations of the entire case.

Cain testified before the Texas court of inquiry and before the McClellan probers to details of the conversation with Estes and Wheeler that Wheeler has emphatically denied. According to Cain, Estes made these remarks in the presence of Wheeler during their Sunday-morning breakfast:

"They [Commercial Solvents] want to put me in business in Brazil.

"You know Mr. Wheeler has been just like a father to me; he put me in this ammonia business.

"They [Commercial Solvents] sent me $400,000 just a few days ago."

According to Cain, Wheeler contributed the thought that, in Switzerland, numbered bank accounts protect the depositor from annoyance and—"If Billie Sol gets too involved, we can always use him as a consultant in Switzerland." To which Billie Sol demurred, saying: "Well, I think Brazil will be better."

Cain also quoted Wheeler as saying: "We have established ourselves firmly in the ammonia market here, and we intend to keep that market. . . . Furthermore, if we have to, we can step in and take the place of Billie Sol. . . . We can keep those grain-storage tanks full, too."

Wheeler later admitted that Commercial Solvents did send Billie Sol $400,000 on February 28 (the very day that Billie Sol in his lawyer's office was telling Cain and Irion "There are no tanks"), but he denied emphatically ever mentioning the Swiss banking system, ever discussing sending Billie Sol to Brazil, ever indicating to Cain that Billie Sol meant more to Commercial Solvents than just another fertilizer customer. Obviously, someone

was lying, and this clash of direct, sworn testimony was referred
to the Justice Department for examination.

The meeting of Estes' creditors took place in the board room
of the Mercantile National Bank in Dallas on March 27 (a full
month after Estes' original confession to Cain and Irion) and was
attended by thirty-three executives and attorneys of the victimized
finance companies. Cain and Irion explained just how Estes had
mulcted them of $22 million. Estes himself put in a brief appear-
ance. According to *Fortune,* "he seemed, in turn, arrogant, dis-
consolate, and deflated. On the whole, he did not leave the
financiers optimistic about their prospects of getting any money
out of him."

This was a disastrous impression to create in the minds of the
financiers. Even at this late date, even in the full light of revelation, virtually the only consideration that seems to have weighed
with them was: Could they possibly get their money back out of
Estes? The implication is that, if they could have, they wouldn't
have cared about anything else; but, when they became convinced
that Estes couldn't pay, they became righteous and turned to the
law. When they did, events marched swiftly. The next day the FBI
arrested Estes on a charge of having transported false mortgages
across state borders, a federal offense. From that point on, the fat
was in the fire.

<h2 style="text-align:center">6</h2>

The arrest of Estes, followed swiftly by his indictment on both
state and federal charges, quickly blew up a scandal of national
proportions. A great and suggestive mystery revolved about the
influence the wheeler-dealer from the Pecos had apparently exerted
in Washington. Though the Manwaring memorandum of December 1960 had scowled at the kind of cotton-acreage swindles
Estes was pulling off, the Kennedy administration's Department of
Agriculture in all the intervening months had taken no positive
action to curb Estes' manipulations. Instead, it had actually honored Billie Sol by elevating him to membership on the department's National Cotton Stabilization Advisory Committee. The

pattern was a paradoxical one, to say the least. Here was the big operator from the Pecos, who had been circumventing the law through the illegal transfer of cotton acreage allotments, named to membership on the very committee that was supposed to give the department advice and help in preventing just such deals from happening! How had Billie Sol Estes managed to be on both sides of the law at the same time?

The answers involve the kind of influence that almost everyone knows money exerts in the corrupt society. Estes' cash talked for him more loudly than any principle talked for government. The truth is as simple as that.

All through 1961, consideration of Estes' cotton-land deals dragged along at a snail's pace through the bureaucratic echelons of the Department of Agriculture. The McClellan committee never could pinpoint responsibility for this sluggishness and inaction; indeed, in trying to do so, it almost lost itself in a bewildering maze of conferences, rationalizations, changed tactics, backing and filling through all of which ran the suggestion that many members of the Department's operating personnel recognized that Estes could flex the kind of muscle to justify a prudent man's treading warily in his presence.

Estes's ruthlessness in using his power was demonstrated in the events of late October 1961, a period of crisis in the continuing wrangle over his swindled cotton-acreage allotments. After some ten months of temporizing, the Department appeared to be working up its nerve to cancel the allotments on the more than 3000 acres Estes had finagled; if this happened, there was the distinct possibility that Estes might be held liable for onerous financial penalties. To counter the twin threat, Estes and his attorney, John Dennison, flew to Washington. There, on October 16, they held a long discussion with Joseph A. Moss, Director of the Cotton Division, and other second-echelon officials of the Agriculture Department. Among those taking part in the day-long conference was Wilson Tucker, deputy director of the Cotton Division and a department expert on cotton-transfer transactions.

The results of the discussion apparently were too inconclusive for Estes' taste, for two days later, on the morning of October 18, the door of Wilson Tucker's office blew open and Billie Sol Estes and John Dennison blew in. Estes was in a towering temper. Even Dennison, who insisted afterward to the McClellan committee that he could not remember much of what his client had said, admitted that Estes had lost all control of himself. Wilson Tucker's memory was better than Dennison's, and he testified in explicit detail to threats Estes had made. This is the McClellan committee's summary of his testimony:

He [Tucker] said Estes made some general statements concerning the use of his personal airplane in helping in behalf of the Kennedy–Johnson campaign and mentioned his close association with important people in Texas. Tucker said Estes told him that if the investigation was not stopped he would bring a group of about thirty-eight individuals, including lawyers and accountants, to Washington who would (1) establish offices in Washington, (2) purchase space in newspapers and magazines, and (3) appear on television in order to embarrass the administration and the Department because of their attempted efforts to smear his reputation. He said Estes claimed, however, that he did not want to have to do this. *Tucker said Estes then stated that the pooled allotment matter had already caused the death of one person and then inquired if Tucker knew Henry Marshall.* Tucker said he acknowledged knowing Marshall and no further mention was made of him during the conversation. [Italics added]

Since Marshall had been officially ruled a suicide, this remark of Estes linking his death directly to the cotton finagling certainly seems in retrospect one of the most amazing in this entire affair. But nobody appears to have paid much attention to it at the time. Tucker was so shaken up by Estes' loud rampaging about his office that he quickly told the Pecos magnate the affair was much too big for him; it would have to be handled on higher echelons of the Department. Trying to set up an appointment for Estes, Tucker telephoned Joseph Moss, who was home on leave; and on Moss's instructions, he arranged for Estes and Dennison to meet the next day with Emery E. (Red) Jacobs, the deputy administrator of the Commodity Stabilization Service.

Tucker testified that C. M. Cox, Jacobs' assistant, asked him to brief Jacobs thoroughly on what had happened before Jacobs met with Estes and Dennison. Tucker did. He said he gave Jacobs "a full explanation" of everything that had taken place. Jacobs remarked, Tucker testified, that he knew Estes, and he wondered whether he should meet Estes and Dennison alone. He finally decided to do so; Tucker himself was not present at the meeting— and he was never told what happened.

"Tucker admitted that no one had ever made such a threat to him previously in over 25 years of service with the Department," the McClellan committee subsequently reported. But Tucker did not write out any memorandum on his encounter with Estes and Dennison to be sent upward through Department channels.

Now the mystery deepens. Jacobs testified that he did not get the impression from Tucker's briefing "that Estes was threatening to smear the administration." When he met with Estes and Dennison, Jacobs said, "Estes was very agitated and implored that the investigation be stopped because it was doing tremendous damage to his reputation." Jacobs' testimony was that he took a hard line with Estes; told him the investigation could not be stopped since everyone already knew about it; and insisted that a fair investigation would benefit both Estes and the Department.

If Jacobs' testimony can be believed, the furious Billie Sol Estes who had come to Washington threatening to tear the Kennedy administration apart departed quietly for Pecos, mollified by what would seem to have been far from satisfactory assurances. But perhaps Estes had other reasons for optimism. Just six days after the Estes–Dennison–Jacobs huddle in Washington, Jacobs went to Dallas. The occasion, he said, was a meeting of department hands and field personnel. It just so happened that Billie Sol Estes was in Dallas at the same time, staying in the same hotel that Emery Jacobs had selected—and so, naturally, they "visited" together. And it just so happened that, on the morning of October 25, after a hasty breakfast, Emery Jacobs confided to Billie Sol Estes that he was badly in need of some new haberdashery and intended to pay a little visit to Neiman-Marcus, Dallas' ultrafashionable department store.

Hearing this, Billie Sol, the soul of courtesy and consideration, insisted on coming along on the shopping trip. Emery Jacobs had no reason to deny Billie Sol this pleasure. So they went to Neiman-

Marcus together. According to testimony by Neiman-Marcus employees in the Texas inquiry, Billie Sol was so interested in the problem of Jacobs' attire that he went right into the fitting room with Jacobs; and when Jacobs came out, he had in his hands a roll of cash.

Here was the wardrobe he had acquired in this one morning's shopping, as listed in the McClellan report:

2 suits at $245	$490
1 sport coat	$195
2 pairs of trousers at $65	$130
2 pairs of shoes at $135	$270
4 shirts at $16.95	$ 67.80
1 shirt	$ 22.50
2 belts at $15	$ 30
2 ties at $8.50	$ 17
2 ties at $7.50	$ 15
1 tie	$ 15
1 tie	$ 10
Indistinguishable item	$ 12.95

The total came to $1275.25, and Emery Jacobs, a $16,500-a-year government official, calmly peeled off the bills and paid for it all in cash. Jacobs insisted before the McClellan committee that Estes "gave me no money," that he had paid for the clothes "with money that belonged to me." Chairman McClellan asked a bit skeptically if he was accustomed to paying such fancy prices for his wardrobe. Jacobs acknowledged that he did not often buy this much at one time, but, he said, he had not had a new suit for five years and he had decided to stock up. He conceded that those $135 shoes were a bit out of line with his usual budget. This, he said, "was egotism and extravagance," but, "I wanted a pair of those shoes. I had the money. I thought I could afford it, and I bought them."

Less facile were some of Jacobs' other explanations. That hotel bill in Dallas, for example. He admitted that Estes had paid it for him. He had meant to reimburse Estes, but Estes never forwarded the bill to him and he forgot. Telephone-call slips also established that, following the rendezvous in Dallas, he received a whole series of telephone calls from Estes. Jacobs admitted that, after Estes' arrest, he had called John Dennison, couldn't get him, and had left word for Dennison to call him back, asking for Jacobs under the name "Bill Spriggs" when he did so. Jacobs said he was terribly upset at the time; it had been very foolish of him to use an alias—but he wasn't thinking clearly and he had.

The months following the purchasing spree in Dallas were threaded with traces that seemed to show Jacobs was at times extremely solicitous of Estes' interests. The Department at one point in late December 1961 decided to revoke Estes' cotton allotments, but Estes and Dennison came to Washington, protested, got the action reconsidered. Investigators were sent to Texas to make an on-the-spot report. One of them, Thomas H. Miller, testified that Jacobs called him in and, in the words of the McClellan report, "instructed him to write a memorandum justifying the Department's decision to permit Estes to retain all of the cotton allotments he had acquired at that time." Jacobs denied this, said he had told Miller to be "objective." But the record showed that three investigators went to Texas and that Miller came back and filed a separate report—a report that recommended exactly what he said he had been told to recommend. On another occasion, Jacobs called in Moss, the Cotton Division chief, and together they drafted a memorandum for the acting administrator, Edwin A. Jaenke, to sign. The memorandum would have permitted Estes to keep all the cotton allotments he had finagled. Moss testified that this was Jacobs' idea; he neither opposed it nor approved it—he just "participated"; he just went along with Jacobs. Jaenke, it developed, never did see and never did sign the memorandum that had been prepared for him.

It was a tortuous story, stained throughout its course by yellow-gold tracers left by Estes' cash. When the Department on December 26, 1961, decided to revoke Estes' cotton allotments, the reverberations shook much of official Washington. Senator Yarborough, for whom Estes had worked so industriously, and Congressman James Rutherford appealed to the Department to be fair to Estes, to give him another hearing. So a meeting was held in Washington on January 6, 1962, in the office of Under Secretary Charles S. Murphy. The result: It was decided to cancel the cancellation and to hold another "investigation," the one on which Miller was sent. Emery Jacobs transmitted this word to Texas officials on January 8. "On that same day," the McClellan committee reported, "Billie Sol Estes drew a check in the amount of $1500 payable to 'J. T. Rutherford.' " Though the McClellan committee dropped the matter there, Congressman Rutherford had acknowledged publicly that he did receive this contribution, but he said it was money for his campaign fund and represented donations by others in Pecos besides Estes. No such argument could be advanced for another Estes check made out this same busy January 8. This one was for $1000, and it went to Jerry Holleman, Assistant Secretary of Labor, a man who was not running for any public office.

Estes' money was certainly getting scattered around, and it was curious (a confirmed cynic might almost be excused for believing it was cause and effect) that nothing untoward happened to Estes. Not until the Estes bubble burst in Pecos, not until Estes had actually been arrested and indicted, did the Department of Agriculture act. Then, in a fine burst of righteousness, on April 17, 1962, it canceled all of Estes' illegally acquired cotton-acreage allotments and imposed upon him penalties totaling $554,162.71.

This belated display of rectitude could not still the swirl of scandal. Resignations and dismissals from government service became the order of the day. Assistant Secretary of Labor Holleman, who prior to coming to Washington had been president of the Texas AFL–CIO, protested that he had taken the $1000 Estes check to meet "living expenses" because he could not comport himself socially in the style Washington demands on his $20,000 annual salary. He insisted that the gift had been "personal," that it had "no connection with any of Mr. Estes' interests"; but when press and public did not trample themselves in a headlong rush to embrace this explanation, Holleman resigned and went back to Texas.

In the Department of Agriculture, the center of the storm, Secretary Orville Freeman, who by all the evidence hadn't known about the Estes affair until he read about it in the newspapers, laid about him with his executive decapitating sword. Two of this awesome blade's most prominent victims were Dr. James T. Ralph, Assistant Secretary (for Agriculture Stabilization), and Ralph's assistant, William E. Morris. Testimony at the Texas court of inquiry indicated that both men, like Emery Jacobs, had accompanied Billie Sol Estes on a shopping spree to Neiman-Marcus.

The Texas inquiry showed that $1100 worth of high-priced duds had been billed to Estes after this little excursion on September 8, 1961. Robert Watson, a department-store salesman, testified that two $245 suits were fitted for Dr. Ralph. Another salesman testified that Dr. Ralph tried on a pair of $135 alligator shoes but rejected them in favor of two pairs of calfskin shoes ($36.95 apiece) that were billed to Estes. There were also six shirts priced at from $16.95 to $29.95, and it was testified that Dr. Ralph returned two of the shirts later, trading them in for six lower-priced models.

The Assistant Secretary—there were only three in the Department, and Dr. Ralph, who had served briefly as California Commissioner of Agriculture, was among the first appointees named by President Kennedy on January 21, 1961—emphatically denied the charges. The Texas testimony had been that Neiman-Marcus delivered the purchased articles of attire to Billie Sol Estes at his hotel, and Dr. Ralph swore under oath that he had never received them. He admitted that he had accompanied Estes to Neiman-Marcus; he admitted that he had let himself be measured for the $245 suits and that he had tried on the $135 alligator shoes. He had done all this, he said, because Estes was "an unusual person," and he hadn't wanted to offend. But he had received nothing.

This flat denial stayed the downward stroke of Secretary Freeman's sword, but only temporarily. It was discovered that Dr. Ralph had been charging long-distance telephone calls to Billie Sol Estes' credit card. That did it. The Assistant Secretary was given his walking papers.

The case of his assistant, William E. Morris, was more flagrant. Morris was fired after he failed to appear before the Texas court of inquiry to counter the charges. The testimony indicated that Morris had been too close to Billie Sol for any possible denial to have served him. Morris' wife, who was a secretary on the staff of Representative Edward Edmondson (D., Okla.), had been carried on Estes' payroll, according to his records, at a salary of $300 a month as "Washington columnist" for the Estes newspaper in

Pecos. Correspondence taken from the "Bill Morris" file in Estes' office also indicated that Morris had been helpful in passing along tips to Estes.

One such letter, written in early 1962, suggested to Estes that Representative H. Carl Andersen (R., Minn.) was "the man we need for a good contact in Congress." The letter pointed out that Andersen was the ranking Republican member of the House Agricultural Appropriations Committee. "He is really in a bind," the letter said. "He is really good standing by his friends." The letter added that the congressman was anxious to sell stock in a family-owned coal mine near Seattle, Washington.

Shortly after this, it was disclosed, Morris took Andersen down to Pecos to talk to Estes. The journey resulted in a fine meeting of minds, and Estes invested $5000 in "stock" in the Andersen-owned coal mine. When this transaction came to light, Congressman Andersen made an emotional appeal for understanding in the House. It had been, he said, a pure business deal. "H. Carl Andersen never did anything wrong with the Estes affair," H. Carl Andersen told his fellow congressmen in his almost tearful peroration. "My conscience is clear. So help me God."

It was pointed out, however, that it seemed a trifle strange, if the deal with Estes had been just an ordinary purchase of stock, that Estes never bothered to get any stock certificates showing that he had an interest in the Andersen coal mine. As Ted Lewis, Washington correspondent for the New York *Daily News,* wrote, Congressman Andersen's heart-tugging defense turned out to be "pretty much a dud."

So it went. There seemed almost no end to the trail and the taint left by Billie Sol Estes' cash. In the Department of Agriculture alone, Secretary Freeman forced the resignations or fired, suspended, or reprimanded eight officials and employees, plus twelve county employees in the field service. And almost everywhere one turned, there was new spoor indicating that Estes had made a contribution to some congressman's campaign fund. Frank Cain, the Pacific Finance attorney to whom Estes had first acknowledged "There are no tanks," testified before the Texas court of inquiry that Estes had told him one $40,000 item on his accounts represented a payoff. Estes estimated, Cain testified, that payoffs cost him $100,000 to $200,000 a year, figures that in themselves speak graphically of the widespread susceptibility of man in the corrupt society.

7

There remained only to dispose of Billie Sol Estes, the unscrupulous manipulator who had been responsible for unveiling on such an unprecedented scale the ethics of our times. Once it had become evident that Billie Sol could never possibly "pay out," it became also evident that he could expect scant mercy. The wolf-pack of society was ready to turn upon the wolf on whom so recently it had fawned. Texas indicted Billie Sol on swindling charges; the federal government indicted him for mail fraud and conspiracy. Estes himself evidently figured that the jig was up; and, using to best advantage the month's grace the finance companies gave him while they decided whether to prosecute, he took steps to fortify himself for the bleak future.

A. B. Foster, Jr., general manager of Billie Sol Estes Enterprises, told the McClellan committee that between March 14 and April 6, 1962, Billie Sol withdrew $195,565.27 from his various enterprises. On two occasions in March, Foster said, Estes gave him two stout envelopes to be placed in Estes' safe-deposit box in the bank. Prior to Estes' arrest on March 29, Foster continued, he retrieved these envelopes and gave them to Estes. He said he believed the envelopes contained another $17,600 which Estes had taken from the till. What became of the $213,165 that found its way into Estes' pockets in these last-minute transactions remains a mystery at this writing, more than three years later.

There were signs, however, that Billie Sol, despite his officially bankrupt status, was not really impoverished. After someone fired a shot through the window of his $150,000-waterfall-palm-garden mansion in Pecos, he moved with his family to Abilene, some 250 miles to the east. There he settled down comfortably in a $50,000 tannish limestone home on Lytle Lake. There he sometimes relaxed on the green lawn sloping down to his private dock and fishing pier or occupied himself tending the plants in his vegetable garden. And when he went out about town, he rode in an air-conditioned

Cadillac. The court had ruled he was entitled to a home and one car free from the claims of his creditors, and this home and this car represented his exemptions from bankruptcy.

Some captious individuals wondered how Billie Sol, who had wound up owing $36 million on a business empire that was eventually auctioned off for $5.8 million, could manage to live such a financially uncomplicated life, so remote from the pinch of poverty. To such skeptics it was explained that the lakeside estate had been purchased by one of Estes' lawyers, Jack H. Bryant, of Abilene. Bryant rented it to Estes for $350 a month. Just where did the $350 a month and gas money for the Cadillac come from? Nobody was answering that question.

Estes himself endeavored to create the public impression that he was a changed man, but he didn't seem too greatly changed. A wheeler-dealer in Pecos, he remained a wheeler-dealer when he moved to Abilene. His mind steamed with plans, all grandiose. Since Billie Sol Estes was a name that had acquired a national notoriety, Billie Sol's fertile brain worked overtime on plans to capitalize on this public awareness. He envisioned a great hotel-motel chain; facsimile "Wild West" towns for tourists; franchised shops selling curios from abroad; a national life-insurance company; a scheme to corner outlets for the sale of natural gas to Europe; and, above all, a pet project to be called International Love and Goodwill Corporation.

International Love represented the new, the real Billie Sol Estes, Billie Sol told reporters. "I never saw the real values until after my troubles," he said. He had been "plumb wrong" in concentrating on making money for selfish personal advantage instead of helping others to achieve equal opportunity, and the new Billie Sol Estes, though stuffed to the gills with hotel-motel plans and all the rest of it, was *really* going to be concerned with helping people. As evidence of this new idealism, he scrambled out of his automobile to applaud a group of "freedom walkers" in Georgia, and he continued to preach religious fundamentalism as a lay preacher of the Church of Christ.

There remained, of course, the disturbing problem of his conflicts with the law. He was tried in Texas on the swindling charges, was convicted and sentenced to eight years in prison. He was tried in federal court on the mail fraud and conspiracy charges, was convicted and sentenced to fifteen years in prison. His lawyers kept him out of jail with appeals, and Billie Sol went whirling ahead with his grandiose plans as if no fateful tomorrow would ever come.

On June 27, 1964, he flew to El Paso for the unveiling of the first souvenir shop in his new line of business ventures. A twenty-four-foot-high neon sign on the roof of the shop displayed a likeness of Billie Sol inside a sunburst. *Sol* is "sun" in Spanish, Billie Sol explained, watching the sun-sign as it radiated flashes of golden sunbeams. In tall yellow letters, at one side of the sign was the legend BILLIE SOL ESTES, IMPORTER AND EXPORTER OF FINE PRODUCTS SHIPPED TO ALL PARTS OF THE WORLD.

The store, formerly a pawnshop, was located only a few paces from the Mexican border, and its flashing sign shone down on tourists crossing the bridge from Juarez, the largest Mexican border city. The shop itself was stocked with bright serapes and Mexican metal and leather goods. Its proprietor was Paul W. Slone, a young promoter who told reporters that similar Estes novelty shops would be opened in every one of the fifty states. How had bankrupt Billie Sol managed to get back so swiftly into business? Well, it was really very simple. Slone and his wife and Samuel Burke, the man who designed the sunburst sign, owned the corporation; Billie Sol was just "an associate" who had graciously permitted them to use his name for "publicity purposes."

The publicity angle turned a bit sour in January 1965 when the U.S. Supreme Court rejected Billie Sol's appeal from his federal conviction. In a 5–4 decision on June 7, however, the court threw out his Texas conviction on swindling charges because portions of the trial had been televised over Estes' objections. The majority held that televising court proceedings might affect witnesses' testimony because of their knowledge they were on camera, it might influence the judge's conduct, and it represented for the defendant "a form of mental if not physical harassment. . . ." The decision did not affect the 15-year federal term Estes had already begun to serve in Leavenworth, nor did it bar the possibility he could be tried again in Texas state courts on the swindling charge—but without television.

8

What did it all show?

It showed quite clearly what few persons seemed willing to recognize—the in-depth corruption of contemporary American society.

Prodigious amounts of energy were expended trying to turn the Billie Sol Estes fraud into something that it was not, a great national political scandal. During the 1964 Presidential campaign, Republican gumshoes covered the West Texas prairie like locusts, trying to ferret out some clinching evidence that would tie Billie Sol to the coattails of President Lyndon Johnson. They never found the damning bit of detail that they sought, apparently for the simple reason that it never existed. True, on one occasion, Billie Sol had dispatched a crate of cantaloupes to Johnson, then Vice-President, and Johnson had thanked him in effusive Texas terms. But Billie Sol had sent cantaloupes to President Kennedy, to virtually everyone who mattered, and few persons, even in Texas, where Radical-Right prejudice runs deep, would have contended that President Kennedy's actions could have been influenced by the gift of a crate of cantaloupes.

Despite this dearth of evidence, Republican candidate Barry Goldwater tried desperately to make a national political issue of Billie Sol Estes. But his denunciations had a hollow ring, doubly so because Republicans as well as Democrats had become bogged down in the Estes affair. Billie Sol's first grain-storage contracts had come from the Agriculture Department under the regime of Ezra Taft Benson, an ardent Goldwater supporter, and the largest stockholder and controlling influence in Commercial Solvents was Jeremiah Milbank, Jr., the New York financier who was Goldwater's assistant campaign treasurer. For Goldwater to try to make political capital of the Estes scandal under these circumstances was patently ridiculous.

Yet Goldwater was right in his fumbling belief that the Billie Sol Estes affair was a great scandal and that it did, indeed, have a significant meaning for America. That meaning was simply this: Billie Sol Estes in his multiple and unscrupulous machinations had touched virtually every level of American life, and on every level he had found willing accomplices. Everywhere there had been just one glaring, missing ingredient: the incorruptible man.

It had been Billie Sol's scheming mind that devised what a federal judge called "one of the most gigantic swindles in the nation's history," but it had not been Billie Sol alone who had made that swindle so gigantic. Virtually every spectrum of American society had participated in that deed—the farmer who could not resist his 10 per cent on an obviously fishy, something-for-nothing deal; workers and helpers who did whatever they were told without question, phoneying tank-car serial numbers in a palpable fraud; accountants who certified to inflated balance sheets they had not even examined; legal brains who devised the fraudulent cotton-acreage-transfer scheme; bankers who winked at Estes' fast shuffles and certified him as a man of sterling character; bureaucrats who couldn't resist the lure of $245 suits and $135 alligator shoes; rulers of industry who cared only about expanding their business, at whatever ruthless cost; great financiers who cared virtually nothing about patent evidences of fraud if only they could get "paid out." Name any segment of American society you wish, and you'll find it represented—and tainted and shamed—in the Billie Sol Estes scandal.

What the Billie Sol Estes case, then, best and most clearly illustrates is the virtual drying up of that "sea of ethics" Chief Justice Warren stressed as the prime requisite of a law-abiding society. Here enthroned was the profit ethic, sufficient unto itself; here enshrined, the motivations of the inevitable result—the racket society in which any mere man is entitled to anything he can swindle from the mass. In Billie Sol Estes, for a time at least, the larceny of man outmatched the larceny of great corporations, and it says much about our times that most people, on every level of life, not only didn't care—many of them seemed positively inclined to cheer.

6

The TV Quiz Shows

THE TELEVISION QUIZ-SHOW scandal was a national orgy of the something-for-nothing society and a glaring revelation of the extent to which an ocean of non-ethics had enveloped American life. The television quiz shows were a fraud perpetrated on the TV screens of every viewing home in the nation. Presented as legitimate contests of the intellect, they were rigged with answers, and grunts and groans and gestures, worse than any wrestling bout. Yet a nation sat enthralled at the weekly contests of obscure and impecunious intellectual giants on the make; and when it all blew up, when the public fraud of the performance led to public lies and deceit and even deliberate perjuries under oath, nobody seemed to care. "What difference does it make anyway?" was the question you heard on every side.

If Billie Sol Estes stood as a symbol of the in-depth corruption of American society, of the across-the-board susceptibility of modern man to a hard bit of well-placed cash, the quiz-show scandal complemented the picture by holding up a mirror to an entire nation and reflecting the face of a society in which all conception of ethics had been smothered in a pervasive venality, each man wishing that *he* had had the opportunity to grab all that TV pot of gold. It was a society that had lost all ability to care about the means, a society that no longer possessed the saving grace of indignation.

I well remember one of the more frustrating conversations of my life. It took place in the aftermath of the Charles Van Doren episode. I was seated in a dentist's office on New York's lower Broadway, and a dental technician was cleaning and examining my teeth. She was intelligent, far above average, but when we got on the subject of the TV quiz shows, I suddenly found that we couldn't communicate.

"I think it's terrible," she said, "all this fuss they're making. What harm did it do to anybody?"

"But it was all a fake," I said. "It was all phony."

"Well," she argued, "it was just *entertainment*. A lot of people, old people, shut-ins, all kinds of people, got a lot of good out of it, just sitting and watching—and now it's all spoiled for them, it's all taken away."

"But they were being duped," I said. "They thought they were seeing something that was on the level—and they weren't. Doesn't that make any difference?"

"I don't see that it matters much," she told me. "They enjoyed it. It was fun for them. And nobody was being hurt really."

"What about lying before a grand jury?" I asked.

For the first time she hesitated.

"Well, they shouldn't have done that," she conceded. "But they were in a spot, and the whole thing had been blown up all out of proportion. I think it's all a shame, really."

To me it seemed clear that deceit and fraud were *per se* evil, that inevitably they would lead to perjury and perhaps to other crimes as well; but the lady couldn't see it. All that registered with her was that a lot of entertainment had been spoiled by the intrusion of unpleasant truths, and it would have been better all around if truth had not raised its ugly head. She was, I am sure, much more representative of the times than I was.

A number of surveys showed this quite clearly. In one random, on-the-street newspaper study, most of the persons questioned said they would have grabbed some of that TV prize money on rigged shows if they had had the chance. College classes were questioned. Most of the students sympathized with Charles Van Doren and saw him as a victim of circumstance; most, asked if they would shun the products of sponsors of the rigged shows, said they would not. The staff of *Look* magazine did some cross-continent questioning of the American public, and everywhere they found the same prevailing general attitudes. One major sentiment seemed to be "Who am I to say what's right or wrong?" William Attwood, a *Look* editor who summed up the findings, wrote that most considered morality "a vague, unrealistic code which they should be familiar with, but which does not affect themselves." Since this was so, "Moral indignation is out of fashion: It isn't smart to get mad." *Look* found that there was a wide public tolerance for quiz rigging and payola. It was justified under this operational code of ethics: "Whatever you do is all right if it's legal or if you disapprove of the law. It's all right if it doesn't hurt anybody. And it's all right if it's a part of accepted business practice."

Ethics? This was a society that had turned its back on the very conception.

I

The fraud was as obvious to many persons as Billie Sol Estes' phony tank-car deal had been to the Pecos farmers, and if the masterminds of the great networks didn't know about it years before they read about themselves in newspaper headlines, about all that can be said for them is that they were as willfully blind as many of the geniuses of the great finance companies had been.

I well remember how, a few years before the scandal broke, a reporter friend was assigned to dig into rumors that the fix was in on some of the popular quiz shows. He was a good sleuth, and he discovered that in truth the fix was in. His series never saw the light of day at the time, of course, probably because it would have stepped on too many important toes and been too "dangerous" for the paper, but I'll never forget one anecdote produced by his investigation.

There was a certain master of ceremonies who had been given the well-rewarded chore of conducting a quiz show rigged to its eyeteeth. Housewives, ditchdiggers, truck drivers, the most obscure and unlikely persons appeared on the show and regularly demonstrated the marvelous capacity of the human brain and the amazing spread of esoteric knowledge in this great free country of ours. Day after day, with infinite variations on the same theme, the performance went on and on, enthralling its captured public, and the master of ceremonies, who knew it was all a fraud, felt his gorge rise until it was almost choking him.

Finally, there came the day when it all got to be just too much for him. A well-coached housewife who was preening herself on her intelligence as if she really had it came on the show to demonstrate her encyclopedic knowledge of the era of the Pharaohs. She batted out the answers to the most obscure and difficult questions with hardly the flicker of an eyelash, and the phoniness of it all overwhelmed the M.C. Spurred on by the moment's rebellion, he decided to break up the order of the questions by slipping in one of his own.

"Who," he asked sonorously, "was the Vice-President under the tenth President of the United States?"

"The Sphinx," the lady answered promptly.

There was, naturally, the very devil to pay. The M.C., whose misguided sense of ethics had led him to expose his superiors' lack of the virtue, was fired on the spot, and though he eventually went on to better things, he suffered through a time of trial when he had as much trouble getting a job as a man afflicted with a bad dose of leprosy. The tiny splash the incident made in the great communications pond rapidly faded away until the last ripple was no longer discernible, and life fell back into its placid rut. Indeed, things got even better, for it was after the incident of the Sphinx that the major quiz shows really caught on and became a national fetish. Trendex ratings soared; sponsors made millions; and contestants' winnings climbed at times into six figures.

Across this happy world of the fraud that was making everybody bushels of money, there wafted in December 1956 the first faint portentous black cloud. Miss Dale Logue, a Las Vegas chorus girl who was supposedly an expert on astronomy as well as anatomy, filed a suit in New York Federal District Court against the producers and sponsors of *The Big Surprise*. She claimed that she had been dropped from the program after being unable to answer a question she had flunked in a private "warm-up" session just before air time.

The Big Surprise was a television quiz show produced by Entertainment Productions, Inc., headed by S. R. Carlin. The chorus girl's suit stirred a mild curiosity on the part of *Variety,* which interviewed Carlin and evidently took his word for it that EPI, "with top prestige and a great stake in quiz shows, tried to exercise unusual caution in seeing to it that its properties do not fall into disrepute, discredit or dishonor. . . ."

This world of sensitive honor was a highly peculiar one, however, as subsequent events were to demonstrate. On June 1, 1959, after hanging fire for nearly two and a half years, the Logue suit was mysteriously settled out of court. *Variety* tried to find out what had happened, but nobody would talk. One of the attorneys in the case said that his "lips were sealed 'by my clients.'" This lip-sealing seemed rather strange in such an open and aboveboard world, especially in circumstances that left unanswered questions that had decidedly ugly implications.

For Miss Logue, the chorus girl with her eyes on the heavens, had charged that *The Big Surprise* had indulged in warm-up sessions before air time and that, as a consequence, it had not been "a true test of skill between contestants." She had also charged that contestants before they went on the air were compelled to sign a release, absolving the producers of the responsibility for paying them any of the prizes that the TV audiences were deluded into believing they had won. The Federal Trade Commission, to which Miss Logue had also complained, obtained a photostatic copy of this release form. It read: "I understand that you [EPI] shall be under no obligation to afford me an opportunity to answer any question or win any prizes and further that *you shall be under no obligation to award me any specific prize or prizes even if I answer all questions correctly, any announcements on the program to the contrary notwithstanding.* I agree that your sole obligation is to award me any prize or prizes, cash or otherwise, that you in your absolute and uncontrolled discretion may determine." (Italics added.) Under that blanket provision, a contestant the audience might think had won thousands of dollars could in reality have been laboring for nothing more munificent than a few hundred as an entertainer's fee.

It would appear that in the truly ethical society somebody, somewhere, might have been interested in learning the truth about such sensitive issues. But not in this society. Miss Logue's suit was settled quietly out of court; *The Big Surprise* just as quietly went off the air; and neither federal agencies nor the press charged with any great vigor along the trail that had been opened.

True, the mysterious showgirl suit, plus ugly and recurrent rumors in the trade, did pique the curiosity of some of the nation's foremost publications. *Time, Look, The New York Times,* all poked their noses at one time or another into the basic question "Are the Quiz Shows Fixed?" And all decided—well, not really. Producers, they thought, probably exercised some degree of "control" over the programs through knowledge they had gained of contestants' strengths and weaknesses in preliminary testing, but there was nothing to suggest outright fraud.

It was a verdict that delighted the television industry, for quiz shows were now multimillion-dollar businesses. Two of them dominated the airwaves above all others and fascinated the American viewing public as nothing had since Arthur Godfrey and His Friends abandoned the world of humility. Carlin, the mogul of the departed *Big Surprise,* had come up with a veritable gold mine in the *$64,000 Question.* A property of rival worth was *Twenty-One,* produced by Jack Barry and Dan Enright and aired over the NBC network. On both shows, the most unlikely persons demonstrated their detailed knowledge of the most abstruse subjects, and the great American public watched agog, each viewer saying to himself: "Could I have answered that question? Could *I* have grabbed off that $64,000 jackpot?" Visions of fortunes obtained without labor, for just a bit of right knowledge at the right time, danced in the minds of millions of Americans, each of whom as he watched could almost taste the money.

With such an appeal to mass cupidity working for them, the TV quiz shows seemed likely to run forever, pouring perpetual millions into the laps of the producers and the networks. But it was not to

be. Into this most sublime of worlds came the unwelcome in-
truder—chance.

2

The month of August 1958 can only be compared in the television industry to 1929's Black October in the stock market.
Abruptly, on August 16 of that year, Colgate-Palmolive Peet Corporation and the Columbia Broadcasting System announced without explanation that they were canceling the quiz show *Dotto*.
Reporters scrounged around for days before they got a hint of just
what had caused this sudden and inexplicable decapitation. Finally,
Colgate conceded that the show had been canceled because an
affidavit had been filed on August 7 regarding what Colgate gently
described as "an incident." There was no description of the "incident." CBS would say only that, as a result, it had conducted
its own investigation of all its quiz shows and "had failed to turn
up any 'improper procedures.' " This, of course, made matters
delightfully clear. On the one hand, there had been no "improper
procedures"; on the other, an affidavit about "an incident"—an
affidavit that must have contained something other than a criticism
of motherhood—had been filed and, almost with its filing, *Dotto*
had been axed.

Later inquiries were to show what had happened. On May 20,
1958, Edward Hilgemeier, Jr., an unemployed twenty-four-year-
old actor, had been waiting in the wings as a stand-by contestant
to go on *Dotto*. As it turned out, he wasn't needed on this particular day, but as he waited, he noticed a notebook lying on the
floor. It had been dropped accidentally by a woman contestant
then doing valiant intellectual battle before the cameras with a
competing and equally brainy female. Hilgemeier, leafing through
the notebook, was startled to discover a list of questions that
matched exactly the questions being asked at that moment on the
show. And so he was hardly surprised when the contestant who
had absent-mindedly dropped the telltale notebook finally pulled
off just the right answer to the ultimate question—and walked off
the show the winner of $4000.

What Hilgemeier next did with his discovery writes a poetic chapter in the annals of the corrupt society. Having stumbled by accident upon proof of a racket, he took steps to insure his own reward. His actions were as significant for what he did not do as for what he did do. He did not return the notebook to its rightful owner. He did not run screaming to the District Attorney. Instead, he approached the lady who had just been jobbed on *Dotto* and shared with her his knowledge that she had been the victim of a plot.

The vanquished lady, highly incensed to learn she had been counted out in advance of the contest, promptly banged upon the doors of Frank Cooper Associates, producers of *Dotto*. She would not be appeased, she informed the producers, unless she received a sum equal to what she had been cheated out of by the owner of the tattletale notebook. Cooper Associates, in tacit confession of the error of its ways, paid her $4000. Then Hilgemeier, the discoverer of the fraud, came charging upon the scene, righteously indignant and insistent that the shock to his faith in man deserved some recompense. Cooper Associates evaluated his discomfiture at a mere $1500, a price that so disillusioned Hilgemeier that he promptly filed an affidavit with the Federal Communications Commission, alleging deception on *Dotto*.

Such was the "incident" that killed off *Dotto,* but it was not being explained in all its succulent details at the time. It remained just an "incident," inexplicable in CBS's own version of the fatality and so the father of a mystery that needled the press into pursuing a few tentative inquiries. Reporters questioned some of the contestants on the other top quiz shows. First and foremost on their list of knowledgeable prospects was Charles Van Doren, the star of NBC's *Twenty-One*.

Van Doren, a Columbia University instructor, was young and engaging and obviously brilliant. He was the son of Mark Van Doren and the nephew of Carl Van Doren, the biographer of Benjamin Franklin and a Pulitzer-Prize winning historian. Young Van Doren was the author of three books in his own right, and he was possessed of a boyish, winning smile that qualified him for his rank as the matinée idol of the quiz programs. Combining all of these qualities with what was an apparently encyclopedic range of knowledge, Van Doren had run his earnings up to $129,000. So, naturally, reporters sought him out early in the game and asked him what he knew about quiz-show rigging. Van Doren scoffed at the very idea.

"I never got any kind of hint or help and, as far as I know, nobody ever did on the program," he told *The New York Times* flatly. "I have heard rumors of irregularities on quiz shows, but I never have heard any proof. Most of the shows are absolutely on the up-and-up."

Hank Bloomgarden, another *Twenty-One* contestant, backed Van Doren. Those "warm-up" sessions about which there were such rumors, Bloomgarden said, were held only to see that the lighting and acoustics were right and "to acclimatize new contestants to the program."

The whole atmosphere of the television industry, from top management, through active producers, down to winning contestants, was one of bland reassurance. This was the best of all possible worlds. The TV quiz shows were being produced by distinguished experts in the field; they were being carried by the largest networks, headed by some of the most eminent business executives in America; they had drawn high-caliber contestants, a college instructor, a minister, lawyers, psychologists, even chorus girls. The flower of our society, one might say, was represented here, and so it was unthinkable that anything could be *really wrong*. Such was the pretense; such the mask of high probity. It was a mask that had hardly been donned on the front pages of the nation's press before it began to slip.

3

Herbert Stempel, a full-time college student who was being supported largely by his in-laws, had been the star of *Twenty-One* until he was dethroned by Charles Van Doren. This dethronement had been rigged and fixed the way a bad prize fight is rigged, and Stempel, who had been plunged from celebrity back into campus obscurity, hadn't taken at all kindly to the idea. The thought of the dive he had been compelled to take stewed in him until finally he decided to blow the whistle. In an affidavit that he gave the New York *World-Telegram and Sun* on August 28, 1958, he declared that he had lost to Van Doren because he had been ordered to lose—and he had followed orders.

With the publication of Stempel's affidavit, fuss and fury became unconfined. Barry and Enright, the producers of *Twenty-One,* promptly denied all and announced they were suing Stempel and the *World-Telegram and Sun* for libel. NBC was also righteous. It announced: "The charges made by Herbert Stempel against the quiz show *Twenty-One* first came to our attention over a year ago. At that time we made an investigation and found them to be utterly baseless and untrue. We are completely convinced of the integrity of *Twenty-One* as a program and of the integrity of its producers, Barry & Enright."

The subsequent congressional inquiry was to show the flimsy nature of the "investigation" that convinced NBC of the integrity of all its works. The "probe" consisted of having Dan Enright, *Twenty-One* producer, sit down with Thomas E. Erwin, vice-president and general counsel of NBC. Enright told Erwin he was pure and his show was pure, and that was that.

NBC had a compelling motive for believing what it wanted to believe. In early May 1957 it had purchased five hot-property quiz shows, including *Twenty-One,* from Barry and Enright for $2.2 million. Barry and Enright had remained on as producers of the shows under the NBC banner, at handsome retainers. But NBC needed time to get back its multimillion-dollar capital investment, and now, just fifteen months later, it was faced with the prospect that it might have purchased tainted goods. Its perturbation was understandable.

Whenever a fat sum like $2.2 million is at stake, the in-fighting becomes vicious. NBC and Barry and Enright lost no time training their heavy batteries on Stempel. Dan Enright disclosed that Stempel, who had won $49,000 on *Twenty-One* before being counted out, had come to his office on March 1, 1957, and threatened to kick up a public scandal by charging he had been given questions on the show. Stempel wanted $50,000 as the price of silence.

Unknown to Stempel, the entire conversation had been tape-recorded, and Enright now played the tape for the press. On March 7, in a return bout, Enright said, Stempel had signed a statement denying he had ever been given questions on the show; the *quid pro quo* for this denial, according to Stempel, was the promise of a job on the producing staff of *Tic Tac Dough,* another Barry and Enright enterprise. But once Stempel had affixed his signature to the denial, the job prospect had evaporated.

Any way one looks at this sequence, it seems clear that here was a fine ethical bouillabaisse. This was a stew in which only money counted, and the doublecross and the double-doublecross were its principal ingredients. At the top, blinkers covering their unseeing eyes, sat the emperors of the communications kingdom, ignorance of the odoriferous pot brewing on the lower echelons, one of their cardinal qualifications for command. For only by such doublecross and such ignorance could the whole flimsy structure be kept together in one functioning piece.

There can be no question that Stempel came out of this first round with the Goliath of NBC a badly splattered man. His initial revelations had been discredited as being motivated by crass impulses rather than high principle, and the all-too-easy assumption was that NBC held a corner on virtue. But Stempel's charges, considered against the background of the inexplicable demise of *Dotto,* had been too explicit to be so cavalierly ignored. At least District Attorney Frank S. Hogan of New York thought so. He order an investigation—this time, a real investigation. And down in Washington the Special Committee on Legislative Oversight, headed by Representative Oren Harris (D., Ark.), announced that it, too, would look into the quiz-show mess.

Hogan's inquiry was the first to document the fraud. Some 200 witnesses were called before the New York County grand jury. One of them, Richard Snodgrass, hurled another bombshell. He had been a contestant on *Twenty-One,* had had winnings at one time of $73,000, and had been compelled to depart only $4000 richer. After appearing before the grand jury on September 27, 1958, Snodgrass met reporters and held up for them to see three unopened registered letters he had addressed to himself. The envelopes, all postmarked prior to his appearances on *Twenty-One,* contained the specific questions and answers later used on the show.

Here, it would seem, was proof of a substantial nature. NBC reacted with virtuous shock. "This comes as a complete surprise to us," the network announced, promising a "prompt and thorough investigation of the charges." This "prompt and thorough" investigation resulted in nothing more conclusive than NBC's announcement eight days later that it was relieving Barry and Enright of their duties as producers so that they could devote full time to defending themselves. As for Barry and Enright, they proclaimed that "our absolute integrity will be clearly and finally established. . . ."

This business of establishing integrity turned out to be exceedingly difficult under the circumstances. Albert Freedman, who had been in direct charge of *Twenty-One* under Barry and Enright, testified before the grand jury on October 2 and denied that he had ever given any contestant questions and answers in advance. Charles Van Doren testified on October 10, and subsequently, repeating what he had told the grand jury, he insisted to reporters that he had not been given questions and answers before appearing on *Twenty-One*. Charges made by others, he said, caused him "surprise and disbelief."

Van Doren's "surprise and disbelief" must have turned into shock when Albert Freedman was indicted for perjury and when Barry and Enright, invited to appear before the grand jury to establish their "absolute integrity," refused to testify on the advice of counsel. Without their assistance, the grand jury finished its work. It had established, as some of its members later said, that the quiz shows had been rigged, and it drew up a 12,000-word presentment describing the mechanics and the extent of the rigging. This document, handed up to Judge Mitchell D. Schweitzer, was promptly impounded in an action unprecedented in New York courts.

The very purpose of a presentment is to call public attention to nauseous ethical situations that may stop just short of the boundary line of indictable illegality. Since 1869, New York grand juries had handed up 497 presentments. All had been made public. But this presentment was somehow different. Evidently anticipating the grand jury's action, attorneys for *The $64,000 Question* and *The*

$64,000 Challenge had filed suit to suppress publication of the presentment, and Judge Schweitzer declared he would bottle up the document until this legal issue was resolved. The cause of "absolute integrity" seemed to be requiring a devious defense.

District Attorney Hogan, a calm man whose temper rarely reaches the boiling point, now became aroused. Judge Schweitzer might smother the grand jury presentment, but he couldn't prevent Hogan from saying what he wanted to say in defense of that suppressed document. On July 13, 1959, the District Attorney filed with the court a twenty-page brief arguing for the release of the presentment. The brief was more than just a legal argument; it was also a disclosure of what the grand jury had found.

Hogan left no doubt that the quiz shows had been rigged. He referred to "a national fraud whereby television quiz shows have been constantly misrepresented to millions of citizens as honest tests of the contestants' knowledge and skill." He added: "It is hardly disputable that millions of viewers would feel shamefully cheated by a hoax which stole many hours of their time. Nor could the justice of their position and the basic immorality involved be sloughed off by protestations that the only deprivation was that of the viewing public's 'leisure time,' and that in any event, the public received 'entertainment' even though its character was misrepresented. The very essence of the quiz program's appeal lies in its implied representation of honesty. Were it generally understood that these programs do not present honest tests of the contestants' knowledge and intellectual skills, they would be utterly ineffectual in acquiring the public's 'time.' "

Judge Schweitzer still refused to release the presentment, but it didn't matter so much now. District Attorney Hogan—and he alone—had put the issue in its proper focus and called the fraud by its proper name. He had set the stage for the congressional hearings that were soon to open in Washington.

4

The first day of the Harris committee hearings, October 6, 1959, should go down in the history of the TV-quiz scandal as Herbert Stempel Day. It was Stempel's chance to get even, and he made the most of it. He described how he had applied as a contestant on *Twenty-One* in the fall of 1956 and how Dan Enright, the protesting purist, had come to his home and coached him on his role in the fraud. Enright, he said, had brought a bunch of cards with him, the kind of category cards that were used on *Twenty-One,* and he used these cards in asking Stempel questions. Stempel testified:

"I managed to answer the bulk of the questions and those which I did not know, he helped me on and supplied the answers. After having done this, he very, very bluntly sat back and said with a smile, 'How would you like to win $25,000?' I said to him, 'Who wouldn't?' "

Enright coached Stempel, Stempel testified, on the fine points of acting:

"He showed me how to bite my lip to show extreme tension. How to mop my brow. He told me specifically not to smear my brow, but rather to pat for optimum effect, as that created a more tense atmosphere. He told me how to breathe heavily into the microphone and sigh. . . . He taught me how to stutter and say in a very plaintive voice: 'I will take nine, nine points.' "

Stempel became such a skilled actor that for seven weeks the riggers of *Twenty-One* were content with him as champion. But then, on Tuesday, December 4, 1956, Dan Enright told Stempel that he was to be "defeated" by Van Doren the next evening. Even the two questions he was to "miss" were picked out. Stempel at the time had $69,500 to his credit, but he was to "lose" $20,000 of this before going down to defeat.

All the next day, Stempel said, NBC kept running spot announcements at almost half-hour intervals, asking, "Will Herb Stempel crack the $100,000 mark tonight?"

All the time, Stempel said, "I was sitting at home and saying very, very bluntly, 'No, he is not going to crack the $100,000 mark, because he is going to take a dive tonight.' "

And take the dive he did.

Stempel's story, told under oath in the full glare of nationwide publicity, prepared the way for the final act in the Van Doren drama. The most famous alumnus of the quiz programs, who had been elevated by NBC into a $50,000-a-year job, was subpoenaed to tell his version. For a couple of days, Van Doren disappeared completely, and headlines were rife with agitated speculation about what might have happened to him. But then Van Doren returned; he took the witness stand; and the story he told now, under oath, at long last, proved to be the complete opposite of the stories he had told previously.

The man who had pretended to "surprise and disbelief" at reports the TV quizzes were fixed acknowledged that he had known they were fixed, that his performance on *Twenty-One* had been charted along the lines of fraud before he ever stepped before the cameras. Right from the first, Albert Freedman, acting under the authority of Enright, had told him how it was to be.

"He told me that Herbert Stempel, the current champion, was an unbeatable contestant because he knew too much," Van Doren testified. "He said that Stempel was unpopular and was defeating opponents right and left to the detriment of the program. He asked me if, as a favor to him, I would agree to make an arrangement whereby I would tie Stempel and thus increase the entertainment value of the program.

"I asked him to let me go on the program honestly, without receiving help. He said that was impossible. . . . He also told me that the show was merely entertainment and that giving help to quiz contestants was common practice and merely a part of show business. . . . Freedman guaranteed me $1000 if I would appear for one night. . . . I was sick at heart. Yet the fact is that I unfortunately agreed, after some time, to his proposal.

"I met him next at his office, where he explained how the program would be controlled. He told me the questions I was to be asked, and then asked me if I could answer them. Many of them I could. But he was dissatisfied with my answers. They were not 'entertaining' enough. He instructed me how to answer the questions: to pause before certain of the answers, to skip certain parts and return to them, to hesitate and build up suspense and so forth. On this first occasion and on several subsequent ones he gave me a script to memorize, and before the program he took back the script and rehearsed me in my part."

Van Doren, it was clear, had been an actor, not a human repository of knowledge. Once hooked into the fraud, he contended, he had had no choice but to continue. He had defeated Stempel; for the next three months, he had reigned as the champion of all the quiz-show stars. Several times, he said, he had begged Freedman to release him from the bargain, but he had become such a personable champion it was difficult to set up just the right set of circumstances for his dethronement. Freedman, he said, told him that "I had to be defeated in a dramatic manner." Finally, the drama was concocted. Van Doren was to lose, after playing a series of tie games, to Mrs. Vivienne Nearing, a charming lawyer. When told he was to be defeated, Van Doren testified, "I said: 'Thank God.' "

Such was Van Doren's story. It was told, not simply and straightforwardly, but with much weeping and wailing and beating of the breast. He had come to realize, Van Doren said, that he had made "millions of friends" by his television performances; he had come to realize that he could not let them down; and, just at the crucial moment, when he was wrestling with conscience on the very brink of decision, a letter had come to him—a letter from a woman he did not even know, urging him to tell the simple truth, whatever it might be. It might seem that long before this, long before lying to press and public and committing perjury before a New York grand jury, a man of Van Doren's intellectual attainments might have recognized the virtue of simple truth, but the complicated truth appeared to be that he had not. It took this letter from a humble, unknown, worshipful little woman to open his eyes. "Suddenly I knew she was right," he testified. And so he had decided to make his statement because of his "millions of friends" and in the hope that "my being here will serve them well and lastingly."

This was certainly a virtuoso performance. It is to be doubted whether, in all the annals of the corrupt society, the meaningless rite of expiation had ever been more brilliantly performed. Members of the congressional committee who heard Van Doren's heart-tugging recital of man in the toils of overwhelming temptation were almost in tears; they accepted his confession with almost humble gratitude and lauded him for his candor and his courage; and so, having performed well before his last great audience, Charles Van Doren walked out of the hearing room, once more almost a national hero.

There was, it seemed, in all America—in the hearing room, in the press, among the general public—just one raucous voice. It belonged to William V. Shannon, then Washington columnist for the New York *Post.* Shannon pointed out acidly that, in the first place, "no one has 'millions' of friends" and, in the second place, "much more offensively, Van Doren did not appear before the Harris committee because he hoped 'my being here will serve them well and lastingly.' He appeared because he was handed a legally binding subpoena and had no choice under the law except to appear. He made a statement because he wanted to put himself in the best possible light. It was a self-serving act and, as such, entirely legitimate. But let's cut out the claptrap about his doing it for his fans."

For Shannon, Van Doren's closing line topped all. Van Doren was describing how he had broken the news to his lawyer that he had decided, after all, the path of simple truth was best. "He has been very worried about my health," Van Doren testified. ". . . He was happy. . . . He said: 'God bless you.' " To which Shannon commented: "Dim the lights. Music, Maestro, please."

Shannon's final verdict was that he could not care less whether Van Doren had made $10 or $129,000 on *Twenty-One;* he did not think Van Doren should be severely punished—"but dignity, self-respect, restraint and detachment are civilized values we should cherish. Van Doren affronted those values as much yesterday as he ever did on *Twenty-One.*"

5

The fraud of *Twenty-One* on NBC had been matched by the fraud of its two great rivals, *The $64,000 Question* and *The $64,000 Challenge,* on the rival CBS network. The congressional hearings established that both of these shows had been thoroughly rigged and that knowledge of the rigging had gone high, very high indeed.

The $64,000 Question was the brainchild of Louis G. Cowan, who subsequently had gone on to better things as president of the CBS–TV network. Upon being elevated to this command post with CBS in 1958 after three years in lesser executive roles, Cowan had severed all relations with his old firm, Entertainment Productions, Inc., by returning to it the 42 per cent of stock he still held. EPI continued under the active direction of Steve Carlin, whose *Big Surprise* had supplied the first mysterious big surprise of the quiz-show scandals. Under Carlin, each of the big $64,000 shows had its own producer, Merton Koplin for the *Question,* Shirley Bernstein for the *Challenge.*

Cowan had originated *The $64,000 Question* in June 1955, only a couple of months before he left EPI to join the CBS network, and it had become an almost instantaneous success, the first of the huge quiz-show money winners. Sponsor of both the *Question* and the *Challenge* was Revlon, Inc., the cosmetics manufacturer. Sociologist Meyer Weinberg, who made the most exhaustive analysis of the TV scandal, has stressed the enormous stake Revlon came to have in the shows. His study points out that, from 1950 to 1954 inclusive, Revlon's net profit averaged $1.2 million a year. After it tied its fortunes to the two $64,000 TV quizzes, its sales soared and its profits leaped to an average of $7.68 million a year. Even after scandal killed off the quiz shows, Revlon continued to capitalize on the notoriety it had achieved, and its net profits leaped above the $10-million-a-year mark. Its sales were more than double those of its nearest competitors, and it began using its flood of excess cash to buy into other businesses. From all of this, Weinberg concludes that the TV quizzes really made Revlon, catapulting the firm into a dominant position in its industry.

Under the circumstances, in view of these tremendous stakes, certain questions inevitably arise. Did Revlon know what was going on in the shows to which its fortunes were tied? Did it actively participate in the hanky-panky?

There was, of course, the usual fuss and feathers, the usual desperate pretense that nothing so crass as a fix could ever possibly have taken place, could ever possibly have been countenanced in this pure world of intellectual combat via television. In 1957, in the initial flurry over the showgirl suit against *The Big Surprise,* a skeptical *New York Times* reporter had remarked to Carlin that some of the contestants on the shows appeared just "too good to be true." And Carlin had replied unctuously: "Well, the typical American has many facets, and those who doubt it show little faith in the American way."

The complexion of the American way had changed quite decidedly by the time the Harris committee got Carlin on the witness stand a little more than two years later.

Koplin had preceded Carlin as a witness and had testified quite frankly about his activities as a rigger. He described in considerable detail the manner in which he had set up questions for Xavier Cugat, the popular orchestra leader. Cugat himself testified that he went on the show because he thought it would be good publicity, but that he had hesitated when the proposition was first broached to him because it wouldn't be good publicity if he were made to look bad. Koplin took care of Cugat's image. He interviewed Cugat in great detail about his life and pitched many questions so that they dealt, though not obviously, with events and personalities that had been a part of Cugat's experience. Cugat testified that, in addition, he was briefed before he appeared on the show by a member of the producer's staff. "When I didn't know the answers, he gave me the answers and the questions," Cugat testified. Against the background woven by this record, Carlin had little chance to wave the flag and expound the glories of the American way.

Robert Lishman, committee counsel, referring to Koplin's testimony, asked:

"Do you disagree with his testimony that the extent of the control was such that when you wanted a contestant to continue on either program you could generally assure his doing so with a degree of accuracy about 80 per cent of the time?"

CARLIN: I do not disagree.

LISHMAN: Do you agree with that?

CARLIN: I do agree.

Could this 80 per cent control have been exercised with Revlon remaining in utter ignorance? It appeared highly improbable at first glance. The Harris committee in its probe showed that weekly executive-suite meetings were held from August 1955 to October 1958 on the handling of the *64s*. Several high Revlon officers attended; Carlin and Koplin regularly represented EPI.

Martin Revson, brother of Revlon's president, Charles Revson, instinctively upholding the holy image of big business that must remain forever undefiled regardless of the debasing nature of its acts, insisted through hours of testimony that Revlon, despite the weekly huddles, had no idea its shows were being rigged. "After all," Martin Revson told the committee, "Revlon's reputation was staked on the integrity of our programs." He said he had asked EPI three times whether the *64s* were rigged—and three times EPI had denied it. As in the case of NBC with *Twenty-One,* a denial by the accused was obviously considered irrefutable evidence.

Other witnesses gave detailed and corroborating testimony that offered less challenge to common sense. Here is the exchange between Carlin and Lishman:

LISHMAN: At any of these meetings did the sponsor indicate its desire that certain contestants should be continued on the program?

CARLIN: Yes, sir.

LISHMAN: How often would this happen, approximately?

CARLIN: It would happen virtually every meeting. At every meeting we would have some discussion about futures. What would happen on the next show, what would happen in two weeks.

LISHMAN: At any of these meetings did the sponsor ever indicate that certain contestants must be gotten rid of?

CARLIN: He made an urgent suggestion that certain contestants leave the show.

Carlin's testimony was backed up by that of George Abrams, who had been Revlon's own man in charge of advertising. Abrams, who had left Revlon before the hearings were held, declared in a sworn statement that Revlon's executives had been up to their necks in the quiz-rigging. The "primary purpose" of the weekly meetings, Abrams said, had been to keep the ratings high. "Charts were maintained which showed the contestants then on the program and the 'audience draw' while they were appearing," he said. He added: "If a contestant was interesting, it was generally the consensus of opinion that he should continue on the show. If he was dull, *we* would suggest to the producer that it would be desirable that the contestant not continue in the future." (Italics added.)

The fix did not always work to perfection. There were occasions when the wrong "personality" won, the right one lost. When this happened, Revlon's blood pressure mounted. "If a contestant or match did not come out as we had suggested," Abrams deposed, "the sponsor and agency representatives would be upset and express displeasure—often in a very heated fashion." The result was that "the producers carried out the sponsors' wishes most of the time. . . ."

Abrams said that Revlon did not know precisely how the fix was engineered. "Although we were unaware that the producers ever told a contestant the exact answers to the questions he was to be asked on the program," he said, "we did know that through intensive preliminary screening the producers found out what a contestant knew, and asked him about it." At one point, he said, "it was decided that there be more losers on the 'Question' show, because it was too boring having all winners"—and, presto, there were more losers.

A sidelight on the ethical climate in the executive suite was shed by one paragraph in Abrams' affidavit. It read:

"Memos were made of these meetings and later circulated. At one time, a memorandum was circulated which, in effect, said bluntly what had been decided was that a certain match would end next week, and another contestant would advance to another plateau on the 'Question' show. This famous last memo was a crude translation into plain language of what had been the general purport of the meetings. Mr. Martin Revson was quite upset at this memo, and ordered that there be no more memos, because he did not want to be bound by what anyone put down on paper. He thought it a foolish thing to put down on paper."

This sensitivity to plain language that might possibly reveal the truth—a reaction reminiscent of the attitude of huge corporations in the great electrical conspiracy—also comes through in an excerpt from Carlin's testimony. On one occasion, a quiz-show contestant protested to Abrams that the show had been rigged, and this protest, with its implied threat of public disclosure, rattled the executive suite of Revlon the way a temblor rattles windows. A summit conference was scheduled to discuss the unmentionable, and this was the way it went, according to Carlin's testimony:

LISHMAN: What did you discuss at that meeting?

CARLIN: They wanted to know how it happened. In regard to that, I attempted to explain it and I was not completely candid.

LISHMAN: If they knew you were controlling the show, why were you not candid?

CARLIN: Well, I don't know how you describe this, but you get yourself involved in a sort of psychological game, Mr. Lishman, in which everybody seems to know but no one is willing to admit, or no one is willing to ask, or if they know they don't want to confirm it. We just kept playing the psychological game.

LISHMAN: In other words, there was a general understanding that controls were going on to accomplish desired results, yet no one would come out and talk across the table about it?

CARLIN: More or less. That would be a correct summary.

This background of tacitly acknowledged fraud and hypocritical pretense becomes doubly revealing when one realizes the extremes to which the *64s* went to deceive the viewing public into the belief that the fix that was couldn't be. The highest kind of prestige images were used in this calculated campaign of flaunted probity.

On the one hand there was the lofty professorial image; on the other the bank-vault security device. Bergen Evans, professor of English at Northwestern University, fulfilled the first image requirement, and the Chase Manhattan Bank and the Manufacturers Trust Co., two of the nation's largest banking institutions, collaborated in providing the second.

The *64s* implanted the belief in the viewing audience that the questions used on the shows were drawn up by Professor Evans; that they went directly into the vaults of the two banks; and that they were untouched and untainted by producing hands until two burly guards marched onstage before the cameras, carrying a locked strongbox. A bank vice-president accompanied the guards and assured the viewing audience that no one previously had seen the questions except their editors.

The mechanics of this phony façade were exposed in testimony before the Harris committee. The committee itself, perhaps showing proper deference to ultrarespectable images, issued no subpoenas for Professor Evans or for any bank officials to explain their views of the ethics of the matter; but, one way and another, despite this considerate reticence, a lot of revealing testimony did creep out from under the rug.

After the first series of hearings devoted to the sins of *Twenty-One,* there was a pause for almost a month before the Harris committee, in the first week of November 1959, plunged on into the touchy topic of the *64s.* In this pause, a lot of people began to ask a lot of questions. Professor Evans, to answer some of them, wrote an article for *Life* in which he explained how he had researched subjects for the shows and drawn up questions to be used on them. "I have no reason," he wrote, "to believe the shows I worked for were rigged. If I had thought so, I would have disassociated myself from them at once."

In this same period of calm before the storm, the Manufacturers Trust Co. said producers of the *Question,* its wing of the image endeavor, had usually followed the procedure of handing over sealed envelopes that presumably contained the vital questions. A bank spokesman explained: "We accepted the assurance, given us by the program producers, and so stated on the telecast, that no one, except for the editors, had seen the questions before they were placed in the vault." Just as one never questions an accused producer when he says his show is pure, no bank official obviously would ever question such assurances before committing the prestige of his institution to a public proclamation of their validity.

Unfortunately, when the Harris committee put producers of the *Question* and the *Challenge* to the test, the picture that rapidly emerged was the reverse of all the lofty pretensions. Merton Koplin, the producer of the *Question* under Carlin, was questioned closely by Richard N. Goodwin, a special consultant to the Harris committee.

GOODWIN: Were questions often rewritten or modified a few days before the show, or at least on one occasion on the day of the show itself in light of the screenings that you would have with the contestants?

KOPLIN: Yes.

GOODWIN: With those questions, did you then rush down and place them in the vault so that they could be back up in time for the show?

KOPLIN: Yes.

GOODWIN: Did the producers have a copy of these questions at all times?

KOPLIN: Yes.

GOODWIN: In fact, the bank, while a useful bit of show business, afforded no security whatsoever; is that correct, against any type of control that any producer might desire to exercise?

KOPLIN: That is correct.

Shirley Bernstein, Koplin's counterpart on the *Challenge,* was equally frank. Goodwin read a long statement of hers into the committee's hearing record. It went like this:

Q. What was the purpose of using a reputable bank in which to keep the questions sealed up prior to the show?

A. I knew little about it. I had a key to the safe and I and my assistant would go in to get the questions.

Q. In the light of how the show was conducted, do you think the use of the bank was a little phony?

A. Yes, I do. . . .

Q. One of the purposes of the bank was to give the impression that it was impossible for the contestant to get advance help of any kind?

A. Yes.

Q. Was this a false impression?

A. Yes.

Q. Deliberate, in your opinion?

A. Yes.

6

With professors, banks, industrial executives, advertising agencies and the greatest networks in the country all participating happily in the rigging or being perversely blind to the obviousness of its existence, the ethical climate of the nation at the summit stood once more revealed as that of the racket society advancing into the future under this noble motto: *Use any gimmick that makes you a buck.*

The television industry, one might have thought, would have been a little special. It was constantly bragging of its great educational potential, of its power to guide and set standards. Yet what kind of standards had it been setting? They differed not from the deeply corruptive practices of the electrical industry, of the packaging industry, of the construction industry, of that entrepreneur in fraud, Billie Sol Estes. With television, as with all the other elements of this corrupted society, the money obviously had come first and the manner of its minting hadn't counted. As Billie Sol Estes' adventures in larceny had demonstrated, there is a great public awareness of the real nature of the motivating forces in American life, and among the farmers and the people of Pecos this recognition of the reality had gone hand in hand with the creed that, since it's all a racket, the wise man carves out a piece of the racket for himself. What the television quiz-show scandal did was to transform the face of Pecos into the face of the nation. It broadened the screen. And it mirrored an entire people in frantic pursuit of individual slices of the racket.

As with Charles Van Doren, so with virtually all contestants who were drawn into the web of the quiz-show fraud. In the entire lot, there was only one exception; only *one man* whose conscience absolutely rebelled at the acceptance of tainted money.

Some contestants, it is true, had qualms about the deed; but even these, in the end, had found it impossible to say "No." Typical was the case of Richard Jackman, who had appeared on *Twenty-One* on October 3, 1956. He testified that Dan Enright gave him a list of questions the week before he appeared, though he did not know at the time that these were the same questions he was to be asked on the show, and that, just before he went on stage, Enright came to his dressing room and gave him minute instructions about just how many points he was to bid. Jackman followed orders so expertly that all his friends acclaimed his marvelous performance. This caused Jackman to feel a certain revulsion, he testified.

"Of course," he said, "that was excruciating for me when I realized there had been fraud involved. So I was just sick about the whole business."

Jackman had won $24,500 on the show, but he was so disturbed by the manner of his winning that he flew to Buffalo to consult with his mother about the ethics of the matter. She advised him not to touch the filthy lucre, and Jackman returned to New York primed to throw Dan Enright's dirty money in his face. But the throwing turned out to be not so easy.

Enright urged him to continue on the show; the reaction to his performance, Enright said, had been so good "that he could guarantee me $100 a week for the rest of my life" if Jackman would just continue. Jackman refused. There was much discussion about whether he should take any of the $24,500. Enright assured him the money was his; he had won it. And Jackman finally agreed to take $15,000. Why did he do this? Why not all or nothing? Why $15,000? Jackman had considerable difficulty explaining.

Congressman Peter F. Mack, Jr., questioned him.

JACKMAN: I do not consider that I had any moral claim to the money, sir.

MACK: But you did accept $15,000?

JACKMAN: Yes.

MACK: You accepted that as reimbursement for your participation in the show?

JACKMAN: I guess that clears it up for my own conscience, yes. That was for the evening's sacrifice.

While $15,000 might seem a fairly generous price for one evening's "sacrifice" of rectitude, members of the Harris committee were greatly impressed with Jackman. After all, he had rejected $9500, and this was unique in their experience. He was the first man they had met who had turned down a penny. So there was much admiring chitchat, and Jackman was complimented effusively. Carried away by it all, Jackman commented at one point: "I suppose I could subsequently have brought suit for it [the remaining $9500] after I thought it over." His nobility in firmly turning his back on such legal recourse practically overwhelmed the committee, and Jackman left the stand to a chorus of praise.

The committee might have played a different tune had it been aware at the time of one hidden factor. The truth was that, almost a year previously, Jackman *had* filed suit for the $9500 he had initially refused; and, more than three months before he took the stand before the Harris committee, he had won the suit and collected the money! As Meyer Weinberg commented in his study of the case: "Even the market for righteousness was rigged!"

The children's market was rigged, too. One of the sensations on the *$64,000 Challenge* had been Patty Duke, child actress, age eleven. Patty had been so precocious she had answered the most difficult questions and had won $32,000. Of course, she was so precocious and so successful because she was briefed with the questions and answers before every show. All of this came out when Patty's manager, John Ross, who had collected a 15 per cent commission on her $32,000, appeared before the Harris committee. Ross testified that he had been aware of the preshow briefing sessions but that he had never asked Patty what went on. "Perhaps I was afraid if I pursued it I might find out the truth," he acknowledged.

The congressmen became quite incensed at the idea of a child actress, age eleven, being initiated into the intricacies of the fix, and Representative Steven B. Derounian took out after Ross.

DEROUNIAN: Do you think it is healthy for . . . young children [to get] into situations like this where they are taught to cheat and lie for money?

ROSS: No, sir.

DEROUNIAN: Is this not rather a tawdry thing for the youth of this country to be brought up with a scummy foundation, as this protégée has now? What respect can she have for truth?

ROSS: I have been trying, in every way, to make up to her if it would ever be at all possible. I hope I am succeeding.

DEROUNIAN: Would you have done this to your daughter if she had received the same opportunity?

ROSS: It may not say much for me. I don't know, sir.

At the close of his testimony, Ross agreed that, the more money Patty Duke made, the more he made.

"Would that possibly be the reason that you were not concerned about the information you got that she received the answers to the questions in advance?" he was asked.

"It might be, sir," Ross admitted.

Even a minister, it developed, had not been impervious to the allure of tainted cash. The Reverend Charles E. Jackson, Jr., of Tennessee, twice appeared as a contestant on *The $64,000 Question,* posing as an expert on great love stories. Each time he was given questions in advance—the same questions, it turned out, he was later asked on the show. He won $16,000, was told to quit— and did. Nothing about this performance seems greatly to have disturbed the Reverend Jackson's sensibilities; it remained for an experience that was less happy financially to arouse him to indignation.

In September 1957 he was invited to appear on *The $64,000 Challenge.* Once more, he received an advance screening, this time from Miss Bernstein. During it, he was asked a question he did not know about an obscure nineteenth-century poem written by Thomas Hood. On the show, Jackson's opponent was asked the Thomas Hood question; she didn't know it; and, under the rules, this ended the game for both of them.

Testifying before the Harris committee, the Reverend Jackson gave a very melodramatic description of the emotions that assailed him when he heard his opponent get the Thomas Hood question and realized they were both being jobbed. He said:

"When I heard her get the Thomas Hood question and be unable to answer it . . . my first reaction was to say, 'No, Ralph—yes, I know this answer but I got it on a screening' and I could see visions not only of about six cases of apoplexy there, but I could see my bullet-riddled body as I passed an alley somewhere. I decided against that plan and when I got out on the stage I even considered in my mind saying, 'Well, I don't think I ought to take this check.' "

Reverend Jackson "considered," but he didn't do it. He took the check for the $4000 he had won.

Later, however, when he thought about the potential winnings he had missed, he began to feel the indignation of the greatly wronged. It was one of the ironies of the quiz-show fixes that the sensibilities of contestants like Jackson and Herbert Stempel seem not to have been greatly exercised so long as they were winning; but when the fix turned against them and they were counted out, they felt indignant—they felt as if they could have gone right on winning on their own. It was at this point that the quiz-rigging was always placed in jeopardy, for there is no vengeance like that of the aggrieved when deprived of hard cash. In the Reverend Jackson's case:

"I called Miss Goostree [his opponent]. I asked her what had happened in her screening. She said she had been led to believe that the questions for the night would be on Shakespeare. Here is a nice little fix. They didn't ask me if I wanted this answer. They didn't ask her anything. But they fixed it so we were both going to be through at $4000.

"You will have to accept my word. I was even angry at her being gypped and me profiting from being gypped as I was denied my chance to do better . . . I feel I was gypped; I could have gone much further."

The righteous outrage that possessed Jackson at this thought impelled him to send denunciations of the *Challenge* to *Time*, *The New York Times,* and the *Nashville Tennessean;* but, though he told them all that he had been fed questions and answers on the *Challenge,* none of them cared or dared to touch the story.

In the entire history of the quiz-show fix, there was just one person who had the fortitude to turn down money. He was Arthur Cohn, Jr., a New York car-card advertising salesman. Cohn appeared on *The $64,000 Challenge* on March 23, 1958. His opponent was Wilton J. Springer. Cohn and Springer had met previously when they appeared for preliminary testing; they knew and liked each other. On the evening of their big test before the cameras, they were waiting around to go on the air, and Miss Bernstein, spotting Cohn, asked him if he would send Springer to see her in a dressing room. Springer went, and there he received a very thorough briefing on the questions that were to be asked that night.

Immediately after this warmup session, Springer walked over to Cohn and told him what had happened. Both men were disturbed by the implications, but it was now showtime and they were on the air. When the questions were asked, they turned out to be the identical ones Springer had been given in the warmup session. He had the answers pat, of course, and won $4000. Cohn didn't get a chance. How did Cohn feel? He described his emotions later to the Harris committee:

"There were only a few seconds to have feelings. I was nervous. I did feel that I was going to blurt out the entire thing. At the risk of being goody-goody—and I hate holier-than-thou people—it was just cheating. I was terribly upset, and I was going to blurt it out. Then I thought nobody wants a troublemaker, and I made up my mind then and there, at the risk of sounding a goody-goody, I would complain immediately after the show."

Cohn stuck to this resolve. An hour after the show ended, he telephoned Miss Bernstein and accused her bluntly of rigging the performance. She tried to deny it, but Cohn informed her that his wife and a couple of guests had been present, they had heard Springer tell him what had happened, they would make good witnesses. This threat raised merry hob in the executive suites of Entertainment Productions and Revlon. Mutual agitation kept the telephone wires humming, and finally George Abrams of Revlon, who had known Cohn for years, called him and asked him if he wouldn't please come to the Revlon offices and talk things over.

Reluctantly, Cohn went. He described to Abrams and another Revlon executive exactly what had happened.

". . . They apparently believed me. They were upset," Cohn told the Harris committee. ". . . They were going to raise the devil with Entertainment Productions because they said it smelled bad as far as they were concerned. I said again at the risk of my halo being tight, I don't want the $250 [this was the consolation prize he had won], not that I am so rich, but it is dirty money and I have to live with myself. . . .

"I told them I didn't want the $250. They insisted it would upset their bookkeeping."

They kept pleading with Cohn to please take the $250, if only for the sake of the bookkeeping, but he wouldn't. He finally told them that, if the cause of their bookkeeping was so sacred, they could send his $250 check to the National Society for Crippled Children. But Cohn himself accepted no money. He was the only man in the entire quiz-show mess who did not.

It was this session with Cohn that led to the meeting between Revlon and Carlin in which, Carlin told the committee, everybody played "the psychological game," pretending that what everybody knew was happening wasn't happening at all. Later, when the whole story unfolded before the Harris committee, Cohn himself seemed almost apologetic. Like Douglas Johnson in the case of the Brinks cash, he had done the honest thing, but he seemed to recognize that it was the kind of thing that isn't done very often anymore, he seemed positively worried that people might attribute to him some special virtue.

When Committee Counsel Lishman told him, "Unlike anyone that has so far appeared before us, you did something with the $250 check besides putting it in your pocket," Cohn protested:

"May I say just one thing. Again I say, I don't want to be goody-goody or holier than thou. I don't deserve the credit. In all sincerity I think it is due to my background and my upbringing and my good wife, that it was very easy for me to decide to do what I wanted to do, as I saw things the right way. Because I was brought up that way. So it really was no reflection on me."

It says much about our society when the upright man—the lone upright man in the entire smelly mess—feels he must protest against being considered upright.

7

The Harris committee hearings sent the quiz-show scandal into its final spiral. When the dam broke under congressional pressure, evasion became no longer possible, and only the truth would serve. But this truth, told to the Harris committee under oath, was in many instances in irreconcilable, perjurious conflict with the testimony that had been given under oath to District Attorney Hogan's New York grand jury months previously. The offense was public, unforgivable. There was no help for it; action had to be taken.

District Attorney Hogan summoned a new grand jury into session, submitted the new evidence to it, and secured a flock of twenty perjury indictments. Included in the list were most of the headline prize-winners of the TV quiz shows: Charles Van Doren;

Mrs. Vivienne Nearing, the attractive lawyer who had defeated him but had won only $5500; Hank Bloomgarden, the medical research consultant who had bested Mrs. Nearing and had taken home $98,500; and Elfrida Van Nardroff, the champ of them all, winner of $237,500. All, without exception, pleaded guilty and threw themselves upon the mercy of the court; and all, without exception, received that mercy—nothing worse than scolding lectures and suspended sentences.

Now perjury, the deliberate lying to a grand jury, is no mere peccadillo of a crime. Condoned, it can lead only to the thwarting of the law and the undermining of all justice. Regardless of the moral issues involved in the TV quiz fixes; there can be no real excuse or justification for perjury; there can be no question that, as an offense, it expresses contempt for the whole system of law that is the foundation stone of a law-abiding society. Yet the attitude of the court and public toward this offense and these defendants was an almost complaisant one.

Everyone realized, of course, that the big advertisers who had sponsored the shows, the producers who had organized them, the advertising agencies who in many instances had had a hand in the rigging, the millionaire network executives who had run the shows in defiance of all kinds of ugly rumors and who had been obdurately and purposely blind—none of these untouchables was ever going to have to suffer. Only the vulnerable smaller fry—the $50- to $100-a-week laborers in the vineyards of the corrupt society who had found great, rigged wealth irresistible—were going to have to pay the forfeit; and so the mood was not to punish but to pity and exculpate. The rite of expiation would be performed. In meaningless words, proper obeisance would be made to our dead ideals.

Typical was the performance in New York's Special Sessions Court on January 17, 1962, when Charles Van Doren, gaunt and trembling, led a parade of ten TV-quiz contestants before Justice Edward F. Breslin. The Justice looked down sternly from the bench, but his words were compassionate and understanding.

"I understand you were one of the first who wanted to throw himself on the mercy of the court," the Justice told Van Doren.

"The punishment began the day the matter was exposed to the press.

"I see in your eyes, as I've seen in the eyes of others who have pleaded in this investigation, how humiliated and contrite you are and they were. . . . You are entitled to a chance."

And so Van Doren and the others, sentences suspended, faded from the limelight. Confession made, absolution given, they had served their purpose in their last appearance as public figures; with their help, the amenities had been observed and a ritual that changed nothing and meant little had been performed.

It appeared that this was the end, that all could now be conveniently forgotten; but it was not, in the final analysis, to be quite that easy. Barry and Enright, the producers of the rigged *Twenty-One* and *Tic Tac Dough,* were also the proprietors of WGMA, a radio station in Hollywood, Florida. And so the Federal Communications Commission in early 1963 was confronted with a delicate problem: What should it do about renewing their broadcasting license? Were men who had rigged network TV shows over a period of years the kind of men who should be privileged to operate a radio station?

Miss Elizabeth C. Smith, an examiner for the FCC, pondered this ethical issue and responded with a resounding "Yes." Her reasoning, as Jack Gould commented in *The New York Times,* made "a particularly distinctive contribution to the enticing rationalization of contemporary morality." For what Miss Smith said, in effect, was: "Since everything is a racket, what's wrong with Barry and Enright?" She did not, of course, express it so crudely. She phrased it this way:

"Barry and Enright held no copyright for, or exclusivity of use of, the practice of rigging television quiz programs. It was in the public domain and used by others. This fact does not, of course, give Barry and Enright, collectively or individually, absolution for their misdeeds, but it does place in better perspective their actions. . . .

"The same general type of controls was used on other television quiz programs and their use was somewhat symptomatic of the moral climate . . . shown to exist in the television industry."

Though Barry and Enright shouldn't have lied in denying publicly that any of their shows were rigged, there was no evidence, Miss Smith wrote, that they had encouraged any of the perjuries committed on their behalf by Van Doren, Mrs. Nearing, Bloomgarden, and others. Besides, she reasoned, the two producers doubtless had passed through a searing personal ordeal as the result of the exposure of their activities.

"There is less likelihood they will repeat actions in any way similar to those here under censure than would one who has not gone through their soul-searching experience," Miss Smith wrote. "Mistakes which were made in the past—and gross mistakes of judgment there were—have indelibly left their imprint on these men. Steel which has been through the crucible of a fiery furnace is stronger than ever."

Here one feels impelled to recall William Shannon's line on the congressional testimony of Van Doren: "Dim the lights. Music, Maestro, please."

Miss Smith's conclusion was that, though the activities of Barry and Enright reflected "adversely upon their character qualifications to run a radio station," this should not absolutely disqualify them; this should not prevent the renewal of their license.

Her recommendation, and even more the reasoning used to justify it, caused a considerable editorial uproar. The FCC's own broadcast bureau fought Miss Smith's views in an appeal to the full commission, and the commission, in the end, overruled the examiner and refused to renew the Barry–Enright radio license. Though this action upheld standards of probity in broadcasting, the battle had been something of a squeaker, and the mere fact that an FCC examiner could endorse the flimsy rationale—if everyone else is doing it, it's all right, or at least it's forgivable—seemed itself one of the most significant tributes that could be given to the prevailing dearth of ethics in the corrupt society. As Jack Gould wrote: "The idea that an erosion of values can be overlooked so long as it is sufficiently widespread might yet prove to be the most controversial aspect of the entire quiz case."

7

Everybody Joins the Game

THE TELEVISION QUIZ-SHOW scandal claims a unique niche in the annals of the corrupt society, not because it was such a racket but because of the breadth of exposure it gave to an entire people's fascination with rackets. One of the more perceptive analysts of the time, evaluating its significance, wrote:

For some years it has been the writer's conviction that in modern American society there is a secret understanding, shared by almost everyone . . . that all public life and all public institutions are a fraud. Contemporary society itself is widely assumed to be fixed.

Among those who are deprived of a share in the institutionalized fraud, there is likely to be a feeling of resentment, coupled with cynicism and delight in the downfall of the upper-frauds. None of this precludes a vicarious, and equally common, enjoyment of the fruits of that fraud once it has been exposed. . . .

At the same time, those on or near the top are privately willing to concede that public life is a fraud, but they hug to themselves and *entre nous,* among the few intimates in their milieu, the pleasantly guilty secret. The essence of this secret is that they have mastered the sales, public relations, personality and administrative tricks of "beating the system" while publicly extolling its virtues. Their cynicism is practical.

Practical it may be for those who pull the strings at the top of the mass society, but for the millions of individuals lost and hopeless on the lower or bottom rungs of the ladder such cynicism is a deeply corruptive force. The ideal that any man, by honesty and thrift and hard work, can carve out for himself a secure and rewarding niche has been buried along with the dinosaur; and individual man, crushed in the pressures and insecurities of the mass society, recognizing the non-ethics of that society, turns as all his betters have turned to the arts of manipulation, to the techniques of the racket.

But for him such imitative endeavor is an ugly trap. Racket skills can be exercised with impunity only by those at the top of the rackets. Only they have the wealth and power and prestige that, if they are found out, can still guarantee immunity. If they fall, the system falls, God forbid—a calamity that, naturally, cannot be allowed to happen. For them the racket is two-edged. It is a racket that protects itself by being a racket, for its extent can never be acknowledged, must never be recognized.

The average man, trying to participate in the system he sees in operation all around him, deals from no such peak of prestige and power. If he gets caught, he must be exposed and humiliated and punished, if only as a lesson to the rest of us, if only as reassurance that we are not what indubitably we are. The racket, then, will not work—or it will work for only a limited time before catastrophe— for the little man who, because he is insignificant, is frozen out of the juicier rewards of the inequitable tax system and the other corruptions of the racket society. If the little man were blind, he might be safe. But he is not blind, and he is not exactly a fool. He sees what he sees, and he knows what he knows; and, finding in the widely prevalent non-ethics of his time no other standard to follow, no other way out of the trap, he convinces himself that it must be all right because "everyone else is doing it" and he turns to the racket handiest to him in the hope of making his fortune. He turns to it even when, in the long run, common sense must tell him he can end only in ruining himself.

I

Awareness begins early—in grade and high school.

In Los Angeles, in 1961, a poll was conducted among the 1174 students in the seventh, eighth, and ninth grades of the Bancroft Junior High School. This key question was asked:

"You are in your teacher's office. He is called out of the room, leaving you there alone. You see on his desk the answers to the test you will be taking later. Would you look at these answers?"

Only 6 per cent of the B–7 pupils (the first semester of seventh grade) said they would peek, but 41 per cent of the A–9 students (last semester of the ninth grade) admitted they would take advantage of the opportunity and cheat.

One ninth grader, precocious indeed, gave succinct and almost perfect expression to the prevailing ethics of the age.

"I think anyone given the chance to cheat and not get caught would take it," he wrote. "If it's there for the taking, take it."

Yet ironically—and again in perfect tune with our times—from 74 to 94 per cent of the students questioned in the different classes (including, of course, that high percentage of those who said they would cheat) rated themselves as "basically honest" and unwilling to "compromise ideals for power, money or prestige." This belief in their ability not to compromise when they had already compromised is typical of the schizophrenia of the corrupt society. Many of the students justified their willingness to cheat because, they said, the pressure was on them from home to "get those grades up—no matter what!" High grades would be needed for college admission, and the "no matter what" came as virtually a corollary to the need. So the students yielded to the pressure, they met the necessity by cheating if they could; but this did not tarnish their opinions of themselves. "I am honest most of the time," one twelve-year-old boy wrote, giving the attitude its perfect expression. Another philosophized: "There should be a place for sometimes."

How serious was the situation reflected in the Los Angeles survey? Hasn't there always been some cheating in grade and high schools—even in colleges?

Certainly there has. As one of an older generation (high school '28, college '32—an unforgettable year), I know there was cheating in my day, but the atmosphere, the methods and the intent were, I think, quite different. We had no strict honor codes; nobody gave his word that he wouldn't cheat, given the opportunity. It was

fairly well understood that it was part of the teacher's job to prevent cheating and the corollary to that was that, kids being kids,
they would cheat a bit if they could. If you had a good teacher, one
with eyes in her head, there was precious little cutting of ethical
corners. But if you had a teacher who was so blind she couldn't
see what was happening six inches in front of her nose, the whole
class was likely to have a field day. Football players, of course,
almost always had to be helped.

Nobody considered such lapses from the proper code of conduct signs of acute moral depravity. It was simply a question of
kids being kids. And the difference, I think, was that most of us
really were kids. There was very little cold calculation in what we
did; cheating with us was not an organized racket. Most of us, I
think, did our best to make it on our own. We felt better that way,
and it never occurred to us (except the football players, who were
special hardship cases, intellectually speaking) to *rely* on cheating.
If caught out, most of us would have felt guilty and been properly
abashed, and I doubt if we could have coined a justification for our
lapses like that of the Los Angeles ninth-grader who wrote: "If it's
there for the taking, take it."

The academic world I remember was certainly more innocent of
purpose than the world of today. I cannot recall an instance of
those years in which anyone ever set out deliberately to steal
examination papers and sell them for a price to fellow students or
in which students blackmailed instructors to get their grades raised.
Yet these are precisely the kind of scandals that today have rocked
the foundations of major colleges.

The year 1965 was ushered in by an unparalleled cheating
racket at the august Air Force Academy in Colorado Springs. By
the time the investigation ended, 105 cadets had been dismissed
for direct participation in the plot. Both the high caliber of the
institution and the low caliber of the racket in which the students
had become involved made the Air Force Academy scandal of
particular and striking significance.

The Academy, the Air Force's counterpart of West Point and
Annapolis, had been especially proud of its high standards and the

quality of its recruits. Unless one were an especially promising football player, in which circumstances it becomes conceivable that special dispensations could be arranged, to hope for appointment to the Academy a high school graduate was expected to be truly outstanding, sound physically, in the very top level of his class scholastically, possessed of school leadership qualities and high standards of personal conduct. Most candidates are thoroughly checked out by Air Force Reserve officers familiar with their hometown environments. The object is to weed out all but the best. And so it was a sizable segment of "the best" who were on exhibit in the Air Force cheating scandal.

According to officials of the Academy, it all started when a cadet acquired a key to a cabinet in which semester final-examination papers were kept. He stole the papers, had them copied, and then recruited about a dozen other cadets to help him sell them.

Now the Air Force Academy has a very high and strict honor code. It says specifically: "We will not lie, steal or cheat, nor tolerate among us anyone who does." A cadet under these rules is obligated to inform on another who, like himself, has given his word of honor and then by his conduct demonstrated that his word is worthless.

Under the circumstances, the development of a profitable racket in the sale of stolen examination papers required deft management. But the cadets in the inner circle were equal to the challenge. They would approach a cadet most circumspectly and feel him out in general terms to determine what his reaction would be to the actual proposition. Only if a cadet exhibited some positive eagerness would the ringleaders approach him a second time, broach their offer and make the cash deal for the stolen examination papers.

When the scandal broke out in headlines through the forced, piecemeal resignations of some of the cadets involved, cries of righteous outrage and indignation went up from both the young men and their parents. "I didn't raise my son to be a tattletale, an informer" became the usual self-serving explanation. The hypocritical pretense was that a lot of cadets had been cashiered, not because they had cheated but because they hadn't informed on others, thus violating the Academy's strict honor code.

The Academy met this counterattack by putting on the record the basic facts uncovered by its investigation. In a press conference on February 3, 1965, Maj. Gen. Robert H. Warren, commandant of the Air Force Academy, said explicitly that every one of the dismissed 105 cadets had been directly involved in the theft, sale, or use of the examination papers. Not one had been dismissed for "tolerating," he said, explaining that those who had broken the Academy's honor code in this respect would be dealt with separately by the Cadet Honor Board.

In defense of the honor system, General Warren said: "It is a good system, a sound system and an effective system." It was perhaps significant that forty of the dismissed 105 cadets were athletes and that twenty of them had been counted on for the 1965 varsity football team. But General Warren denied a bit heatedly that the Academy had been accepting cadets who were swifties on the gridiron but not so fast in class. "It's anything but true . . . ," he said. "There is no basis to reports that these men had to cheat to get through here."

Yet cheat they had; and they had not only cheated—they had made a racket out of the cheating.

It says much about the uncritical and imperceptive world in which we live that this racket aspect of the case, its most vital feature, was virtually ignored in all the heated public discussions sparked by the cheating scandal. There was a great tendency to exculpate, to belittle the significance of what had happened, to attribute part of the trouble to the Air Force's superhumanly lofty code. Even *The National Observer* argued in one editorial that, while it didn't condone cheating, perhaps the cadets should not be too severely blamed, considering the atmosphere of the times and the example their elders were setting them. All such rationalizations avoided coming to grips with the hard facts of what had actually happened. The sequence was clear. The Air Force cadets had pledged their honor not to cheat, and then had shown they didn't know what the word *honor* meant by going out and cheating. And they had not just simply cheated. They had stolen. They had organized to make a profit out of their theft; and some had sold and some had bought the stolen goods. The mores of the racket society, by these deeds, had found expression on one of the most austere campuses in the land—among young men supposedly chosen from the elite of the rising generation.

The Air Force Academy was not alone. Four years earlier the students of Rider College in Trenton, New Jersey, had given a similar demonstration of the use of the cutthroat principles of the racket society in the academic world. Rider was a ninety-seven-year-old business college; it numbered among its alumni bank executives, corporation partners, top business leaders in many fields. It endeavored, in the words of its Dean of Students, Robert A. McBane, to teach its undergraduates "to be honest business-men," to teach them that "there is such a thing as business ethics." It was a battle of instruction that Rider lost in shocking fashion when, in March 1961, it was forced to expel twenty-two juniors and seniors for running a blackmail racket to upgrade failing or unsatisfactory marks.

A "friendly" recorder, it developed, had been persuaded to upgrade a few failing marks. Other students learned of his action and threatened to expose him unless he gave them higher marks. Virtually all of the students involved in this hijacking of grades were business-administration majors and came, according to Mc-Bane, from "solid, respectable families." Their fathers included a doctor, a corporation president, the owner of a Manhattan credit clothing chain. When the cheating was exposed, these students from excellent backgrounds showed not the slightest signs of either comprehension or remorse.

"The thing that alarmed me," Dean McBane said, "was the complete absence of the feeling in some cases that they had done anything wrong. There was no feeling of moral guilt in them."

So far removed from any sensation of guilt was one student that he tried to work on the college the same blackmailing technique he had employed on the "friendly" recorder. If any disciplinary action was taken against him, he threatened, he would go to the news-papers. "Be nice to me and I won't start a scandal," he brazenly told school officials.

Others, less brash, seemed simply unable to comprehend what they had done that was so heinous. One argued that the course in which he had obtained a fraudulent grade wasn't important ("I'll never use it") and therefore no real crime had been committed. Another said he had wanted a higher grade to become eligible for fraternity pledging; still another—he had had a *C* raised to a *B*—couldn't understand what all the fuss was about, then argued that everything should have been settled amicably by giving him his *C* back. Most significant of all, the scandal found its way into the newspapers only because some of the expelled students, feeling *they* had been wronged, tipped off the press.

A most disturbing feature of such scandals is that they are taking place in one of the more idealistic atmospheres of our culture. The market place traditionally has been a field of sharp practice, but the more cloistered precincts of the college campus usually led to loftier ideals. That these are now being marred by the practices and outlook of the racket society speaks much about the deep corruption of our time.

The extent of both cheating practices and complacent administrative attitudes toward them were detailed in a college survey made by Philip Jacob, professor of political science at the University of Pennsylvania. In a broad poll of college students, he found that, at many colleges, frequent cheating is admitted by 40 per cent or more of the students "often with no apology or sense of wrong-doing." Most revealing of the students' ethical attitudes was their response to Jacob's question about whether they would report another student's cheating under the honor code. Most of those questioned said they wouldn't tattle if the cheater were a friend, *unless* it became clear he was going to be caught; *then* they would tell to protect their own self-interest and advancement. In the racket society, what else matters?

As shocking as the attitudes of the students was the tolerance of many administrators. Two deans, for example, told Jacob that honesty must be judged by "extenuating circumstances." Their students, they said, were not basically dishonest, but they often "backed themselves into a corner" with heavy workloads, social activities, dependence on cramming—then looked for a way out.

Why did the students do this? Experts agreed that pressure was on them to obtain good grades so that they could get a degree and win social approval, essential springboards to the "good" job and the "good" marriage. What they learned really didn't matter so long as these ultimate aims were advanced. Even some college faculties seemed to go along with this interpretation of educational purposes. At one eastern school for women, Jacob found, the faculty had drawn up a list of the fifteen traits the "ideal" student should possess. Intellectual integrity was on their list—in *last* place.

In an atmosphere in which intellectual integrity is so downgraded, novel rackets inevitably begin to flourish. New York City and New York State, in recent years, have provided a couple of shining examples of the non-ethics of the racket society corrupting the field of education.

In 1960, the New York *World-Telegram and Sun* exposed a flourishing bucket-shop operation. Unscrupulous research agencies had put educational fraud on a business basis. For a set schedule of fees, they would provide sit-ins to take critical tests, or they would write term papers, or they would even prepare the master's or the doctor's thesis so vital to an advanced degree—and the greater emoluments that go with it. Frequently the arrangements for such factory-made frauds would be concluded, not by the students but by parents eager to see their children "get ahead," no matter how. The attitude of the parents seemed to be that they were making a business investment; they were buying their offspring degrees, just the way one might buy a plumber's license. What was the difference?

The answer, if one were really needed, was supplied in graphic fashion by the second wing of the New York scandals. In June 1961, the New York State Board of Regents discovered that a racket had been conducted in the licensing of physicians and that a number of medical students who had actually failed to pass their tests nevertheless had been licensed and allowed to go out into the world treating patients.

There had been two facets to the medical-license trafficking racket. The June 1961 licensing test to be taken by some 600 medical students had been squirreled out well in advance and had been hocked by a three-doctor sales ring. Some $10,000 had been collected from the sale of the examination questions before the racket was discovered and a substitute test drawn up in time to thwart the purchasers who had expected to benefit.

In the resulting flareup, Dr. Stiles D. Ezell resigned as secretary of the New York State Board of Medical Examiners. Subsequently, in November 1962, he pleaded guilty to unauthorized possession of the examination papers and admitted he had passed the purloined test along to one of the doctors in the marketing ring. Though quick action prevented damage in this instance, discovery that such a racket had operated on such a level led inevitably to the question: What had gone on previously?

The answer was *Plenty.* The Board of Regents in its probe discovered that twenty-four doctors who "did not receive passing grades in medical licensing examinations" had nevertheless managed to have their grades raised—and had been licensed as qualified physicians. Some of them had been practicing on an unsuspecting public from their foundations of inadequacy for nearly four years. The Board of Regents voted unanimously to cancel all twenty-four licenses. One of the licenses revoked belonged to the son of a doctor who sat on the Board of Regents. The father voted with the other twelve members of the board to void his son's license.

2

A society is threatened with disintegration when its best, not its worst, elements turn to crime. In America today, society faces this pivotal threat from those very sources that are the main reliance of ethical and healthy cultures.

The lax standards among undergraduates and faculty on many a college campus are only one symptom of the times, only one example of the weakening moral fiber of those forces that traditionally sustain a civilization. On a broader scale, throughout the nation, the same dearth of standards may be seen working out in everyday life, reflected most clearly in the changing pattern of crime statistics. For it must be judged immensely significant that some of our fastest-growing crimes today are not those committed by hardened criminals, but those that are the work of some of the "better" elements of our society. Executive-suite embezzlements, employee thefts, shoplifting, bank robberies by rank amateurs— these are the types of "noncriminal" crimes that have achieved shocking importance in the postwar years.

All are crimes of the mass society. Reflected in all, in varying degrees and with varying emphasis, is the common denominator of individual man at war with the amorphous mass pressures of his time. Man no longer deals with man as an individual in the business world; his life is dominated by an entire galaxy of power complexes: by the corporation, large or small, for which he works; by the chain stores in which he shops; by the huge and impersonal banking systems and insurance systems and health plans on which so much of his welfare depends. Since man in so much of his life no longer deals with fellow man but with a vast and impersonal *them,* his ethics based on a code of man-to-man honor no longer apply; each to himself becomes a David pitted against the all-powerful Goliath of *them*—and, in this climate, no means of getting his, of getting even, carries with it a moral stain. The most dishonorable deeds can be committed, but so long as only one of the mass power structures is the victim, the man who commits the deed can come away from it not only without the slightest twinge of guilt, but almost with a sense of positive and honorable accomplishment. This perversion of all values is a hallmark of our time in the rapidly mushrooming field of white-collar crime.

The business atmosphere in which this perversion takes place was examined by *Modern Office Procedures* in 1964 in a broad survey of key office and business executives. Most agreed that the ethics at the top were going to be reflected through every echelon of an organization. Warren C. Stevens, editor of the magazine, wrote:

"As one top man put it, 'The president who vacations in Europe and bills it as a business trip shouldn't be upset when his secretary calls in sick and he finds out she couldn't be healthier. He's only getting what he asked for.'

"Nearly all the men we talked with believe that the moral tone in the offices and upper echelons of the nation's business firms isn't always what it should be. But just how bad it is, they can't agree.

" 'Business ethics have gone to the dogs,' one middle management man said emphatically. 'Most companies are out to make a big profit in the easiest way possible, no matter who is hurt or what they have to do. As a result, the people in their offices play all sorts of crazy games trying to get by with as much as possible.' "

At the other extreme were businessmen who insisted that competition today is cleaner than it was thirty years ago and that the moral tone in the offices is much higher. Most of the executives questioned believed, indeed, that the cutthroat aspects of competition between businesses were less vicious today than in the past, but when it came to the inner-office moral tone, even those loyal to the image of business purity had to concede that the climate isn't all it should be.

"The truth is that there seems to be a double standard of morality in the office," *Modern Office Procedures* wrote. "Most executives feel that anything they do is above reproach, but woe to the employee they discover in any questionable activity. Unfortunately, the indiscretions of the few foster those of the many. . . .

"Most of the people we surveyed believe that the real problem of ethics is in the day-to-day operation of the office: inter-business throatcutting may be on the decline, but petty immorality is mushrooming.

" 'The trouble,' said one controller, 'is that there's a constant current of undeclared war between management and employees. This is particularly true in large companies. Management believes it isn't getting a day's work for a day's pay, while the employees feel that the company is trying to take advantage of them. There's a constant round of petty thievery, unjust rulings and decisions, backbiting and maneuvering.' "

This "petty thievery" really isn't petty. It is today one of our major crimes. So widespread has the practice become that the most conservative estimates put the total cost to business at a staggering $1 billion a year, and some authorities insist the true figure is closer to $3 billion. Embezzlements in the executive suite and wholesale looting by employees on lower levels have literally wrecked many banks and businesses.

Norman Jaspan, the New York management consultant who has built a multimillion-dollar business on his skill in ferreting out embezzlers, emphasized in a speech to marketing executives in the winter of 1961 how the standards at the top in one large department store became everybody's standards. Originally, said Jaspan, the store was well-managed and prosperous. Then the manager "buys himself a house in the suburbs and sends a couple of his store's maintenance men over to redo the interior for him. He figures, what's a little company time and a little company paint? But his employees get the principle of the thing. A few years later, $200,000 worth of goods is disappearing in a twelve-month period. He's a professor this fellow—he gave them a short course in dishonesty, and they all graduated *cum laude*."

Jaspan paused, smacked the lectern with his hand, and drove home his major point:

"It means that when you have dishonesty at the top, it spreads downward like a catching disease."

As Jaspan pointed out in his book *The Thief in the White Collar,* this particular type of crime raises a more delicate social issue than any other. He quotes Edwin H. Sutherland, the eminent sociologist, to this effect: "White-collar crime violates trust and, therefore, creates distrust; this lowers social morale and produces social disorganization." The point, of course, is that one expects criminals to be criminals; to find them practicing their arts does not undermine faith in the social structure. But when distinguished executives begin to loot the corporate till, the president of the woman's club turns to shoplifting, and the cop on the beat becomes a burglar, society is really shocked and rocked to its foundations.

The extent of the shock, the nature of the social damage, may perhaps be gauged if one studies the portrait of the typical embezzler as drawn by *Fortune:*

"The typical defaulter is in his thirties, is married, has one or two children. He lives in a respectable neighborhood, drives a medium-priced car, and once in a while travels on the weekend. Whatever his secret life, he usually looks like a good mixer and is active in the community; often as not, he's a church officer. Temperately, he takes an occasional drink. Usually, he's had a couple of job promotions, partly because he's been around the firm for a while, and partly because he has slightly better than average ability, works hard, and seems willing to accept responsibility. In one study of 1,001 cases, 270 of the embezzlers held supervisory or executive positions."

It is the picture, one might think, of the really "good guy"— the solid, respectable, valued citizen, the salt of our civilization. But it has become, given the ethical pressures and the lassitude of the mass society, the portrait of the "bad guy," the secret thief.

As shocking as the portrait itself is the attitude of today's society toward the suave embezzler once exposed. Indicative of the fact that we attach no opprobrium to thefts that victimize *institutions* rather than *individuals* is the fact that the embezzler is often treated almost as a hero, a kind of Robin Hood. Take, for example, the case of one charming former manager of the Manufacturer's Trust Company branch in New York's Greenwich Village. A personable, go-getter type, he was liked by all, did favors for all—but all the time he was embezzling money from the bank in pursuit of his own get-rich-quick scheme, a risky venture involving heavy betting on the harness races. Naturally, the horses took his money as fast as he could "borrow" it from the bank, and by the time bank examiners became aware of what was happening, the embezzlement amounted to a whopping sum. While the case was pending in the courts, the cashiered bank manager went to work in a Seventh Avenue bar in which he had a secret interest, and before long business was booming. Longshoremen and neighbors flocked in; everyone, it seemed, wanted to hoist a toast to their good old pal who had hoodwinked all the power complexes of the mass society so long and so successfully.

A similar attitude colors one of Norman Jaspan's most shocking anecdotes, involving a youth whom he identifies only as Roger, "the son of a minister in a large mission." Roger, after serving a three-year hitch in the Navy, went to work as a stock clerk with a wholesale drug and sundry company. His position left him free to roam the warehouse, checking inventories. Roger's take-home pay was only $172 a month; he was paying out $81 a month for a second-hand Pontiac, which also ate up $40 a month for gas and oil. Roger, as can be seen, had himself painted into a financial corner, and to work his way out of it, he soon began to help himself to the drug firm's wares.

At first he simply took free samples of vitamins and medicines which he gave to the charges that passed through his father's mission. This was so easy that Roger was soon helping himself to other merchandise. Soon he was swapping goods he had stolen for goods that other fellow employees had stolen—items like cameras and prescription drugs that were not available to him in his section of the warehouse. Fearing that the stolen goods would be missed, he falsified the stock-card records—and did it so skillfully that he remained undetected. Roger ultimately came to grief when an honest store-owner complained to the wholesale firm that other stores were selling its goods (some of the stolen goods, naturally) at impossibly low prices. An investigation resulted. It showed that Roger, in six months, had stolen more than $6000 worth of merchandise.

The theft itself wasn't what disturbed Norman Jaspan most, but the attitude of the youth's father, the minister. Listen to this direct quote from Roger:

"My father told me that it's none of my business to discuss with the company what the other boys were doing and that the company should handle their own problems and that it wasn't for me to tell them anything other than what I, myself, personally took. My mother knew that I was stealing. She told me last night that she knew the stuff I was bringing home wasn't given out for nothing by the company. She is a little disturbed, but my father is used to these things and it doesn't seem to bother him!"

When one finds even a minister taking such a casual attitude toward so serious a dereliction on the part of his son, one begins to understand the true dimensions of the ethical debacle in modern

American life. It is a debacle founded upon a cynical lack of faith in the existence of standards at the top, compounded by the conviction that "everybody's doing it" and a man is a fool if he doesn't, as business does, "look out for No. 1." Added to all this, there is often the deep-seated and smoldering resentment of many individuals against the corporate "trap" in which they find themselves; they rebel against the overwhelming and ruthless and impersonal corporate power that uses and drains and discards men. This burning resentment of the corporate monster often underlies embezzlement by an executive who feels he has been double-crossed or misused.

Take for example the celebrated case of Richard Crowe, assistant manager of the 195 Broadway branch of the First National City Bank of New York, who walked off with $883,660 worth of cash from the bank vault. Crowe had long been regarded in the bank as "a comer." He had started out as a clearance clerk, risen to teller, then note teller, loan teller, and finally chief clerk. In 1932, National City, which had acquired a Staten Island bank in a merger, sent Crowe there to take charge because he was well-acquainted on the island. Crowe's salary at the time was $1800 a year, less than he had made working for the Miami *Herald* before he went to college. But he was, of course, "a comer"; his reward waited in the future.

Subsequently, in an article in *Cosmopolitan,* Crowe revealed what happened to this bright prospect. During the war, he was asked to help raise funds for the USO. He checked with the bank management. Sure, they told him; go right ahead; wonderful. The first campaign was a great success, and soon Crowe was a man in much demand. Every charity drive, every civic organization wanted him to help in its financial campaign. Always Crowe checked with his superiors to see if he should go ahead; always they told him the same thing—sure, wonderful. After all, every time Crowe's name appeared in the paper, National City's did, too.

Crowe was becoming a valuable personality boy for National City; he was getting it much favorable publicity. But many of the expenses were coming out of his own pocket. As he later wrote, he sometimes had to take a party to lunch or to dinner:

"The check would be, say, $40. Sometimes I got the full amount back from the bank; sometimes I didn't. And many times I took a customer to an $8 lunch and presented the bank with an expense item of about $3.50—which, I knew well, was about all they would allow.

"Don't misunderstand me. I was living high and enjoying it to the hilt. I guess I got cocky and big-headed; the public-servant business went to my head. But I was never home at night—I had too many places to go to—and when I was home, I was irritable with my wife and children. I suppose the out-of-pocket expenses were worrying me. They were terrific. Some nights, going to a formal dinner, I had to spend $25 or more for flowers for the hostess, getting my tails and white tie in shape, cab fares, tips, etc. Before long, I had to begin borrowing (don't forget, during the war I was making only about a hundred dollars a week). At that time, too, I was trying to pay off the mortgage on my house."

When the war ended, National City called Crowe in and suggested he take a transfer to the larger Broadway branch as assistant manager. He was promised a raise and was given the understanding that, before long, he would be made manager of the branch. He promptly agreed.

The raise came through, but he soon discovered that the branch manager was a man about his own age, apparently capable, with no thought of retiring; there was little prospect that Crowe was going much further up the ladder. As long as he had been able to feel that he was "a comer," he would scrimp and wait for his reward; but the effect on him was quite different when he began to fear he might be a "has-been." He still had the burden of his fourteen-room house in Staten Island on which he had to pay the mortgage; in all, he still had to scramble to carry a debt load that totaled some $35,000. On his salary of $7250 a year he simply couldn't make it. At forty-one, Richard Crowe was trapped; blocked off on the advancement ladder; burdened with debts from the front he had put up during his climb.

"So you can see what a mess I was in," he wrote. "And, after months of keeping everything bottled up inside me, I found out I couldn't do it any more. One day—that Wednesday in March, as

I stood there in Lawler's bar—everything exploded. I suddenly got disgusted with myself for leading such a phony life, trying to keep up with the Joneses. And I transferred the blame from myself to the bank—I somehow held the bank responsible for the situation I was in.

"I thought, What am I going to do?

"And then I thought, I'll fix their wagon, good.

"And that was how I decided to take the money."

On Friday night, March 25, 1949, after everyone had left the bank, Crowe scooped up nearly a million dollars in cash, stuffed it into a new suitcase and took off for Florida. Nine days later he was arrested in the washroom of a small Daytona Beach nightclub. Brought back to New York, Crowe was tried, convicted, sentenced to three years in prison. A model prisoner, he was released after thirteen months. Norman Jaspan later described the outcome in these words:

"When he returned home, he was not only warmly greeted by his family but his neighbors as well. The only people who no longer spoke to Richard Crowe were those he had worked with for some twenty years. Officials at the bank told their employees, including the best man at his wedding, never to see Richard Crowe again. Every one of them obeyed."

Like the deed and its motivation, these conflicting reactions to it speak sharply of the war between corporate dictates and the instincts of man.

This is a war that, in the intervening years, has grown in intensity. A few statistics show what has been happening. During the past two decades, embezzlements forced 105 banks to close their doors. Between January 1, 1958, and June 30, 1960, according to the *Digest of Bank Insurance* published by the Insurance and Protective Committee of the American Bankers Association, roughly $20 million was embezzled by bank officials and employees. The losses occurred in an incredible number of banks— 12,350 across the nation.

Who had been responsible for this shocking wave of inside thefts? Menial employees exclusively? By no means. An FBI breakdown showed that 42.7 per cent of the thefts were the work of bank tellers, clerks, or lesser help. The rest, the bulk, were the handiwork of the banking hierarchy—30 per cent by bank cashiers; 12.7 per cent by bank managers; 8.6 per cent by bank presidents; 6 per cent by vice-presidents. Some 531 banks had been victimized by their own cashiers, 152 by their own presidents.

Significantly too, and another symptom of the moral inversion so typical of the times, surveys have shown that the perpetrators of this particular type of white-collar crime are far less disturbed by sensations of guilt than they used to be. Two studies, each of 1001 embezzlers, made by the United States Fidelity and Guarantee Company, showed the contrast. In the first study, covering cases that occurred before 1935, thirty embezzlers committed suicide; in the second, all occurring in the postwar era, the suicides numbered only nine. The figures, like the individual cases, seemed to say that guilt was becoming an obsolete emotion in an America in which the transgressions of the power structures absolved the individual for his own derelictions.

3

When the institutions that dominate so much of American life are considered fair game, it stands to reason that outsiders as well as insiders are going to join in the merry hunt. In recent years, they have been doing just that—and with great gusto.

Shoplifting is one of the fastest-rising crimes in the nation—up 81 per cent in the last six years, according to a 1964 FBI report. Best trade estimates are that shoplifting costs between half a billion and a billion dollars annually. In supermarkets, at least one out of every fifty-two customers is a thief, and the trade magazine *Progressive Grocer* estimated after an exhaustive survey that shoplifting in food stores in 1960 came to $260 million, more than the annual food bill for the entire city of San Francisco. And the looting today is far worse than it was then.

Who are the shoplifters? It is estimated that about half of them are professionals, narcotics addicts, cheap criminals, the dregs of the underworld. But the other half! These are housewives with no need to steal, women with family incomes in the $100–$200-a-week category.

One study was made in Oakland, California, of 197 shoplifting arrests. Of the total, 56 cases involved professors, doctors, teachers, engineers, salesmen, office workers, military officers—and their wives. In their thefts, luxury items outranked staples 137 to 60. Oakland's experience was typical. William F. Alexander, a protection expert, has said: "In one city I surveyed I found that some 50 per cent of those apprehended represented the better-fed, better-clothed and better-housed."

As one baffled chain supermarket executive put it:

"What do you do when you find the wife of the biggest surgeon in town stealing?"

The techniques employed in the thefts demonstrate larcenous calculation worthy of the truly criminal. In Michigan, a "pregnant" supermarket customer was halted and promptly gave "birth" to a varied assortment: one pound of butter, a chuck roast, two packages of cube steaks, a package of dried beef, a large bottle of pancake syrup, and candy, hair tonic, and toothpaste. In California, a plain-clothes detective watched a mother proceeding along the aisles of a supermarket. She tapped various items with her finger. Trailing her, her two children picked off the shelves the items she had designated and stuffed them in their pockets. When the trio was halted at the checkout counter and the children compelled to disgorge, the mother flew into a righteous tirade, berating her children for being so light-fingered.

Why do such persons, ostensibly the "good" people of our society, embark upon such careers of petty crime? Why do they become cheap, common shoplifters?

Industry sources believe that the proliferation of self-service stores is largely responsible. Whereas in the past goods were kept behind counters or in glass cases, today they are stacked on open shelves, packaged and designed to tempt the customer, pleading to be picked up. As the manager of one chain explained, "We try to tempt people into buying and we tempt them into stealing." Theft has been made easy.

Granting that this is so, it can hardly be the entire explanation.

Are we to suppose that professional people and their wives—surgeons, military officers, teachers, engineers—are seduced by brightly decorated packages on shelves just an arm's length away? After all, they are not stealing the wealth of Fort Knox. They are filching, many of them, just a pair of nylons or a few candy bars or a long-playing record, items they could well afford to buy. Is their ethical sense so weak they cannot resist such minor temptations? Apparently it is.

Some store managers see what they believe to be signs of widespread moral decay in the attitude of teen-agers. Such youngsters exhibit, all sources agree, a growing boldness and cynicism in shoplifting. When apprehended they are defiant, rarely showing any signs of guilt or remorse. One merchant in a high-income suburb reported that, out of several hundred shoplifting teen-agers he had caught, *only one* seemed to feel guilt. Most adopted the casual attitude that everything could be straightened out by paying for the stolen goods.

Just as the "better" elements of our society have turned to shoplifting, so have they given impetus to a new wave of bank robberies. Time was when a bank robber like Willie Sutton stood at the apex of the criminal profession. He was a specialist, a member of the underworld elite. Today this elite has been supplanted by an army of amateurs. Scientific protective devices and intensified activity by local police and the FBI have all but eliminated the Willie Suttons; but the amateurs, for the most part law-abiding citizens with no previous criminal records, have taken over and have been robbing at a pace that even the old-line, hardened criminals might envy.

A few figures show the trend. In the depression-ridden 1930s, criminal gangs perpetrated a wave of sensational bank burglaries and holdups. In 1932, they set an all-time record, pulling 554 jobs with a resulting take of $3,384,117. Newspaper headlines were filled with the deeds of bank-robbing desperados like John Dillinger and "Pretty Boy" Floyd and "Machine Gun" Kelly. But police, private protective agencies and the FBI curbed the wave of lawlessness. By 1941, there were only fifty-eight holdups, with a loss of $150,275; by 1943, only six burglaries with a piddling take of $270. Bank robbery, it seemed, had been virtually eliminated; but then came the postwar era—and the amateurs took over.

Throughout the decade of the 1950s, bank robberies climbed steeply. By 1959 there were 346, with a take of $1,407,000, more than three times the total of losses just nine years earlier. And the figures were still soaring. More appalling than the steep rise, however, was the changed nature of the crime. Professional criminals weren't doing the robbing; it was, almost exclusively, the work of ordinary citizens who saw nothing particularly heinous about straightening out their personal financial problems at the expense of big and wealthy institutions.

By far the great majority of these new citizen-robbers had no previous police records, no criminal associates, and so for several years, before banks began installing hidden television cameras and other devices, approximately four out of five were escaping with their loot, even though their techniques were relatively simple and crude.

Unlike the old-time professional who spent days casing a bank, plotting his raid like a military campaign with lookouts stationed and getaway cars ready, the new thieves were lone-wolf operators who frequently were not even armed. They would walk into a bank clutching in one hand a toy pistol, half-concealed, which they tried to make look like a menacing weapon, or they would show a startled teller a small vial of colored water they would pretend was nitroglycerine. Trading on such menaces, they would shove through the window a typed note demanding a specific sum and threatening the teller with immediate extinction if he didn't hand it over. Since many tellers had been advised by their banks not to risk their lives being foolish heroes (after all, the banks were protected by insurance), the brash but amateurish approach of the new citizen-bandits worked more often than not; and, booty clutched in hot hands, they would walk quickly out into the city streets and get lost in the crowds or in the nearest subway.

A common and distinguishing feature of such crimes was that most of the amateurs seemed to consider they had committed no crime at all. They had robbed to meet definite and, to them, critical family needs, and what was wrong with getting the necessary money from a bank? They hadn't demanded any more money than they had actually needed, and, besides, the bank was protected by insurance, wasn't it?

Some of the individual cases show the motivations and the perverse reasoning. In one Los Angeles case, a young man was arrested after he had held up banks for a total of $4095. His motive? He had robbed to pay his mother's medical bills. A compassionate judge ordered him to repay $2474 in five years and released him on probation, convinced that his schoolteacher wife could keep him out of further trouble.

In Brooklyn, a twenty-five-year-old bride-to-be tried to rob a bank to get money for her trousseau; in Illinois, a prominent forty-seven-year-old businessman and civic leader needed money for his personal expenses; in Michigan, a twenty-eight-year-old pregnant woman turned to bank robbery as the only means of getting the money to cover worthless checks she had issued.

Typical of the attitudes of this new bank-robber breed was that of a young man arrested in New York. He had shoved a note demanding $3000 under the nose of a woman teller; instead of giving, she ran screaming. The young man ran, too—out of the bank and into the arms of the law. He explained, with a virtuous air, that he had merely wanted enough money to pay his debts. Said he: "Everybody's robbing banks these days. I'm an honest, law-abiding citizen."

The idea that robbing a bank did not tarnish a man's reputation for honesty ran like a thread through many of the stories. *Fortune* observed:

". . . the bandits themselves have a casual attitude; many seem to regard banditry as only a slightly unorthodox business transaction. One criminologist notes that some bank bandits are the sort of men who would not dream of holding up a taxi driver, a poor fellow who might have four children to support. The idea seems to be that robbing a bank hurts nobody, and may even be in accordance with general ethical guidelines. Not paying one's debts is bad, and many bank bandits say they rob to pay for things bought on the installment plan. . . . One highly successful bank robber had a most bankerlike explanation for his activities: 'I was determined,' he said, 'to protect my credit rating.' "

4

From coast to coast, in cities large and small, America has been rocked in these mid-years of the twentieth century by the kind of scandals most indicative of the utter ethical collapse of a civilization—cops turned robbers.

Historically it has been true that civilizations are in deep trouble when the forces of the law become lawless. Such an inversion of values is usually the final sign that internal rot has bitten so deeply into the fabric of society that the pattern of disintegration is virtually irreversible. In America today, this danger signal flies plain for all to see.

Burglars in blue have turned up in police force after police force in such numbers that they cannot be dismissed with the comfortable old rationalization that "there are always a few bad apples in the barrel." These burglars in uniform have been organized into such bands that they have often constituted 8 to 10 per cent of a city's entire constabulary. Traditionally, especially since the corruption of the Prohibition era, American cities have wrestled with the problem of police corruption, with the kind of widespread graft that has protected prostitution and gambling and flagrant violations of city ordinances. "Honest graft" policemen sometimes call it, though there is of course nothing honest about it. Nevertheless, it is far removed from what has been happening in recent years—from cops turning active burglars, casing their jobs like burglars, stationing lookouts, cracking safes with burglar's tools in planned campaigns of crime. This final step across the ethical boundary line from guardian to destroyer of the law is something utterly new and shocking in the American experience. And yet, perhaps, it should not be so surprising in a society that on so many levels sanctions theft.

What has perverted the forces of the law and turned cops into burglars? This question, asked in city after city, usually produces the same, invariable answers. In essence, cops become burglars because they see at close hand, constantly and repetitively, the internal mechanisms of the racket society; and in the end, their resistance, battered on every hand, begins to weaken and they wind up reasoning, since nobody else cares, why should they? Typical experiences repeat themselves in the stories of cops turned robbers. A policeman, starting out honest and idealistic, makes the mistake of apprehending a flagrant violator who turns out to be the cousin of the mayor or the brother of the racketeer who helped to bankroll the mayor's last political campaign. The honest cop instantly becomes the victim of his own zeal, is reprimanded and banished to the boondocks, there presumably to learn better the lessons of discretion, but all too often to stew in corroding inner resentment at the injustice that has been done to him. Soon he sees the absolute corruption of it all. Store-owners who have been victimized by real, professional burglars—often businessmen who consider themselves among the elite of the community—are almost happy that their stores were looted; they write up losses they never had so that they can collect more on their insurance, and to keep the cops happy they press upon them as gifts articles of value that weren't stolen but that can be added to the insurance claim. If the cop refuses to go along with the deal, there is always that threat that the businessman, with his contacts, can do him in at City Hall. After years of such experiences, a man who was dedicated when he joined the force begins to figure that it's stupid to be so strait-laced: he might as well join the racket and become a burglar himself—and make the merchants really happy.

Sometimes, such is the nature of the policeman's trade, temptation keeps creeping up on a man, and in the atmosphere of the times, it is a temptation that is not so easily shoved aside. A Los Angeles policeman put it this way:

"It's three in the morning and you're on patrol and you hear a burglar alarm. You find the back door of a jewelry store open, and inside the place is turned upside down. Someone has taken a lot of stuff, but he had to leave in a hurry and there's a lot more lying around. There's nobody within six blocks to see what you're doing. You know the stuff's insured anyway. So what do you do?"

The question, as he asked it, was purely rhetorical. But it should be obvious that, once a cop sweeps up some loose "lying-around" loot from a real burglary, rationalizing the deed by the reflection that nobody will suffer because "it's insured," it becomes easier for him to take the next step—to pull off burglaries himself, again fortified by the comforting thought that it's only the insurance company that pays.

In Denver, the stimulus was even more direct. Colorado's Queen City of the Rockies was plagued in the late 1950s by a wave of burglaries. Supermarkets, drugstores, businesses of all kinds were being broken into; safes were being carted away and looted. But the proprietors were not too concerned. Time and again, a store-owner would suggest to police who had been called to investigate: "Why not take something nice home for your wife? It's all covered by insurance anyway."

The merchants who made such suggestions had no idea, of course, that they were sometimes talking to the very men who had looted their stores the night before. What they were really doing was pressing a little extra bounty on the crooks, a reward for the robbery, as it were; a gift to make the gods rock with ironical laughter.

In this atmosphere of non-ethics and total corruption, it is little wonder that the Denver Police Department eventually became riddled with some fifty-five burglars in uniform, nearly 8 per cent of its entire force. Paradox heightened the significance of the Denver experience. The city itself was not a cesspool of under-world intrigue and corruption; it did not harbor, as Chicago and New York have harbored, major underworld gangs reaping millions of dollars of illicit loot that can be used to corrupt police and erode the standards of the force. Denver, by contrast, was a "clean" city. As one of the guilty policemen later complained, "There isn't any graft. Nobody pays off for anything." Yet in Denver, in this atmosphere of non-ethics and insurance morality, there developed one of the major police scandals in the nation's recent history.

It began, apparently, with one policeman on the force who was known among his fellows as "a guy always out for a buck." This hustler became the natural criminal leader in a local atmosphere so complacent and indifferent. "Lying-around" loot was too sparse and infrequent for his taste, and so he began to consider helping matters along with a supermarket burglary. In uniform, on routine patrol, he "cased" the supermarket, then induced some of his buddies on the force to go in with him.

Everything was carefully planned. The actual burglars were all off-duty policemen. For one of their lookouts, they had a patrolman on duty, stationed in his police car just across the street from the supermarket. Further down the street in a private car, one of the off-duty cop-burglars kept watch; another lookout was stationed just inside the store at a window. This left two cop-safecrackers to punch and rip open the safe. It was a task that took them ninety sweating minutes; but when it was done, they had marvelous loot—nearly $40,000 in cash and about $25,000 in checks.

This first sip of burglars' tea proved so enticing—and everything had gone so smoothly—that the criminals in uniform couldn't resist trying it again and again. Success bred imitation. Soon other policemen were burglarizing; the ring grew and spread. In one transfer of personnel from the South Denver area, where the plot originated, the original members of the burglary ring were split up and scattered among different squads in the department. But all that happened was that the veteran burglars indoctrinated new recruits into the art and started up new burglary cells in the districts to which they had been assigned. In time, much of the Denver department became honeycombed with burglars.

The technique these cops-turned-robbers developed was nearly foolproof. Off-duty policemen would do the actual jobs. Their buddies on active patrol would ferry them to the site, carrying the burglar's tools in the police car. Then the police car would stand by, covering the burglars. Sometimes a second police car would be stationed about a block away, at a location where flashlight signals could be exchanged with the burglars inside the building. If an interloper appeared, if any alarm flashed over the police radio from headquarters, the guarding officers in the prowl cars would warn their buddies inside the burglarized building to decamp fast. Rarely did this happen. Most jobs were pulled off swiftly and smoothly, and the burglars, their tools, and their loot were picked up by the patrol cars and driven to safety.

In most instances, the very policemen who had pulled off the burglary would be among those assigned to investigate it the following morning. This made everything very convenient; for, if they had overlooked anything and left clues behind them in their haste to depart, they could now in their role of investigators remove the evidence. An elaborate system of payoffs was devised to keep other patrolmen in the burglarized areas happy and noninquisitive; and so, protected on all sides, the happy burglars in uniform burgled away.

Eventually, of course, something had to happen to disrupt this most perfect of all criminal worlds. It occurred early in 1960, when a couple of the thieving patrolmen, evidently carried away by their own greed, departed from the system and tried to pull a job on their own, without the usual patrol-car protection. Two Denver cops, who didn't happen to be in on the act, spotted their car fleeing from the burglary of a coffee shop and gave chase. A safe fell out of the rear of the fleeing car, and the cop-pursuers got close enough for one of them, John D. Bates, to recognize the fugitives as two fellow officers of the law.

What happened to Bates in the role of honest cop makes a fascinating chapter in the saga of the corrupt society. His eyes opened by the coffee-shop incident, Bates did a little sleuthing and became convinced that a really large uniformed burglary ring was operating in the department. He reported both his facts and his suspicions to his superiors. He identified by name the two policemen he had found fleeing from the burglarized coffee shop, and he added the names of a dozen others he thought to be in the ring. The reaction of his superiors was one of shock and outrage—but not against the accused policemen, against Bates! Bates was put on sick leave and ordered to go see a psychiatrist. He obeyed. The psychiatrist reported that Bates didn't seem to be mentally disturbed at all; on the contrary, he appeared to be telling the truth. Only then did the police hierarchy of Denver reluctantly concede that it might have some problem children on its force.

The concession was made, however, with the greatest reluctance, and there was still no passion to learn the whole truth. The two policemen whom Bates had named were arrested, tried and convicted. Bates himself testified against them, but he felt so jittery about his own safety that he went into hiding across the state line. After their convictions, the two imprisoned cops "sang" and implicated seven other members of the Denver force. Still the official attitude was one of unconcern and sweet reassurance. The Queen City's mayor went on television and dished out to the public that syrupy old "few rotten apples" line. Then came June 1961—and catastrophe.

Police in a suburban village got a tip from a mysterious informant that a supermarket in their territory was going to be burglarized. And so on the night of June 29 the suburban cops hid inside the supermarket and waited. Before long, the burglars obligingly put in their appearance. They cut through the roof, dropped to the floor and went to work on the safe, using chilled milk from the refrigerator to cool their power saw. Having let matters proceed to this point, the suburban cops moved in and nabbed the burglars in the act. All three turned out to be Denver policemen.

There was now no stopping the scandal. Soon the sheriff of the adjoining county, a former FBI agent, was arrested, charged with plotting the suburban supermarket theft in which the Denver cops had been arrested and acting as their lookout. The police chief of Denver resigned "for reasons of health," and Governor Stephen L. R. McNichols was asked to step in and probe the Denver department to see just how bad things really were. McNichols and his investigator, A. S. Reeder, another former FBI agent, found that they were plenty bad indeed. The Denver cop-burglars, the Governor later reported, had pulled so many jobs during their years-long career in crime that they couldn't remember them all; but, said the Governor, they had committed at least 120 burglaries and their loot, at a minimum, had been $250,000.

After the arrests and convictions came the probing question: Why? Several of the guilty cops talked, trying to explain their motivations. From their stories, there emerged the familiar rationalization that only the big chains and insurance companies, institutions that could afford it, had been hurt by their depredations. Supporting this cardinal tenet of subversive non-ethics were other reasons. "I went along because I wanted to be a good Joe and not get anyone into trouble," said one. Said another: "They [his superior officers] told me they'd give me a poor mark if I don't go along." Several growled in self-justification about the relatively low pay of Denver police. Still others indicated they had turned to theft out of resentment of political influence. One patrolman joined the burglars after he had been disciplined for cracking down on the relative of a local bigwig; another, after he had been denied promotion following his attempt to arrest the relative of a city official for a law violation.

Quite obviously, such excuses do not excuse or explain. Clearly, none of these Denver policemen had in his character any deep-seated, inviolate sense of right or wrong, and so they were willing to involve themselves in flagrant crimes on the flimsiest of rationalizations—even that of wanting to be "a good Joe." The climate in which they had operated in Denver had been the antithesis of that "sea of ethics" Chief Justice Warren had prescribed as the first essential of a law-abiding civilization; it had been, on the contrary, in perfect harmony with Ruth Benedict's judgment that ours is no longer a "guilt" culture but a "shame" culture—one in which man holds no strong convictions, in which conscience no longer self-imposes control of wrongdoing.

Had Denver been alone, an isolated island of non-ethics, the experience would have been shattering enough. But Denver was not alone; its cops-turned-robbers scandal was typical—and all too common. In any number of cities from coast to coast, the American public was being treated to the same spectacle of the law turned lawless. In Chicago, a major scandal involved a large number of policemen who had allied themselves with underworld burglars and, for years, had pulled off jewel and fur robberies and looted drug, appliance, and furniture stores. In Reno, seven

policemen were suspended for participating in a burglary ring
that had ransacked ten stores. In Des Moines, an on-the-force
burglary scandal led to the suspension or resignation of twenty-
two members of the department. Nashville and Memphis were
rocked by similar disclosures. Cleveland was jolted by the confession of an eleven-year police-force veteran that he had committed twenty burglaries and had been aided by ten fellow policemen. In Nassau County on Long Island, seven cops were involved
in a burglary ring that had looted appliance stores of some
$10,000 worth of merchandise, and up in Connecticut the manu-
facturing town of Bristol was shaken by the disclosure that ten of
its fifty-nine policemen had been doubling as burglars. One of
the first policemen to resign in the scandal was a lieutenant, a
twenty-three-year veteran on the force and a man who only recently had been a leading candidate for promotion to police chief.
Even college towns were not safe. In November 1962, Stanford
University was plagued by an outbreak of campus burglaries in
which several thousand dollars worth of tape recorders and other
equipment were stolen. Investigation showed that the burglars
were the very patrolmen who had been hired by the university to
protect its campus. And up in Burlington, Vermont, home of the
University of Vermont, a picturesque community proud of its
tradition of Yankee integrity, two patrolmen were nabbed returning from the looting of a downtown restaurant; and before the
scandal ended, five patrolmen of Burlington's fifty-man force had
been implicated as members of the uniformed burglary ring.

Such was the sweep of the cop-burglar wave; such the repeti-
tive warnings that it flashed of the deep malaise gnawing away at
the fabric of American society. The manner in which this social
sickness works on a cop until it finally gets him down and makes
a burglar of him has been most vividly told by Ralph Lee Smith
in his book *The Tarnished Badge.*

Smith interviewed two cop-burglars who had been convicted
and sentenced to prison. Clad in blue dungarees with prison
numbers stenciled on them, the men stood tall and straight, the
image of stalwart cops. Smith called them Blake and Hastings,

and in candid talk he drew from them the picture of the corrupted society that corrupts a cop.

Blake, who said he had always wanted to be a policeman, described himself as "a pretty eager beaver cop" at the outset, but he had hardly joined the force as a probationary patrolman before some of the eagerness began to be drained out of him. Right away, he caught two burglars stealing a generator from a warehouse. They turned out to be veteran cops on his own force. "What could I do?" he said. "I was a rookie on probation and it would have been my word against theirs. On the force, if you don't shut up and go along, you don't last out your probation."

Blake went along. He and a partner were assigned to one of the toughest beats in town. They did such a good job that Blake was slated for promotion to detective, but then it happened. In breaking up a disturbance in a bar, he arrested the sister-in-law of a councilman. The court promptly dismissed the case, and Blake was told his appointment to the detective bureau had been canceled.

The next step involved some of that "lying-around" loot. Blake and his partner were on patrol one night when they noticed a shop door open. They radioed headquarters, then went in, guns drawn. Nobody was there. Blake's partner went over to the safe and started fiddling carefully with the dial. The door opened.

"I thought so," he said. "They left it on day lock. When they do that, all you have to do is turn it to one right number and she opens."

He reached inside and pulled out a bundle of money, then looked at Blake.

"You know, John," he said, "they don't lose a thing. They will claim it on their insurance—in fact, they'll claim more than they lost, and they'll get it without question. Now don't tell me that you can't use a little of this."

As Blake told Ralph Lee Smith:

"We ended up splitting it, and we gave some to the sergeant who came down to cover the case. He needed some too. It was the first money I took. I wasn't 'hooked' yet—that is, I wasn't a regular thief or burglar. But I had taken my first stolen money."

A few nights later, Blake and his partner surprised a couple of men hauling some stolen merchandise out of a warehouse. They turned out to be cops. "My partner and I put up our guns," Blake said. "I suddenly realized that I probably didn't care very much any more."

The thing that really "hooked" Blake occurred shortly afterwards. He and his partner on patrol found the back door of a fur warehouse slightly ajar. They stopped their car, and Blake went in while his partner called for help. No one was inside the warehouse, and the furs and coats on the racks seemed to have been untouched. Probably, Blake thought, the door had been left open by accident or had become accidentally unlatched.

In a few minutes [he told Ralph Lee Smith], the lieutenant pulled up in a second car, and he had the owner of the place with him. The owner came in and walked halfway down the center aisle. Suddenly he gasped.

"My God!" he said. "They're gone!"

"What's gone?" I asked.

"Over against the wall there," he said excitedly. "I had piles of skin on pallets. They're gone!"

"Pallets and all?"

He didn't bat an eyelash. "Pallets and all!" he said.

"How many skins were there?"

"A couple of hundred of them."

"What were they worth?"

"Between $6 and $7.50 each."

This meant a loss of $1,200 to $1,500. I was skeptical. "Look," I said, "I don't think anybody took anything here. There's no sign that the door was forced. It's been snowing since about 8 P.M., and there were no footprints or car tracks of any kind anywhere in the alley before my partner and I pulled in here."

He turned on me furiously. "Are you doubting my word?" he shouted. Then he looked at me and his tone changed. "By the way," he said, with a smile, "do you fellows know your wives' sizes? We're grateful to you for the protection you give us. I'd like to give you each a coat for what you've done here."

I don't know if you can understand it. But somehow that was the end. "Yes," I said, "I know my wife's size and I'll take one."

"What about your patrol partner?" the man asked.

"He'll take one, too," I said.

"And how about the lieutenant outside?"

"I *know* he'll take one," I said, and I was right.

After we had all gotten our coats, the lieutenant said to me, "Fill out a loss report." I filled it out, describing the loss just the way the man told me, and the man signed it.

The next day the loss report went through the detective bureau and a detective called me in. "Do you think that stuff was really stolen?" he asked me. "I don't know," I told him. "All I know is, if you want a nice new fur coat for your wife you can go over there and get one." The detective promptly went over and got himself a coat. The loss report went into the insurance company and the insurance company paid off with no muss or fuss.

So Blake said to himself, in effect, what the hell, and became a burglar.

Hastings' story paralleled Blake's almost detail for detail, only at the end he added a special fillip.

"After we got going regularly on our burglaries," he told Ralph Lee Smith, "businessmen would come to us and would make it clear that they wouldn't mind if somebody came along and broke into their places. They would even tell us how much money a thief could expect to find if he broke in on a given night. When we would crack the places, sure enough, there would be just the amount of money they said. It was sort of our pay. The owners of the places would then file insurance claims for amounts larger than they had lost, and the claims would always be paid. We used to be able to compare what we actually got with the claims that the owners made."

And there you have it—the picture of a society so badly corrupted that the "honest" businessman asks the cop on the beat to break into his place and steal so that he can swindle the insurance company out of a few thousand dollars! Could the perversion of morals and ethics be more complete?

~~ 8 ~~

Bobby Baker

THE CAPITOL OF the United States at night is an awe-inspiring sight. Seen against the black backdrop of the sky, floodlights illuminating its majestic contours, the dome rises in a kind of august yet human splendor, its slender spire seeming to flirt with the stars. It is a temple of shimmering white, pure and undefiled, symbolizing the loftiest aspirations of man. No matter how many times one sees it, to see it again, majestic sentinel and symbol in the night, is stimulus sufficient to start an electric prickling of the nerve ends. The American who can look unmoved at this monument to the lofty ideal of a government founded on freedom and justice for all must be lacking in the capacity to understand, to feel, to respond. I have seen this soaring dome many times from the vantage point of the Skyline Inn out South Capitol Street, and the sight never wears, never fails to bring me the sense of renewal and dedication, the feeling that the ideal lives on, a reality for all Americans, a heritage to be treasured and preserved.

And yet it was beneath this majestic dome, in the chamber and the cloakroom, in the corridors and the offices of the United States Senate, that the poisons of the corrupt society combined to produce the Bobby Baker scandal.

It was here, on hallowed ground, that the wheeling and dealing rose to its most frenzied pitch; here that the manipulators did multibillion-dollar business in influence and contracts. It was here that $100 bills were stashed in nice green mounds on the desk and in the safe of the powerful Secretary of the Senate Majority; here, according to Republicans at least, that government telephone lines were used to send call girls to their assignations.

Girls, liquor, parties, contacts, inside knowledge, influence, favors—all the devices and corruptions of the corrupt society conjoined at the apex, under the very dome of the Capitol, in the career of Bobby Gene Baker. A poor boy from Pickens, South Carolina, in the upland pine country, Bobby Gene pulled together and united in his person all the webs of conspiracy and manipulation. He was bankrolled in his single most important business venture by gamblers from Las Vegas, for whom ever after he assiduously fronted. He was bankrolled in other fortune-making deals by emissaries of the vast Murchison empire that had so stirred Billie Sol Estes to emulation. He was the alter ego of Lyndon B. Johnson, now President of the United States. He was the virtual "godson" of the late Senator Robert B. Kerr, "the uncrowned king of the Senate," a man whose tips and whose banks helped further the Baker fortunes. He was a founder and officer of the Quorum Club, the exclusive hideaway a stone's throw from the Capitol where succulently fashioned waitresses, scanty black net hardly concealing nature's bountiful endowments, served the drinks and soothed the careworn brows of legislators, brass hats, lobbyists, and businessmen. It all added up, for Bobby Gene Baker, to a $2 million paper fortune, amassed in less than nine years on a salary that never exceeded $19,600 a year!

Such are the fruits of knowledge, position, influence in the corrupt society; such the rewards of manipulation when the racket ethic—get it when you can, how you can, any way you can—dominates the conduct of man.

What follows is an account of what is known about the Bobby Baker scandal. One of the most disturbing things about it is that necessary qualification "what is known." For this is only part of the story. In one of the lamest and most halting investigations in congressional history, the Senate of the United States probed into the ashes of the Bobby Gene Baker case with the gingerliness of men fearful that at any moment they might trigger a time bomb. "We're not investigating Senators," declared the chairman of the investigating committee, so no Senators were investigated. "Are you suggesting that personal and sexual peccadillos would be within the framework of this committee?" one Democratic Senator asked in shock, and so the matter of call girls who reportedly earned as much as $800 a week (and not all of it just from lobbyists and businessmen) was never investigated. With so many doors so firmly barred, with Senators dragging their feet along so many avenues of suggested and obvious inquiry, the "what is known" about the Bobby Gene Baker case represents only the tip of the iceberg. What remains hidden beneath the waters, man can only conjecture, but the reluctant-dragon performance of the Senate of the United States suggests inescapably that the Senate thought it would be more than either the Senate or the American people could endure.

I

The Senate of the United States helped vastly to mold the character and shape the destiny of Bobby Gene Baker. Only fourteen when he was appointed a page, he literally grew up in the Senate; it was his job, his school, his home. What he became, the Senate largely helped to make him. It is not a happy reflection.

Bobby Gene was the oldest of eight children born to a Pickens postal worker who later became the town postmaster. Though he signed his name Robert G. Baker after titles and affluence came his way, he was really named after his father's sports heroes— Bobby Jones, the champion golfer, and Gene Tunney, the heavyweight boxing king.

Washington, when Bobby Gene arrived in 1944, was an awesome place. The boy from Pickens was a rustic from the hinterlands dumped down in the middle of a capital that was the seat of world power. Victory over the Germans and Japanese was imminent, and the wartime, frenzied pace in this nerve center of it all overwhelmed the lad from the pine lands. Until he received his appointment as a Senate page from the late Senator Burnet Maybank, Bobby Gene had never even been on a railroad train, and to prepare himself for the trip to Washington, "just so I could say I'd been on a train before," he took a ride from the town of Easely, down the road a piece from Pickens, a whole ten miles to Greenville in an adjoining county.

In Washington, Bobby Gene, like other pages, roomed in a boardinghouse. He was at first desperately homesick, but when a former schoolteacher wrote him, urging him to buck up and have courage, Bobby sent back a reply more notable for its spirit than its grammar. "Bobby Baker don't quit," he wrote.

Nor did he. Old-timers in Pickens were to recall years later that Bobby had always been extremely mature for his age. At thirteen, he had clerked behind the soda fountain in a drugstore, and in a short time he knew everybody in town and virtually everything about the business of the store. In rapid fashion, he took over the front of the store and "did everything but fill prescriptions." The same drive and talent for knowing everyone and learning all was to carry Bobby far in the Senate; and the time was to come when he would do everything but vote. He would even do that by proxy because, as he himself once bragged to the Chicago *Daily News:* "On any issue I have at least ten Senators in the palm of my hand."

Bobby as a youth was on the short, slender side, and he walked always like a man in a hurry, shoulders hunched forward, head a little bent. This attitude led some members of the Capitol press corps to dub him "The Mole," and like the mole he burrowed deep.

He knew all the secrets. He knew who slept with whom and where, who drank too much and his favorite brand of poison, who had special interests in special legislation and what they were—in other words, he knew where all the skeletons were buried and how the levers of pressure could be applied. With this knowledge he coupled discretion. He always acted as if it all went in one ear and out the other, but it didn't. Not a particle of useful knowledge ever escaped the brain of Bobby Baker.

All the time he was soaking up this varied information the way a sponge soaks up water, young Bobby was racing up the Senatorial promotional ladder. At seventeen, he became chief Senate page.

Then he was second assistant in the Senate Document Room, messenger to the Senate minority, assistant to the Senate door-keeper, chief telephone page to the Senate majority, and assistant clerk to the majority conference. He was holding this last clerical post in 1949 when he attracted the attention of the new junior Senator from Texas, Lyndon Baines Johnson. They quickly became a team. Under Johnson's sponsorship, Bobby Gene became assistant minority secretary; and when the Congressional elections of 1954 gave the Democrats control of the Senate, Johnson became the majority leader and Bobby Baker, his protégé, was catapulted into the post of Secretary to the Senate Majority. He was only twenty-six, the youngest man ever to hold the office.

Probably not one American in a thousand had ever heard, before the Bobby Baker case broke, of the Secretary to the Senate Majority. Just what was the job? And what made it so influential?

You won't find the answer in the Senate rules. They provide simply that the Secretary to the Majority shall provide information and messenger service to Senators on the floor and that he shall substitute for the Sergeant at Arms in the latter's absence. It sounds innocuous enough, but there are special political factors that give the job a lot more weight than would at first appear.

In the first place, the Secretary is the personal choice of the Majority Leader. He becomes the leader's right-hand man in dealing with Senators; he is the leader's eyes and ears on the floor, and when he speaks, if he has the full confidence of the leader as Bobby Baker did, he speaks with the authority of the leader behind him. With a man like Lyndon Johnson running the Senate almost like his own private club, Bobby Baker wielded more authority than most Senators and a good many members of the Cabinet.

He conveyed to Senators the party line on all issues.

He sounded them out on how they would vote and reported their attitudes to the Majority Leader.

He forecast the lineup of votes on hot issues in both parties so that the Majority Leader always knew precisely where he stood, who might kick over the traces, who needed to be persuaded.

He kept the Majority Leader informed of the interests, needs, and weaknesses of individual Senators.

He kept detailed records of each Senator's vote from the time he entered the Senate.

He organized and managed the Capitol staff serving the party leadership and handled the details of arranging party conferences.

He arranged and kept track of "pairs"—the system of matching up pro and con votes of Senators who were absent but wished to have their views recorded on a certain issue.

Take a good look at that long list of services performed by Bobby Baker as the Majority Leader's Man Friday on the Senate floor. It explains much. Lyndon Johnson made his reputation as unquestionably the strongest leader of the Senate in modern times. He always knew the exact lineup of the Senate on every vital issue. When the passage of a bill hinged on the swing of half-a-dozen votes, he had what was considered an unerring instinct for the weaklings in the camp of the opposition; he always seemed to know just who could be persuaded and, if it came to that, just whose arm could be twisted and how. Behind a lot of that almost uncanny knowledge lay the industrious, unceasing sleuthing of Bobby Baker.

Bobby was so helpful to LBJ that he quickly became an almost indispensable man to "the Establishment," the closely knit inner clique that in hard reality virtually runs the affairs of the Senate. It is a predominantly conservative coalition composed of Southern Democrats and like-minded Republicans, and it has been the dominating power in the Senate ever since it was formed back in 1938 to block any further radical experimentation by the New Deal. In recent years, first under Johnson and later under Senator Kerr, the Establishment has come to full flower as virtually a law unto itself. Through its medium, a few giants in both parties saw to it that "safe" conservatives dominated the makeup of key committees; that dangerous innovations like Kennedy's "Spartan" expense code in his proposed income tax revision were scrapped; that the 27½ per cent oil-depletion allowance was protected as if it represented one of the stars in the flag; that, in a word, the votes were mustered to kill any measure inimical to the Establishment and the vested interests that lurked behind it.

Who belongs to the Establishment? An occasional liberal like Hubert Humphrey or a mild, middle-of-the-roader like Mike Mansfield is sometimes admitted into the foyer; but the hard inner core is always safely conservative. One Senator who looks at the Establishment with the disenchantment of an outsider described it to *Life* magazine as "around fifteen like-minded Senators on the inside—the heart of it—twenty-five more around the periphery, and eleven or twelve anxious fellows who'd like to be on the inside." Those three categories represent more than a majority of the Senate, and control of them seems always to be retained by the conservative coalition.

It is significant that, after Johnson was elevated to the Vice-Presidency, Mike Mansfield was chosen as the new Majority Leader, a title he held without the real power that had been Johnson's. That power continued to reside in the inner circle of the Establishment, and it was wielded with such authority by Senator Kerr that the press was soon calling him "the uncrowned king of the Senate." After Kerr died on New Year's Day, 1963, control of the Establishment's power was considerably diffused, but note the kind of hands that held and wielded pieces of it: Senator Harry Byrd, the arch-conservative Virginia Democrat; Senator George Smathers of Florida, equally "safe" on money-business issues; Senator Richard Russell of Georgia, one of the ablest of the conservative Democrats; and Senator Everett Dirksen of Illinois, the Republican Minority Leader, noted for occasional and unpredictable somersaults, but like the others predominantly conservative.

As errand boy for Lyndon Johnson, Bobby Baker performed invaluable services for the Establishment. He cultivated the art of settling freshman Senators into their jobs with such solicitude for their welfare that many were forever grateful. Bobby would show the neophyte to his desk, explain the procedures and customs of the Senate to him, offer help in securing housing accommodations or a loan if the Senator needed either, and by these and other attentions impress upon the new solon that Bobby Baker had just one desire in life—to serve him. Senator B. Everett Jordan, the North Carolina Democrat who was later to head the committee investigating Baker, recalled on one occasion that, on his first day in the Senate, he went and sat where Bobby Baker told him to sit

and stayed until Bobby said it was all right to leave. While in-
itiating such newcomers to the pitfalls of the Senate, shrewd Bobby
would size up his men, and when he spotted a likely prospect, he
became a kind of recruiting sergeant for the Establishment. "You
get along if you go along," he would counsel, and many listened.
Bobby's services to the Establishment extended, however, far
beyond such blandishments. He was at times the agent of devious
Machiavellian plots that disposed of the ambitions of Senators not
in the inner circle, and under Lyndon Johnson he served from
1955 to 1961 as secretary of the Democratic Senatorial Campaign
Committee, his the hand that dispensed or withheld finances to
bankroll expensive Senatorial campaigns.

In his first function as the Establishment's hatchet man, insiders
recalled the devious stratagem by which he disposed of the aspirations of two liberal Senators for vacant spots on the key Judiciary
Committee. Leading candidates for the posts in January 1961 were
Senator Quentin Burdick of North Dakota and Stephen Young of
Ohio. Baker appeared before the powerful Democratic Steering
Committee, which decides such assignments, and informed it that
both Burdick and Young had changed their minds; neither any
longer wanted a seat on Judiciary. Since Baker was supposed to
know the Senators' minds almost better than they knew them
themselves, no one questioned this authoritative report, and two
conservatives, Edward V Long of Missouri and William Blakley
of Texas were named to the vacant spots. Burdick, especially, had
expected the appointment and had been waiting to hear that he
had been named when he learned to his complete surprise that he
hadn't. As one insider remarked, "Burdick was a Kennedy supporter and therefore didn't belong to the Establishment—a com-
bination Lyndon Johnson wasn't likely to forgive. So Bobby Baker
shivved Burdick. It was typical."

It wasn't, however, the end of the shivving. Blakley, who had
been appointed to Johnson's vacated Texas seat when LBJ became
Vice-President, was so arch-conservative that his selection split the
Democratic Party in Texas wide open; and when he ran for election to Johnson's unexpired term, the liberal contingent in the party
stayed home. The result was that a hard right winger, Republican

John Tower, was elected over him. This confronted the Establishment with a delicate situation. First in line for the Judiciary Committee vacancy was Senator Ralph Yarborough of Texas, a leader in the party's liberal wing there and so no favorite of Lyndon Johnson's. It seemed there was no face-saving way of avoiding the appointment of Yarborough. What was the Establishment to do?

Bobby Baker, according to Capitol Hill sources, showed the Steering Committee the way. Yarborough said afterward he was informed Baker told the committee that it "just couldn't afford to let Yarborough have that seat. He would then be in a position to control Texas' judicial patronage, or would be in a position to prevent Lyndon from controlling it." The way to avoid this disaster, Baker pointed out, was to change the composition of the committee. It had consisted of ten Democrats and five Republicans, and at his suggestion the setup was changed to nine Democrats and six Republicans. This self-sacrifice on the part of the Democrats eliminated Yarborough, and so, of course, it was impossible to appoint him.

Such maneuverings earned Bobby Baker the title "The 101st Senator." They were not confined to the Hill, but often affected decisions in the White House as well. There are some indications that even President Kennedy himself was shivved on vital parts of his program by the wily Bobby Baker. Insiders recalled how, on one occasion, Kennedy toyed with the idea of enlarging the Senate Finance Committee to circumvent its ultraconservative majority led by Senator Byrd. Bobby Baker, who had acquired a reputation as an infallible head-counter, was whisked to the White House and demonstrated to the President that, according to his figures, the proposal didn't have a chance. Kennedy believed him and decided not to fight.

Some saw Baker's fine hand in the maneuverings that killed off the Kennedy 1963 medicare proposal. Everyone knew the vote would be close, but Baker's head count in July showed that it then had enough support to squeak through. Baker's estimates were passed up to Majority Leader Mansfield, but Bobby made certain at the same time that a copy went to his new mentor, Senator Kerr, who was leading the fight against medicare. Mansfield and the administration, evidently deceived by the infallible Bobby Baker's forecast of victory, called for a vote, perhaps prematurely; and Senator Kerr, who had spotted a flaw in the Baker figures, trounced and buried the medicare proposal. In the post mortems, the inevitable questions were asked: Had the infallible Bobby Baker slipped and erred in his head count? Or had the mistake been deliberate?

No one had the answer, but Senator Paul Douglas of Illinois, the dean of Senate liberals and one of the most respected members in the chamber, always had his doubts about Bobby Baker. Baker, he said bluntly, had never been a true Secretary to the Senate Majority; he had served almost exclusively the interests of the southern minority in the party, the group that formed the heart and soul of the Establishment. Baker, Douglas said, froze the party liberals out of virtually all information. "I won't say he gave us false information," said Douglas. "He just didn't give us much."

The liberal wing of the party got some help for a time from Jessop I. McDonnell, Assistant Secretary to the Majority and the only northerner on Baker's staff. But in 1962 Baker eliminated this leak by firing McDonnell, and Douglas' protests to Majority Leader Mansfield did no good. Indicative of Baker's Establishment bias, said Douglas, was the way he handled the requests of new Senators for committee assignments. All such requests were funneled through Baker, and invariably, Douglas said, Baker would advise the applicant that he would have to clear his choices with Senator Russell, long a leader of the southern bloc.

Outside Washington, on the broader political battlefronts of the nation, Bobby Baker's services to the Establishment were nakedly obvious. "He'd go around the country putting the arm on those oil men in the Southwest and then he'd hand out the money where it would do the most good—for them," one informant told *Life*. Frank Moss's experience was recalled. In 1958, Moss was running for the Senate in Utah, and an emissary was dispatched from Washington to offer him $10,000 for his campaign. Moss, envisioning the radio and television time he could buy, was delighted. But then, he was told, there was just one little condition. If he was to get this campaign donation, he would have to sign a letter saying he had studied the 27½ per cent oil-depletion allowance and had concluded it should be continued. Moss refused to be bought —and he didn't get the money.

Moss was not alone. Subsequently, in the Baker inquiry, Republicans wanted to call Senator Thomas J. McIntyre of New Hampshire, to question him about "a published report referring to an allegation Baker had offered a sizeable sum of money to meet campaign expenses of a Senator, conditioned on the Senator's voting a certain way on particular legislation." The Democrats were having none of this and threw up another of their protective screens about Bobby Baker. Some things—and the Establishment is one of them—must remain forever sacred.

2

How does a humble servant of the Republic leap to millionaire's status in less than ten years, even while establishing his beauty-queen secretary in a $28,000 town house, complete with $6500 worth of wall-to-wall carpets and lavender furnishings? Admittedly it's a good question. Even the Senate of the United States recognized that.

The answer, as it emerges from the Senate records, is that you do it with others' money. You are obviously just such a lovable cuss that gamblers in Las Vegas and Murchison tycoons and bankers all over the landscape are just eager to put up $100,000 or so, on which oftentimes, so great is their affection, they are willing to take the loss, if there are losses, while guaranteeing you the profits, if there are profits. In this situation, if you were Bobby Baker, you couldn't help but make millions.

It is instructive to trace Baker's meteoric rise in the world of high finance as revealed in some of his own credit statements. These documents, analyzed for Senate investigations by the government's General Accounting Office, show that prior to the love affair with Lyndon Johnson—"The Leader," Bobby always called him, in reverential caps—the Baker fortunes were just about what you would expect those of a civil servant to be. In an appraisal of his net worth filed on May 3, 1954, Bobby set the figure at

$11,025. Even this was not so impressive as it might sound. A major portion of his assets consisted of his mortgaged home. He listed a used car worth $700 and 120 shares of stock valued at $5000. His salary at the time was $9000 a year.

After he became Secretary of the Senate Majority under LBJ in 1955, his prospects brightened. His salary went up gradually until at the end he was making $19,600 a year, and he began to accumulate an astonishing amount of wealth from other sources. By September 1960, after less than five years of intimate collaboration with LBJ, Bobby Baker was listing his worth at $278,476. This was piling it up at a rate of better than $50,000 a year (and Bobby was living high in the meantime, too), quite a feat on a salary of less than $20,000. And even balmier times lay ahead.

When Lyndon Johnson became Vice-President, Bobby nestled himself under the protective wing of Senator Kerr, and it was then, from all the evidence, that everything he touched turned to gold and his bank balance pyramided at a gallop. By February 1, 1963, just two and a half years after his earlier estimate, Bobby was proclaiming that he was worth $2,166,866. The GAO, in studying his figures, found that Bobby evidently had encountered a little difficulty subtracting his liabilities from his assets because he really wasn't worth $2 million plus, just $1,791,186. But why quibble about a paltry $300,000–$400,000 or so? Any way one looked at it, Bobby Gene Baker was a very wealthy man—on paper.

One of Bobby's most remunerative deals began in the Johnson era and carried over into the years when he was playing godson to Senator Kerr. It involved stock in a firm popularly known as Magic—and magic it truly was. The initials, with a vowel added, stood for the Mortgage Guaranty Insurance Corporation of Wisconsin. This was a private firm, its stock closely held, that had been set up in 1957 as a kind of private FHA to insure the top 20 per cent of mortgages. During the first year, Magic lost $63,677; the second, $7567. But then in 1959, when Bobby Baker became interested in it, it turned the corner from loser to big winner and began justifying its nickname. It was a magical performance that was aided greatly by a couple of favorable federal rulings.

The first involved the Internal Revenue Bureau. Under Wis-

consin law, Magic was required to set aside half its premium earnings as a reserve against extraordinary possible future losses. This
reserve had to be maintained untouched for a fifteen-year-period.
Magic contended that, during this period, it should not have to pay
income taxes on earnings so sequestered. Twice Internal Revenue
ruled against it. But Magic was persistent. It went to Representative
John W. Byrnes, Wisconsin Republican, and Byrnes appealed to
Internal Revenue for reconsideration. He also drafted a bill under
which Congress, if Internal Revenue proved obdurate, could grant
Magic its tax exemption. The result was that on May 25, 1960,
Internal Revenue yielded to the pressure and ruled Magic's reserve
should go tax-free.

This was a great boon for Magic. A second federal action favor-
ably affecting its stock was a decision by the Securities and Exchange Commission approving issuance of the stock to the public.
This, of course, gave it wider distribution and helped put a platform under its price. A knowledgeable operator in the Washington
nerve center, catching wind of such developments ahead of time,
naturally had a gilt-edged opportunity to make himself a tidy
fortune. And Bobby Baker was the man with all the contacts.

Lobbyists were always swarming like flies around Baker's office,
and one of them was Glenn Troop, a vice-president of the Savings
and Loan League and the registered Washington lobbyist for the
group. Troop and Baker became close friends, and it was probably
through Troop's influence that Baker was invited to speak at the
annual convention of the Savings and Loan League in San Fran-
cisco in November 1958. There, as chance would have it, Troop
introduced him to Max Karl, president of Magic.

As Karl later recalled it, they just met; they didn't discuss the
affairs of Magic at all; it was all of no significance, really, and he
all but forgot about Bobby Baker. But Baker didn't forget Karl.

In July 1959, with business perking up, Magic directors decided
to split the stock eight for one as of September 1. The sequence of
events would seem to indicate that Bobby Baker, with his ear to
the ground in Washington, heard a rumor of what was coming,
for in August he telephoned Max Karl and questioned him closely
about Magic's prospects. Karl later acknowledged to the Senate

investigating committee that he had told Bobby the split was coming. Bobby promptly said he wanted some stock. Could Karl get him some?

Karl thought he could. In fact, he knew darn well he could. There was a nice plump block of stock that had been allotted to his own brother-in-law, a Dr. Friedman. Now, peculiarly enough, though Max Karl's own brother-in-law must have known the stock was splitting, though he must have had as good information from Max Karl as Max Karl could give over the phone to Bobby Baker, the man he barely knew, Dr. Friedman had become disenchanted and had decided he didn't want to put up the money for the stock. He had told Karl, Karl testified, to sell the stock if he could. So Karl offered it to Bobby Baker for just what his brother-in-law would have paid for it—$28,750. Bobby snapped up the bargain and sent his check for the full amount to Karl on August 21, 1959. Just where Baker got the money, whether he had it himself or borrowed it or got donations from friends, never did become quite clear; but, in any event, he was in under the wire, just ten days before the eight-for-one split—and, with that, Magic was off and running.

Bobby Baker did so well so instantaneously on his first whirl around the dance floor with Magic that he decided to ask the bank to play his favorite waltz again and yet again. His next flirtation came early the following year, in February 1960. Magic had sought SEC approval for registration of a stock issue, and on February 8 the final amendments to the registration statement were filed and SEC approval indicated, though the approval itself wouldn't become effective until February 25. Bobby Baker didn't wait. The events of February 8 were good enough for him, for on that date he bought more stock.

This time he didn't have a cent of his own money invested, though he expected to profit handsomely. This time he was being given a free ride by some good friends.

Bobby and his wife, Dorothy, had known Alfred S. and Gertrude C. Novak since 1955. The two couples had become exceedingly friendly; they visited each other, went on vacation trips together—and finally went into business deals together. Novak, a builder, was to become Bobby Baker's partner in the plush Carousel Motel in Ocean City, Maryland, but that was in the future in February 1960, when Bobby began to talk up Magic to the Novaks.

As Mrs. Novak later told the story to the Senate committee, she and her husband had gone to the hospital to visit Mrs. Baker and see her new baby. Bobby was there, and after the baby had been properly admired, he began to talk about a different kind of baby to Novak. He said "he knew of some stock being available that would be good, and then, of course, we never knew whether it was going to be good or bad. But he asked whether we had any money we could invest in some stock, and as I recall, my husband said 'Yes,' he did have some but he didn't know how much, and then they proceeded from there."

Bobby explained he was short of cash at the moment, "and in talking he wanted to know if he got this stock and we paid for it, if we would share in the profits later, if there would be any profits." The Novaks agreed to risk their money to make themselves and Bobby a profit, share and share alike. There was just a "gentleman's agreement" that Bobby would share the losses, if there were any, but it was all a very free-and-easy understanding—and on this basis the Novaks put up $12,000 in hard cash.

Odd, certainly, but not so odd when one knew what Bobby knew and what, presumably, he must have told Novak. In registering its first public stock issue with the SEC, Magic had reserved 36,340 shares for its officers at $2.50 a share. The officers themselves were not to keep the shares, but were to dispose of them at this price where they would do the most good. Yet when the shares went on sale to the public on February 25, 1960, they were to be priced at $25 a share. An insider who could get a few thousand of those $2.50 shares certainly stood to make a barrel of money— and Bobby Baker knew just where he could get them.

In a letter to Max Karl on February 8, 1960, Bobby wrote that he had purchased a bloc of stock (3680 shares) from "Eddie Adams and Walter Adams." Presumably, from the letter, Max Karl must have been expected to know who the Adamses were, but later, when he testified before the Senate committee, he insisted he had never heard the names until the Baker inquiry started. And he knew, he said, absolutely nothing about them. This seemed most peculiar because, as Baker's letter to Karl had made clear, the Adamses had "previously purchased" this bloc of insider's stock, something they couldn't have done unless they had known someone highly placed in Magic. In buying up these "previously purchased" shares, Baker evidently paid the Adamses a little margin for their trouble, for his price to them for the $2.50 stock was $3.27 a share. Though Senator John J. Williams, the Delaware Republican who caused the investigation, had introduced into the record at the very outset of the hearings a photostat of Baker's letter to Karl and photostats of Baker's own worksheets on the transaction, not a member of the committee asked Karl any searching questions about the Adamses or about what he thought when he got Baker's letter. Senator Williams had speculated that the entire negotiation might have been handled the way it was, through the Adamses as go-betweens, to camouflage Baker's close "insider" relationship with Magic, but nobody on the committee felt impelled to ask a single question that might have shed light on the vital point: Just how *did* Bobby Baker acquire 3680 shares of this dirt-cheap insider's stock—and *why* was he so rewarded?

The tremendous booty involved was made clear by the worksheets introduced earlier by Senator Williams. Baker had the stock registered in the names of the Novaks, who had put up all the money, and they held the stock together for more than a year. Then, in late March and early April 1961, they sold off 3000 shares at a price of $66,889.86. Making an allowance for the cost of the shares they still retained, Bobby and the Novaks had each made $28,539.93 on the deal—and Bobby had made it all with the Novaks' cash, without risking a cent of his own!

Though the Senate committee remained obdurately blind to all the implications in this startling transaction, nothing in the entire Bobby Baker scandal better illustrates the built-in chicanery of the business practices that dominate our times. As Senator Williams had pointed out to the investigating committee earlier, an amazing amount of this $2.50 "insider's" stock had found its way into the hands of officials, especially Wisconsin officials. The state highway commissioner, the state savings and loan commissioner, the state securities commissioner had all been privileged, just like Bobby Baker, to help themselves to stock in this sure-fire, get-rich-quick deal. It had been pointed out to the committee, of course, that most of these officials did not deal with Magic's affairs in their official capacity, but it had been acknowledged that the state securities commissioner did. Only, the committee had been assured, he had "disqualified himself from consideration of these matters by reason of his stock ownership." Conceivably, however, subordinates who had to pass on Magic's application for the pending stock issue might have gotten the idea, from the boss's disqualification of himself, that the boss had an interest and would be pleased if his department acted favorably where Magic was concerned.

The ethical issue posed is obvious. So long as stock regulations permit financiers to offer insiders at $2.50 a share stock that is going to be marketed to the public at $25 a share in a few weeks, we are going to have a society that puts a premium on the racket of manipulation. Such unconscionable price leverage throws wide the door to the purchase of influence and the corruption of public officials. The deal itself (except for possible conflict-of-interest aspects, hard to prove) is all technically legal—the operators have seen to that—but ethically it can be just as much of a payoff as the blood money put into an envelope by a racketeer. Ethically, there isn't a particle of difference, and this particular type of big-business corruption isn't going to be stopped until all stock options and special stock deals are stopped; until it is decided, if it ever is, that there must be just one price for a stock at all times—the price the public has to pay.

To suggest so much is to suggest also, of course, that there are basic frauds in our system, a proposition that no committee of the U.S. Senate could be expected to countenance. Republican members of the committee, who spent a quite enjoyable time barking fiercely at the Democrats, seemed possessed of neither bark nor bite when it came to probing the Magic "insider" deals—and, perhaps, for a very good reason. For it had developed that one of their own stalwarts in the house, Representative Byrnes—he who had wielded the big club with Internal Revenue—had also been privileged to get in on a good thing with Magic. Byrnes didn't get any of that $2.50 stock as Bobby Baker did, but in September 1960, acting on the advice of one of Magic's officers, he invested $2300 in its stock. In a long oration in the House, Byrnes subsequently defended his conduct, insisting he had done nothing wrong, that he had had no idea he was being given a favored price. Actually, it appears that at the time he invested in Magic (some six months after he had introduced tax-saving legislation for the company) the stock had already been scheduled for another split, this time ten for one, on September 30, 1960. In the split and the resulting runup, Representative Byrnes' $2300 worth of Magic had become worth about $28,000 by the time the Bobby Baker scandal broke. Though Byrnes was a piker compared to Bobby Baker, it seems likely that his involvement dampened Republican enthusiasm to make an issue out of Bobby Baker's deals with Magic's president, Max Karl.

These transactions had been numerous and remunerative. On one occasion in November 1959, some three months after he had bought his first bloc of stock, Baker telephoned Karl and asked him to arrange a $15,000 loan on the stock. Karl did, signing the note himself. Later, in June 1960, Baker sold enough of the stock to pay off the loan, but he still had a handsome profit on what he retained, and he was still wheeling and dealing in Magic. And he was still finding kind-hearted souls glad to supply money for his ventures and to let him share in the profits.

The new philanthropist who came to Bobby's aid was a Murchison tycoon. It may or may not be significant that Bobby Baker, the Establishment's man on the Senate floor, seems to have been beloved by the Murchisons; but the fact remains that he *was* the Establishment's man and that his ties with Murchison representatives were multiple and close. In this instance, the Murchison tycoon who took an interest in Bobby's welfare was Robert F. Thompson, executive vice-president of Tecon Corporation of Dallas, the heavy-construction wing of the vast Murchison enterprises.

Thompson subsequently testified that he believed he first met Bobby in the office of Senator Lyndon Johnson. They had known each other "on a social basis," Thompson said, for a number of years. This was the situation when, in late 1960, Thompson got a telephone call from Bobby, who said he thought he had a good stock deal. Parenthetically, it should be noted that Bobby was absolutely certain by this time of the magic in Magic, for with the second stock split his original $28,750 investment, less than a year and a half old, was worth more than $400,000. Even with this runup, Bobby figured there was still more money to be made.

Thompson said he telephoned Karl, checked up on the stock, thought it was a good deal. He and Bobby met in Washington and agreed to buy 5000 shares. Since they didn't have the kind of money needed for such a transaction, Thompson telephoned Robert Stewart, president of the First National Bank in Dallas, and arranged for a loan of $110,000. As it happened, Max Karl could find only 2990 available shares of Magic at the time, and so in the end Thompson borrowed just $64,000 from the Dallas bank to pay for the venture. In all of this Thompson was the active partner; Thompson was taking the responsibility—yet Bobby Baker was to have a 50 per cent stake. The casualness of it all amazed the Senate investigators. Their questioning of Thompson went like this:

Q. Later were certificates for the 2990 shares delivered?

A. Yes.

Q. In whose name were they issued?

A. I don't even remember the name they were in.

Q. Weren't they in your name?

A. I'm not sure, sir.

Q. You can't recall whether any part of that 2990 shares was in Baker's name?

A. No, sir. I don't think they were.

Q. Who executed the note to the bank?

A. I did.

Q. Why didn't Baker sign it?

A. It was a matter of convenience. I was in Dallas, Baker was here, and I just borrowed the money and had a gentleman's agreement with Bobby; that is the way we do business in Texas, that we have got a joint venture and that is the way we did it.

Q. So you had no formal agreement with Baker as to what his interest was in the 2990 shares?

A. Except he had half the losses and half the profits.

Q. But that was just a verbal agreement between you?

A. Yes, sir.

Q. You didn't attach enough importance to it to put it in writing?

A. I didn't think it was necessary.

This was only the first of a series of Thompson–Baker stock adventures. In October 1961 Baker and Thompson bought another 9000 shares of Magic, borrowing $250,000 from the First National Bank of Dallas for the purpose. This time Bobby and his wife signed the note with Thompson. In another deal in April 1961, however, Thompson again took all the responsibility. He borrowed $110,000 on his own signature to buy 500 shares of Investors Diversified Service. The Murchisons, just at this time, grabbed control of IDS after a bitter stock fight; the stock ran up in price; and when Thompson's 500 shares were sold just six months after purchase, the profit was over $26,000. Thompson sent Baker a check for $13,082.44, his half of the winnings, although Baker had invested nothing, signed nothing, had only "a gentleman's agreement" with Thompson!

Bobby Baker made a fortune in Magic. He dealt back and forth, buying and selling, using the names of lawyers, friends, fellow-workers as fronts for some of his deals. The only portion of his endeavor that had not turned out too well at the time of the Senate hearings was his massive stock purchases with Thompson. The price of the stock had run up to $40 a share after they bought it, and they could have cashed in a handsome profit. But they had held on, the Baker scandal broke, and the price of Magic had been adversely affected. They still owned, Thompson testified, 8565 shares which had been pledged to the Dallas bank as collateral for their loans. But, at the current market price when he testified, they were some $40,000 in the hole. On some shares that they had sold earlier, they had made an $18,000 profit, half of which had gone to Baker. Baker had pocketed the cash, not using it to reduce the note; and Thompson still hadn't asked Baker to co-sign that first note. He still had no written agreement with Bobby.

It strains credulity that Bobby Baker could just fall into such deals, getting insider's stock at bargain-basement prices, being bankrolled in stock gambles on another's credit, without anything in return ever having been expected of Bobby Baker. Max Karl insisted vehemently that Bobby never lifted one little finger to help Magic in any way. Karl testified he thought "it was important that MGIC have well-known stockholders who might attract other stockholders. . . ."

Q. And at that time it was your view that Mr. Baker was quite an important person in the world of Washington?

A. I thought he knew a lot of people; yes.

Q. And could be useful to your company?

A. Useful only to the extent that other investors might follow his lead.

The questioning of Thompson didn't even get this far. Thompson conceded that Tecon did a lot of government business.

Q. Can you give the committee some idea of the quantity in terms of dollars at any one time?

A. You mean the total amount?

Q. Yes.

A. I just wouldn't have any idea, but it is a sizable amount; I will say that.

It may seem incredible to some, but obviously not to the Senate committee, that the key official of a multimillion-dollar concern wouldn't have any clearer idea than this of just how much business his firm was doing. Thompson later conceded that "most" of Tecon's business was with the federal government, but he wasn't pressed to define "most" or "sizable." Nor was he pressed at all about what role Bobby Baker might have played in all of this. Had Bobby used his position and influence to help Thompson's firm, considering that Thompson had "helped" him so generously on the stock deals? This, of course, was the key question. And it was the question that wasn't even asked.

3

It wasn't all just making money in the Washington set of Bobby Baker. There were fun and games, too.

A lot of the sport centered around the hideaway for harried officials and brass hats, lobbyists, and businessmen that Bobby Baker helped to organize in the red-brick Carroll Arms Hotel, just across the street from the new Senate Office Building and just two blocks from the Capitol. This special retreat was called the Quorum Club.

The Quorum Club was chartered in 1961, with Bobby Baker its moving spirit. His law partner, Ernest C. Tucker, handled the incorporation details, and Bobby was the No. 3 keyholder and the first secretary of the organization. Located originally in two rooms of the Carroll Arms, the club expanded until it occupied a five-room suite. Over the entrance door was a large *Q,* and inside were lounges, card tables and chairs, a player piano, a well-stocked bar. The dark walls were adorned with paintings of nudes. Members sometimes referred to it as an "intimate luncheon and cocktail hideaway" for the "advise and consent set."

Incorporation papers described the aims of the Q Club as "literary purposes, mutual improvement and social intercourse." The first, unless composition of favored legislation for lobbyists is viewed as a literary endeavor, seems to have been sadly neglected in the actual operation; but there can be no question that a lot of "mutual improvement" and "social intercourse" of one kind or another was indeed promoted.

Membership was limited to 200, with initiation fees of $82.50 and annual dues of $48. These were bargain-basement rates for lobbyists privileged to join an "in" group on the Hill, and they flocked around in such numbers that they overloaded the rolls of the Q Club. Among the other members were two generals, two admirals, a Navy captain, four Democratic Senators, two Republican congressmen, and a couple of aides of the then Vice-President Johnson. The Senators were Brewster of Maryland, Church of Idaho, Edmondson of Oklahoma, and Williams of New Jersey.

The congressmen were Ayres of Ohio and Battin of Montana, and the Johnson aides were Walter Jenkins and George Reedy.

Among the businessmen and lobbyists who hobnobbed with such personages in the Q Club appears virtually every name to figure in the moonlighting business deals of Bobby Baker. A look at some of the most prominent names shows how Baker's private business interests and the "social intercourse" of the Q Club tied together in one neat little package. Here are some of the outstanding names on the Quorum Club roll and their ties to Baker:

Edward M. Bostick. A stout, florid, vigorous business type, he was president of Melpar Corporation of Falls Church, Virginia, a subsidiary of Westinghouse Air Brake and a maker of aerospace components. Bostick was to oblige Baker with a vending-machine contract that helped set Bobby up in one of his most important ventures—and, incidentally, to lead to his downfall.

Glenn Troop. Skillful lobbyist of the U.S. Savings and Loan League and the man who introduced Baker to Max Karl, laying the groundwork for the Magic deal. Troop and Baker were close friends, and they and their wives often went partying together.

Thomas D. Webb, Jr. Washington representative of the vast Murchison interests. Webb's retainer was paid by Thompson's Tecon, but he represented the entire Murchison empire in Washington. He was later to help set up a remunerative deal for Baker in the sale of meat coming from a Murchison packing plant in Haiti; through Webb, Baker met other Murchison tycoons, was a guest at some flamboyant Murchison parties, and enjoyed Murchison hospitality on one vacation to the plush Spanish Cay in the Bahamas and another to the Thousand Islands in the St. Lawrence River.

Scott I. Peek. Administrative assistant to Senator George W. Smathers of Florida and the first president of the Quorum Club. The Peeks and the Bakers often went partying with the Tuckers, Troops, and Webbs; Baker and Peek were partners in one business deal linked to Smathers. Their attractive secretaries shared quarters in the $28,000 lavender-decor town house Bobby Baker provided.

Leonard Lee. Vice-president of the Tennessee Gas Transmission Co. As luck would have it, this was the firm that owned the $125,000 house, in an exclusive section of Washington not far from Vice-President Johnson's home, that Bobby Baker acquired as his family mansion.

Fred Black, Jr. Consultant to North American Aviation Corp., a major defense contractor, at a reported retainer of $14,000 a month. Black was also paid fancy retainers by other major firms because he was the personality type who knew almost everybody who counted. He was to be a partner of Bobby Baker's and a vital cog in the vending-machine deal that was to be, for Baker, more magic than Magic.

These were the kind of men who regularly foregathered in the Quorum Club almost in the shadow of the Capitol dome. They met not alone. Though the club membership was strictly male, there was no prejudice against decorative female guests. And then there were also the hostesses. In the widespread embarrassment caused by the Bobby Baker affair, members of the club insisted that the hostesses were always most decorously clad in black dresses and even, a most improbable garb, in sweaters and skirts. Veterans of Washington high life tell a more titillating tale. They insist that there were occasions, at least, when the hostesses wore the tightest of black tights and black net stockings and that the scenery so put on display did nothing to lessen the attractiveness of the Quorum Club for its male members.

One of the most enchanting black-tights and black-net exhibits was the personal property of Ellen (Elly) Rometsch, twenty-seven, the wife of a West German Army sergeant attached to a military mission in Washington. A dazzling brunette with a high-piled coiffure, Elly Rometsch was afterwards described in lyric terms as a ravishing beauty and an Elizabeth Taylor look-alike, and she was said to have displayed a 36–25–34 form with such devastating effect that, when she paraded about the Quorum Club in scanty wisps of costume, she made tired legislators and businessmen forget all about the nudes on the walls.

Washington, like most capitals, is a swinging city. Girls are all over the place. They outnumber men in the government offices by a large margin; they are available for parties; and a real swinger can swing every day and night of the week. In such an atmosphere, fun and business become so intermixed that it is sometimes hard to tell just where one leaves off and the other begins. One Capitol Hill habitué put it this way to *Life:*

> This is a man's town, a transient's town. . . . It's also an action town —big men, big politics, big egos coming and going, out to make a deal or persuade somebody else to make one, stop a law or try to rig one. It's a social town, lots of parties; and probably more than half the parties are more than half business. No party was ever spoiled by having pretty girls around and damn few deals ever suffered from having pleasant company for the dealers.
>
> And something else. I know girls are not a new invention, but it's surprising how many guys act as though they'd just found out. The discovery tends to improve their dispositions.

The evidence would seem to indicate that Elly Rometsch improved a lot of dispositions. With her endowments, she began capering around the Quorum Club as a hostess, and almost overnight, as it were, she was capering all over town. She would leave her husband and five-year-old son in their suburban Arlington home and take off for the night life of Washington, sometimes returning the next morning in an entirely different dress. If her husband got curious about her long and constant absences, she reminded him that she was a model, and models had to work all kinds of hours, didn't they?

One thing led to another, one party to another, and inevitably Elly Rometsch was thrown into contact, not with just a lot of men, but with a lot of other party girls, too. One of the other girls she met was Nancy Carole Tyler, Bobby Baker's secretary.

Carole, as she was generally called, had come to Washington from Lenoir City, Tennessee, a town of 5000 some twenty miles from Knoxville. She had been a beauty queen, Miss Loudon County of 1957, and she had all the right attributes; fine legs, a curvaceous figure, an attractive face. Her long brown hair came tumbling down to her shoulders; her lips were wide, and when she smiled, they revealed beautifully even teeth; her bright eyes crinkled. So gifted, Carole Tyler went to work on the staff of a congressman. Just how Bobby Baker spotted her the record doesn't say; but spot her he did, and in February 1961 Carole transferred her affections from the lower house of Congress to the upper—and a position on Bobby Baker's staff.

She was listed at first as a telephone page for the majority, a job that paid $5687.56. This wasn't very high take-home pay for a beauty queen, and Carole set out to prove her talents were worth more, much more. She succeeded fantastically. Raise after raise came the way of the twenty-three-year-old Miss Loudon County. Two months after she signed on with Bobby, her pay was boosted to $6052.11; four months later, it was upped to $6538.19; and in August 1961, after just eight months on the job, Carole got a promotion to the post of clerk to the Secretary of the Majority, a kind of administrative assistant, at a salary of $7753.34. Even this wasn't the end. In October 1962 Carole was rewarded again, with a jump to $8296.07, the last of a swift succession of merit increases that seem to say the beauty queen from Loudon must have been a secretary with exceptional skills.

Just a month after this last raise, Carole got a bonus, as it were. Her grateful boss, Bobby Baker, purchased that $28,000 town house in the southwest section of Washington; lavished $6500 on lavender wall-to-wall carpeting, drapes, vinyl floors, fancy French wallpaper, shrubbery, landscaping, and special lighting fixtures; and turned it all over to his beauty-queen secretary. Sharing the quarters with Carole was Mary Alice Martin, secretary to his good friend Scott Peek of Senator Smathers' office.

The town house was part of a cooperative housing development called River Park Mutual Homes. It was a three-story, modernistic, masonry-and-glass building, with attached houses in a row on either side of it. It had four bedrooms, two baths, a basement family room finished off with Philippine-mahogany paneling, and a patio out back. The down payment set Bobby back just $1600, but since the rules of the development provided that a house purchased there had to be lived in by the owner or a member of his family, Bobby had to fudge the truth a bit in making application for the mortgage. The house, he said, would be occupied by "N. C. Tyler, cousin, 23, administrative assistant, U.S. Senate, and M. A. Martin, no relationship, age 22, secretary, U.S. Senate."

Not until N. C. Tyler took possession did anyone realize that those innocent initials stood for Nancy Carole, the bombshell of Loudon County. Then things began to happen.

Nights at the town house were just one long, continuous party, according to the neighbors. Nothing loud and raucous; nothing to bring the cops. But caterers serving good food and drinks, important people coming and going. Naturally, none of the neighbors were ever invited to participate in the jollity; naturally, also, they became curious about the high jinks and kept sharp, neighborly eyes on the town house occupied by two attractive girl secretaries from the U.S. Senate.

"I saw four Senators I recognized," one neighbor later said, describing the various parties. "I saw White House people I recognized. I saw Baker, and I often saw that German girl."

"That German girl" was, of course, Elly Rometsch, the gay romper who had extended her activities from the Quorum Club to the town house and elsewhere about town.

Elly Rometsch, if anyone could have followed her about, doubtless would have been an attractive guide to that "other life" of Washington that Senate probers were so determined not to probe. It was a life in which decorative secretaries from the Hill, officials' mistresses and outright call girls intermingled in a wild melange of bartered influence, power plays, and bedroom bawdiness. From time immemorial, the vital ingredient in such a life has been a beautiful woman's favors, and he who either arranges for the favors or knows of them possesses a lever of knowledge, tinged with the threat of potential blackmail, that can be infinitely persuasive when a law is to be passed or a contract negotiated. From this messy aspect of the Baker case the Senate of the United States averted fastidious eyes, but not everyone was quite so squeamish. There were some who probed, who lifted the veil just a bit.

Life reported that "the rustle of skirts—sometimes in the process of being taken off—rustles like a faint silken obbligato to the uproar over Bobby Baker." *Life*'s reporters talked to some of the call girls who circulated in the Baker social quadrant, and the insights they gave into after-hours life on the Hill were truly fascinating.

One of the party girls recalled a dinner in Aldo's Restaurant, one of the clique's favorite spas. Among those present, she said, were Thomas Webb and Bedford Wynne of the Q Club; other business-men, none of them lonely; and Bobby Baker and Carole Tyler. This particular call girl had known Baker for about eight years, a protracted acquaintance that had not moved her to admiration. In fact, in describing her reactions to Baker she told *Life:*

"I've known gangsters and the difference between Baker and professional hoodlums is that Baker's kind operates with a hunting license. Besides, the hoodlums are nicer. Baker is the kind of guy who would be friendly one time and the next time you saw him in different company, you would think he didn't even know you."

A second call girl, only twenty, told *Life* she was making $800 a week plying her trade, a sum on which, she said proudly, "I pay my taxes." This particular charmer knew Baker well, she said, and she had something like a standing engagement with a key defense contractor in Baker's circle. The defense executive was married and had a family, but the girl "liked him a lot," sometimes met him at the Q Club, and often functioned as a kind of hostess and entertainer at an apartment the executive kept in town for the reception of important guests. The call girl said she kept a tam-bourine and harem pants in the apartment, essential props for the Oriental dances she sometimes performed to add to the jollity of an evening.

So sinuously attractive was this call girl, according to her own account at least, that the appreciation of the guests sometimes burst all bounds, and then she would forget all about her harem attire—or, indeed, any attire at all—as she performed her dances. Other girls at such parties, high spirits being what they are, some-times joined in the act, and on one particularly hot summer night, enthusiasm reached such a pitch that girls were peeling all over the place. Hilarity ruled unconfined, and one thing led to another until the evening reached a climax when some of the girls climbed into a bathtub and began to pour champagne over themselves. The champagne-bathers finally became all tuckered out by their various endeavors, and three of them piled into bed together, exhausted.

The fumes of the champagne were still doing their devilish work, however, and in the early morning hours, one of the girls, rolling over, became annoyed at finding a smooth white buttock practically in her face—and chomped down hard on it.

Victim of the chomp, according to this account, was Elly Rometsch. Elly apparently was something of a trouper; for, though she had been so rudely and painfully awakened, she evidently bore no ill will. Indeed, she took charge of everything when day came and the girls started trying to put themselves together again. One girl, it developed, was in a truly distressing state. Her shoes somehow had disappeared during the evening's frivolity, and her cocktail dress had been torn to shreds. Elly, the Good Samaritan, arranged everything. She decked out the unfortunate girl in a pair of the host's pants, loaned her one of her own sweaters and a pair of shoes, and packed her off home.

As can perhaps be glimpsed from all this, the fun and games in the Bobby Baker set were something to witness, but not much of the view managed to straggle into the Senate record. Senator Hugh Scott of Pennsylvania and some of the other Republicans tried on occasion to cuddle up to the topic, embarrassing the Democrats no end and sometimes embarrassing other personages as well. One of those Scott harassed in this fashion was Edwin M. Bostick of Mount Vernon, Virginia, the boss-man of Melpar, defense-contracting subsidiary of Westinghouse Air Brake. Bostick was connected with virtually all the kingpins in Bobby Baker's Q Club set. Fred Black, North American Aviation consultant and Bobby Baker partner, was also the consultant for Bostick's Melpar at a neat $25,000 a year, and Law and Webb, the Murchison attorneys, were also being retained by Bostick's Melpar at a painless $40,000 annually. Having established so much, Senator Scott switched to the subject of girls:

SCOTT: Can you tell us whether Ruth Sabatini is now or has ever been on the Melpar payroll?

BOSTICK: I can tell you "No," in both cases. . . .

SCOTT: . . . Is she now or has Linda Morrison ever been on the Melpar payroll?

BOSTICK: No, sir.

SCOTT: Do you know someone named Linda Morrison?

BOSTICK: Mr. Chairman, I at this juncture would like to raise the question of whether this is relevant to the proceedings.

This precipitated a long discussion during which the Democratic majority on the committee expressed considerable annoyance with Senator Scott and decided that the question was not "germane," a word Bostick picked up with enthusiasm when Scott, later in the questioning, returned to the subject. Scott had established that Melpar was paying another firm a healthy public relations retainer, and he was anxious to know what might be included under the omnibus term *public relations.*

SCOTT: Do you know whether or not Miss Linda Morrison has received compensation from this firm?

BOSTICK: I do not; no, sir. . . .

SCOTT: Were you introduced to Miss Morrison by Mr. Baker or Mr. Black?

BOSTICK: Senator, no; the answer is "No."

SCOTT: You have had meetings with Mr. Black, Miss Morrison and others, have you not?

BOSTICK: Senator, at this point I would again like to raise the question of germaneness of this question to the inquiry.

Scott kept hammering away, and Bostick finally denied that he had ever "met with Mr. Baker and Mr. Black and Miss Morrison on any occasion." And there it ended.

At just one point in the inquiry did the Senate seem to get much closer to the fascinating subject of Bobby Baker's girls. A committee investigator, Samuel J. Scott, questioned Paul F. Aguirre, a Puerto Rican businessman and Baker associate who had loaned Bobby $60,000 to help bail him out financially after all the trouble broke. Aguirre, probably to his later sorrow, recalled one spicy incident. Scott's account of it, as Aguirre told it to him, was later read into the Senate record. Scott wrote:

Mr. Aguirre said he and Baker met by prearrangement in May 1963 in New Orleans to look for trailer park sites . . . Mr. Aguirre admitted that Baker brought Carole Tyler and Elli Rometsch with him from Washington to New Orleans on the May 1963 trip. Mr. Aguirre said he spent several days partying with them in New Orleans but denied going with them to Dallas and Miami. Mr. Aguirre said he knew Carole Tyler socially and had been to her house at 308 N Street SW, and had seen her many times in San Juan, P.R., with Bobby Baker. Mr. Aguirre said he and Baker were close personal friends and that he didn't want to discuss Baker's private life, saying, "I'm sure Baker is paying dearly at home now for this."

. . . When asked further concerning Elly Rometsch, Carole Tyler, and the alleged "parties," Mr. Aguirre declined to discuss the matter further, stating, "if I am asked by the Committee about this, I will deny it even if they have photographs. My wife is expecting a denial and she will get it. I'll take the First through the Twenty-Eighth."

Called subsequently before the committee, Aguirre was as good as his word, claiming his constitutional privilege against possible self-incrimination. And that just about ended that.

Before events got so out of hand that the American public could be afforded such peeps into harem scenes and champagne baths, Elly Rometsch had long departed from the Washington scene. In the summer of 1963, the frolicsome fräulein frolicked so much that her spectacular cavorting caught the eye of worried West German Embassy officials. Elly was dressing too extravagantly, partying too constantly, and dropping important names too indiscreetly for the wife of a plain Army sergeant attached to the West German military mission. Knowing that Elly had been born in East Germany and that she still had relatives there, Embassy officials began to worry about the possibility of a breach in security. They communicated their fears to the FBI, and together the Embassy and the FBI investigated.

They concluded that Elly Rometsch wasn't in contact with any espionage ring; she was just having fun, if one could call it that. Her fun was the kind of fun that didn't look very proper to officials of the West German Embassy, however, and so they gave Elly and her husband just a week to pack their bags and belongings and depart. On August 21, 1963, the Rometsches left for Germany, where Elly's disillusioned husband promptly divorced her. The loss of Elly and her enchanting black tights cast the first small shadow over the Q Club and its gay habitués; it was the first faint portent, though the American public was not aware of it as yet, of the Bobby Baker scandal so soon to come.

4

The caper that did Bobby Baker in was the caper that had made his fortune blossom. Magic was small magic compared to this. This was a deal that, by Bobby's own estimate, made him $1 million in less than two years. The name of the miracle-worker was Serv-U Corporation, a vending-machine company Bobby and some of his friends had put together in their spare time.

How does a man, beginning from scratch with no capital—and Bobby Baker never had any capital in the real sense of the word —manage to organize and build a company that will make him a millionaire in less than two years? Obviously it cannot be done unless the man has friends, and Bobby Baker—"the most powerful man in the Senate" in the opinion of Lennox P. McLendon, counsel for the probing Senate Rules Committee—had more friends than a witch has broomsticks. There were always people ready to put their money at Bobby Baker's disposal; they just loved him so that they couldn't resist the impulse to risk their cash to make Bobby a fortune. In the Serv-U affair, the vital money men who served Bobby well were the hard-featured, beady-eyed gamblers of Las Vegas. They too loved Bobby so much that they shoveled out money by the bushel to set him up in the vending-machine business.

Now, there has been for decades a deep suspicion, amounting sometimes to virtual conviction, that the underworld buys influence on the highest levels of government. But it is rare, indeed, that the tie becomes so nakedly obvious. In Bobby Baker's case, he owed much to many men, to Lyndon B. Johnson, his first great mentor; to Senator Kerr, the uncrowned king of the Senate and his virtual godfather—and last but not least to the underworld gambling racketeers, gone legitimate in the legal oasis of Nevada. The record would seem to indicate that these unsentimental gentlemen invested in Bobby Baker, the most powerful man in the Senate, fully as much as they did in Serv-U—and that their investment paid off, as was afterward demonstrated by Bobby's willingness to become their emissary.

The beginnings of the Serv-U caper are murky, and this very murkiness was perhaps partially responsible for the upheaval that was to blow Bobby Baker's influence cart sky high.

At the heart of the initial gambit was defense contractor Edwin M. Bostick, the gay caballero of the Q Club, the boss of Melpar and the man who had considered questions about call girls not "germane." Bostick was important in the scheme of things because, as boss of Melpar, he had a great deal to say about where Melpar's vending-machine business went. It went ultimately, of course, to Bobby Baker, but before it did there was an interim shift—the event that was to cause all the trouble, really—to a company known as Capitol Vending, operated by a man named Ralph Lee Hill.

Hill was not one of the privileged insiders in the Q Club circle, but it seems that, like almost everyone else circulating in official Washington, he had met Bobby Gene Baker. He was not, however, a Baker intimate, and so it must have seemed somewhat strange when, in February 1962, he got a telephone call from Baker requesting the pleasure of his company for lunch at the University Club. Hill naturally accepted the invitation, and at the luncheon Baker introduced him to a man named Eugene Hancock of Miami, who was also in the vending-machine business.

One of the mysteries never fully explored in the Senate investigation was what Hill must have thought as the conversation developed. Hill always insisted that he did not know at the time that Bobby Baker was fiddling with a thing called Serv-U, just incorporated in January and not yet ready to grab business. He had no intimation that Hancock, a vending-machine man from Miami, was interested in business in the Washington area. Bobby Baker simply told him, out of the blue as it were, that he had arranged for Hill and Hancock to go together out to the Melpar plant in Virginia that afternoon; they were to ask for Bostick, who would be expecting them; and they were to inquire about Melpar's vending-machine business. Just why had Bobby Baker suddenly interested himself in all this, in getting business for Ralph Lee Hill? Just why had he brought in this stranger, Hancock, to go along with Hill out to Melpar? Didn't Ralph Lee Hill think all that was a little peculiar? These were the kinds of questions that were never really explored.

In any event, Hill and Hancock hotfooted it out to the Melpar plant, where they saw Bostick. Bostick called in his assistant, a Mr. Weid.

McLENDON: When Mr. Weid appeared, what if any statements did Mr. Bostick make with respect to the contract, vending-machine contract, with Melpar?

HILL: He told Mr. Weid to show us all the records and anything pertaining to the vending contract, and that he had promised Mr. Baker the contract.

The swift result was that Melpar's vendor of the moment, G. B. Macke, lost the business and Hill's Capitol Vending walked away with it. It had been a most lucrative trip out into the Virginia countryside, and nobody could have been more amazed than Ralph Lee Hill. "At the time I went to Melpar," he later told the Senate committee, "I did not know that I was seeking vending business. I thought I was just giving Mr. Hancock a ride to Melpar." All unsuspecting, he had wound up with the fattest contract he had ever had in his life. It was truly a world of miracles.

Though the Melpar contract had a thirty-day cancellation clause in it, Melpar officials told Hill not to worry; the clause was there only as a protection in case defense business should be suddenly canceled, but as long as he did a good job he could have the contract for years. On the way back to Washington, Hill and Hancock chatted, but there was no intimation, Hill always insisted, that Hancock or his company would ever have any interest in the Melpar business. Hancock told him, Hill said, that he was only after big stuff—like the vending-machine contract at North American Aviation. Hill insisted that, had he had any hint his happy deal with Melpar might turn sour after a single year, he wouldn't have been interested because Capitol Vending had to undertake an $80,000 equipment expansion to handle the Melpar business and

"I certainly would not have jeopardized the stockholders of Capitol Vending."

In the delusion that the plum that had fallen into his lap would stay there, Hill felt grateful to Bobby Baker, who had been promised the contract by Bostick and who, out of the kindness of his heart, perhaps because Hill was a fellow South Carolinian, had bequeathed the business to Hill. So Hill went to Baker's office, thinking to express his gratitude with a case of liquor, but he found that Bobby Baker had very specific ideas about the kind of reward he deserved. The questioning went this way:

HILL: Well, after the niceties, when we first—when I first had the visit, he wanted part of the profits.

MCLENDON: Tell exactly what was said, please.

HILL: Well, he said if the contract was valuable to us, we were making money out of it, and he wanted a thousand dollars a month. And so we argued back and forth and we settled for $250.

Baker's demand, Hill later explained, posed for him a serious ethical dilemma. He had been fighting such kickback practices "for the last three or four years—because I did not like having to pay or give anybody anything other than good service and what they were supposed to get." He had even sued a competing firm that had obtained business by such means. But when Baker demanded his fee, Hill had already committed Capitol to purchase $80,000 worth of extra equipment. His was a small company, and if he dropped the Melpar contract in preference to paying Baker, his firm would be bankrupted. "So I had to take the less of the two," he testified; he had to pay Baker.

The cash payments to Baker began in April 1962, Hill said, and he handled them all personally.

MCLENDON: Can you tell the committee exactly how you handled it, where you paid it, and how you paid it?

HILL: I usually asked the cashier to prepare the $250 in small bills. The cashier usually would have to go to the bank and cash a check, or change some money to get two large bills, two $100 bills, and a $50 bill. In that case, he would bring it back and place it in an envelope, and then I, in turn, would take it over to Mr. Baker's office, usually having to wait for him. If he was not in the office, go back to my office and come back two or three times. But in each instance I did see somebody in the outer office or Miss Tyler whom I had conversations with before I went in to give it to Mr. Baker. And once I gave the money to Mr. Baker he was very frugal. He made sure that everything was there.

McLENDON: Did he count it in your presence?

HILL: Yes, he did.

After Capitol Vending had been operating at Melpar for some time, Hill wanted to raise the price of drinks from five to ten cents and to put in hot chocolate, which was not then being dispensed. He wrote a memo outlining his plan, took it to Baker's office along with Bobby's $250 monthly payment, and gave both to Bobby. The next day he got the word from Melpar that his recommendations had been approved. Hill was happy because the change boosted Capitol Vending's net by more than $2000 a month. Bobby Baker was happy, too—and expectant.

McLENDON: Did he use the expression, "Now, do I get my $1000 per month?"

HILL: He used the expression, "Now, do I get my $1000 a month?" and I indicated, as I recall, the cost of converting those machines. . . . And so we had another negotiation.

McLENDON: About how much you should be paying him?

HILL: That is correct.

McLENDON: As a result of those negotiations, what amount did you agree on?

HILL: $650 a month.

All the time Bobby Baker was jacking up his price to Hill, he was industriously laying the foundation for Serv-U, the firm that would eventually cut the throat of Capitol Vending. Just who first thought up the Serv-U deal isn't quite clear, but most of the signs point to Bobby Baker. Eugene Hancock, the man from Miami who was to become president of Serv-U, said he first heard about it from Ernest Tucker, Bobby Baker's law partner. Tucker told the Senate committee he first heard about it from Bobby. In November or early December 1961, Tucker testified: "Mr. Baker mentioned to me that there was a possibility that a group would go into the vending-machine business, and would I like to be the counsel for it, and they would pay me a retainer. And I said I would."

So it came about that Tucker handled the details of the incorporation and was made chairman of the board and executive vice-president. Gene Hancock was elected president, though, according to his testimony later, he didn't even know it at the time; James C. Walsh, a prominent Washington physician, was the treasurer; and Charles Baker, Bobby's younger brother, was the secretary. The names that really mattered, however, were the names that didn't appear on the board of directors or among the officers of Serv-U.

Two held stock control of the company; behind them, in the shadows, were the more gamy figures who made it all possible. The majority stock interest, 57 per cent, was divided evenly between Bobby Baker and Fred B. Black, Jr., each of whom held 2850 shares out of a total capitalization of 10,000. Black was, of course, the Washington operator and charter member of the Q Club, the personality boy with all the contacts in the Pentagon and among defense contractors—and so the lad who could bring in the business once Serv-U got rolling.

To get it rolling, money was needed, money in impressive amounts. Neither Bobby Baker nor Fred Black had this kind of ready cash, but the record would seem to indicate that they knew very well just where they could get it. They turned, apparently without a qualm, to the gamblers of Las Vegas, and so was formed the intriguing tie between the powerful Secretary to the Senate Majority and men long connected with the gambling rackets that are the treasure chest of the underworld.

Foremost among the financial angels of Serv-U was Edward Levinson, a lifelong gambler. Short, just a fringe of gray hair ringing his balding dome, Levinson has dark brown eyes, almost opaque in their intensity. He gives the impression of a man sharp and cold-steel hard. His record is dotted with repeated arrests in Detroit, dating back to 1928, all for the operation of gambling houses. In 1950 he was arrested in Miami for bookmaking, and in 1951 he was arrested there again for the possession of gambling equipment. It could hardly have been chance that his brothers were also deeply immersed in the gambling rackets. Louis Levinson, helped by another brother, Mike, operated the Flamingo Club in Newport, Kentucky, just across the Ohio River from Cincinnati, during the years when Newport was one of the most important underworld fiefs in the nation, the vital layoff center for syndicate bookmaking throughout the East. Senator Estes Kefauver focused a spotlight on Newport during his 1950–1951 crime probe, then swung another beam of his lantern on Miami. In both places he lighted up Levinson interests, and the Miami exposure was sufficiently intense to make Edward Levinson pull up stakes and move on.

His next port of call, naturally, was Las Vegas, where he became a part owner of the Sands Hotel. By 1954 he had acquired a 13 per cent interest in the Flamingo, the mob-built and mob-dominated showplace Buggsy Siegel had erected when he pioneered the Nevada desert for the Syndicate. The revenues from these gambling traps were tremendous, and by 1955 Levinson was able to dispose of his interests in them and use the bankroll to set up his own palace of no-chance, the Fremont Hotel, the one emporium of its kind located smack in the heart of downtown Las Vegas. From this and from the Horseshoe Club, in which Levinson held a 27½ per cent interest, the tidal wave of greenbacks and silver dollars rolled in; and, just a little more than ten years after Senator Kefauver had chased him out of Miami, Edward Levinson had the kind of cash to buy himself a secret partnership with the Secretary of the Majority in Kefauver's own Senate.

Not only did he have that kind of cash himself; he knew others who were similarly loaded, and it becomes quite apparent from the testimony that it was Levinson who put the financial props under Serv-U. He bought stock himself, and he got others to buy. He brought in Edward Torres, who was vice-president and the active manager of his Fremont Hotel in Las Vegas; Benjamin B. Sigelbaum, who had been his partner in Miami deals; and Sigelbaum's partner, accountant George M. Simon; and, finally, Jack B. Cooper, a Miami mystery man who had been mixed up in the purchase of American warplanes in Sweden and their resale to the Dominican dictatorship of the late Rafael Leonidas Trujillo Molina.

These were the shadowy figures who bankrolled Serv-U. They were, the record says, not the kind of men to go into the kind of deal they went into without some excellent, ulterior purpose. Consider well the details. Bobby Baker and Fred Black each dealt themselves 1500 shares of Serv-U stock at $1 a share. Eugene Hancock was cut in for 1200 shares at $1 a share. But sharp-eyed Edward Levinson and his partners were not permitted to join the party on any such generous terms. Their stock cost them $16.52 a share and, in addition, for the privilege of being accepted into the lodge, they had to pump additional thousands of dollars of "loan" money into Serv-U to get it rolling. When Levinson brought Sigelbaum into the deal, they each acquired 1350 shares—but at a cost of $22,302 apiece for the stock and $41,806 apiece in loans. Jack Cooper and Simon between them put up $91,000 for stock and loans, and Torres contributed $25,000. In the final analysis, Bobby Baker, Fred Black, and Eugene Hancock invested a total of just $4200 for 4200 shares of Serv-U; but the gamesters from Las Vegas and Miami poured in $245,750 for the remaining 5800 shares.

In a world in which money speaks its own language, untainted by its source, Bobby Baker was now in a position to let others shower him with riches. His Serv-U had financial backing; all it needed in addition was the operator who could bring in the business. And Bobby Baker had seen to that when, in setting up the deal, he had cut Fred Black in as an equal partner.

Black was representative of a new breed of postwar professional —the slick "Washington operator," a man with all the contacts, noted for his lavish hospitality, his supersalesmanship, his "inside" knowledge of the developments and contracts that wait in the future. He was the kind of man whom some of the largest corporations in the land hire at a six-figure salary because he can "get things done." And in this ethic, that is all that counts; no one ever asks "How?"

A poor boy from Missouri who had quit college after a few months because family finances ran out, Black's rise had been meteoric. Forty-nine when the Bobby Baker trouble broke, he was living it up in a mansion right next door to that of Lyndon B.

Johnson in Washington's exclusive Spring Valley section, and just down the street was the imposing residence of his good friend Bobby Baker. Fred Black was obviously the kind of man who knew "the right people."

He had worked at knowing them all his life. After that bad start in depression days in Missouri, he had gone to work for the Works Progress Administration; had caught the eye of Donald Nelson and had been elevated to a job with Nelson's War Production Board; had gone into the Army as a private and come out a sergeant—and then, in postwar Washington, had set up his own public relations business, trading on what he had learned in the Army and WPB about how things got done.

From this point on, prosperity just showered down upon the head of the big, full-faced, jolly personality kid who threw money around as if it were confetti. Fred Black's way of life was symbolized by Cadillac Eldorados, $76-a-day hotel suites, $15,000 worth of front-row seats at the fights, the races, and the ball games. He tipped like Diamond Jim Brady on a spree, on one occasion bestowing a television set on an elevator operator; and he threw deluxe parties for "the right people" all over the national landscape. These intimate little joy-fests averaged out at $200 a throw, and in one year Fred Black threw sixty-four times at such posh watering spots as Club '21' in New York, Antoine's in New Orleans, Chi Chi's Club in Palm Springs, the Macombo in Los Angeles, and L'Espionage in Washington. In 1958, Black's public relations firm, Bylco, reported wages and commissions of $300,000 (not including $54,000 which the government later demonstrated had been overlooked), and it listed expenses of $111,000.

Where did that $111,000 go? Well, a hefty portion of it got spent in the entertainment of high brass in the military establishment, especially in the Air Force. At one big party in Palm Springs in 1958, Black's guest list read like a Who's Who of Air Force purchasing: Lt. Gen. Clarence S. Levine, Deputy Chief of Staff for Air Force Materiel; Lt. Gen. T. P. Garrity, Chief of Staff for Systems and Logistics; Maj. Gen. Robert G. Ruegg, Commander of the Aeronautical Division; Brig. Gen. Harvard W. Powell, then Deputy Director of Procurement and Production, and officers from the Oklahoma Air Materiel Area headquarters in Oklahoma City.

Significantly, a point that could hardly have escaped Bobby Baker's keen eyes, Black seems always to have had a way with the Air Force and its contractors. Some of his lushest fees came from services he performed as the go-between in this area. There was, for instance, the case of the Howard Foundry Co. of Chicago, makers of castings and dies for Air Force contractors. Howard Foundry ran into difficulties with the federal government when the Justice Department accused it of overcharging $3,350,000 on World War II contracts. The foundry protested that this levy would virtually put it out of business, and it endeavored to have the dispute transferred from Justice into the more understanding hands of the Air Force.

Fred Black was enlisted to use his persuasive talents to this end. His efforts were later to become a key item in his income tax-evasion trial, a legal duel that ended in his conviction for failing to pay $91,121 in taxes and that spread on the record considerable detail about the non-ethics of our times. Frank C. Howard, president of the embattled foundry, testified he paid Black $150,000 for his success in getting the World War II claim shuttled from Justice to the Air Force. Just how Black maneuvered it, Howard didn't know, and it would seem he didn't care. He acknowledged that, between January and November 1956, Black billed Howard Foundry $24,190.86 for "expenses." On one occasion he had written Howard that he needed $5100 in thirty days because "I have committed myself in your behalf for this amount." Who had Black "committed" himself to? What did he spend the money for? These intriguing questions were never answered. Frank Howard protested he had no idea. "All I know is the outcome," he testified.

This and similar testimony concerning other firms that paid Black lavish fees and underwrote "expenses" in professed ignorance of what the expense items represented provoked Federal Judge John J. Sirica, who presided at the income tax-evasion trial, to denounce what he called the "dirty work" of some contractors doing business with the government. "Don't you think these companies ought to have some statements showing where their money went?" he asked counsel during one argument at the bench. He added that "it sounds as if these companies are making Mr. Black the scapegoat to cover up their own slimy trail," and he embellished this by saying that if "these companies hired this man to do their dirty work, they should be here in the courtroom with him."

All of this talk of slimy trails and dirty work and top-level culprits who are never prosecuted in the corrupt society was in the unperceived future when Bobby Baker and Fred Black went to work to make Serv-U serve them millions. The service was lightning-fast. Fred Black was, of course, the special Washington "consultant" for North American Aviation at a fee estimated at some $14,000 a month, or, in more luscious terms, $168,000 a year. Clearly, Fred Black was a man with an "in" at North American; and when he used that "in," North American suddenly became enchanted with the idea of having Serv-U serve up candy, soda pop, cigarettes, and coffee to its thousands of employees. The contract was enough to put Serv-U in business in a big way. The huge aerospace contractor, which relies incidentally on the federal government for 95 per cent of its work, has plants in California, Oklahoma, Missouri, Texas, and Nevada. It employs some 80,000 workers in California alone; and when, on January 30, 1962, it signed a contract with Serv-U to install vending machines in its Los Angeles headquarters, where 15,000 labor, it transformed Serv-U by this stroke of the pen from a gleam in the eyes of Bobby Baker and Fred Black into a highly profitable money-maker.

Serv-U at the time had no vending machines, no equipment, no employees—nothing. In fact, Bobby Baker and Fred Black hadn't yet put up the dollar a share they were charging themselves for the stock. Once the North American contract was in their pocket, however, they swiftly remedied this oversight and scurried around buying up vending machines and hiring employees to tend them. Serv-U went into business, and hardly had it done so before it took off into the stratosphere faster than an Atlas rocket. It landed vending machine contracts at Northrup Aviation Corp. and at the Space Technical Laboratories Division of Thompson-Ramo-Wooldridge. All of the aerospace boys, dependent for business on government contracts, seemed somehow to have the idea that it would be good policy to bestow their vending-machine business upon the firm masterminded by the Secretary to the Senate Majority.

There was in this halcyon period just one minor item of unpleasantness. Down in Miami, Jack Cooper, the mysterious international wheeler-dealer in American warplanes, had fallen afoul of the federal income tax sleuths. He was getting some decidedly unhealthy publicity in the Miami press. Fred Black, studying the portents, didn't like what he saw. If anyone should connect Jack Cooper with Serv-U, Black's and Bobby's million-dollar baby might suffer a blow that would cut off the flow of contracts. The record indicates that Black discussed this horrendous prospect with Bobby and Edward Levinson, the Nevada gambler, and they decided it would be best for Serv-U to buy out Cooper and his accountant-partner, Simon. The buying-out, of course, would take money, the kind of money Baker and Black didn't have and that Levinson was apparently unwilling to invest.

Getting a mere $100,000 (this was the sum the partners figured they would give Cooper and Simon for their $91,000 investment) proved no problem. Out in Oklahoma City, waiting with open arms, was the Fidelity National Bank and Trust Co. Now the Kerr-McGee interests (the Kerr was, of course, Senator Robert Kerr, Bobby Baker's virtual godfather) controlled some 25 per cent of the bank stock. Fred Black had been introduced to the president of the bank on one occasion by Senator Kerr himself, and Bobby Baker, of course, was known to one and all as the Senator's fair-haired boy. So Fred Black waltzed out to Oklahoma City and borrowed $100,000 for himself and Bobby. They paid the $100,000 to Serv-U, and Serv-U, with Ed Levinson lowering the boom on Cooper and Simon in a showdown meeting, bought up the Cooper-Simon stock. It was added to the holdings of Black and Baker, giving them jointly their 57 per cent stock control of the company. Serv-U, thus purified of any possible headline taint, for the moment at least, was ready for greater things. More North American Aviation business was coming its way; more equipment was needed for expansion—and out there in Oklahoma was the

Kerr-McGee Fidelity National, eager to loan it. Over a two-year period, Black later estimated, Fidelity National loaned Serv-U more than half a million dollars, keeping Black's and Baker's 57 per cent stock holdings locked up in its vault as security for the loans. The result was that, in the spring of 1963, just a little over a year after Serv-U really got rolling, Ernest Tucker could certify that "our monthly net before taxes will be between $65,000 and $70,000 per month"—in other words, a minimum of $780,000 a year.

With Serv-U vending machines spewing out money faster than a Las Vegas one-arm bandit devours it, one might think that Bobby Baker would have been content to ride along with his good thing and not rock the boat. But the record indicates that Bobby was so avaricious he was never satisfied. Out in Virginia, there was that Melpar contract that Bobby had gotten for Ralph Lee Hill, but that, his influence with Bostick being what it was, he might just as well have for himself. Even though Bobby was being paid off by Hill at the rate of $650 a month (according to Hill's unchallenged testimony), he evidently figured that there was a lot more money than that to be made out of Melpar.

Hill began to hear rumors that Capitol Vending's throat was going to be cut, and he was worried because he needed three years at Melpar to work off the debt Capitol had assumed when it got the contract; if he lost the business after one year, Capitol might go broke. He protested to Bobby, and Bobby was by turns discouraging, evasive, and reassuring. He told Hill on one occasion that Capitol was going to lose Melpar's business because Melpar's officials didn't like Hill or his company. Hill protested he hadn't had a word of complaint, had been told they were doing a good job. Bobby insisted that wasn't the way he heard it. Wouldn't Hill like to sell Capitol Vending to Serv-U? Some discussions were held, but they got nowhere. Then Hill learned that Serv-U had had a lot of new vending machines, just the number required to service the Melpar plant, shipped to a warehouse in Bladensburg. Hill went to the warehouse, saw the machines himself, then went back to Baker. Bobby, bland now, told him to stop worrying; he could have the Melpar contract as long as he did a good job. Hill relaxed a bit, but only momentarily. At the end of August 1963, Melpar served him with a thirty-day notice that it was canceling Capitol Vending's contract. Ralph Lee Hill, who testified that he had paid Bobby Baker $5600 in seventeen months to keep the Melpar business, figured he had been double-crossed, and he decided to sue.

Before he took this final, drastic step, however, he decided to make an effort to see whether matters could not be more amicably arranged. He determined to see Nancy Carole Tyler "because she has always been very nice to me and acted like a lady" and because he had "understood from other sources that Miss Tyler has a tremendous influence on Mr. Baker." Not exactly an innocent in the ways of Washington, Hill didn't want to walk into Nancy Carole's fancy town house alone, and so he asked Capitol Vending's treasurer, a man named Gorrissen, to go with him. He telephoned the town house in advance, and Carole said, well, a couple of friends of hers were there from Tennessee, but if that didn't make any difference to him, it was all right with her. Come on over. So Hill and Gorrissen went. What happened is told this way in the Senate committee record:

SENATOR SCOTT: You arrived. She met you at the door, and what impression did you get there when she saw Mr. Gorrissen with you?

HILL: She seemed a little surprised.

SCOTT: Then you introduced Mr. Gorrissen as someone from your company?

HILL: Then I introduced Mr. Gorrissen to her after trying to eliminate the shock from her face. . . .

SCOTT: And then you told her that you understood certain things from reliable sources to the effect that "Bobby was double-crossing me." Did you then ask her anything about using her influence to help?

HILL: Well, she told me—I suggested that she use her influence to talk to Bobby, and she told me words to this effect. She says, "You can talk to him. You can tell him what you are going to do. He will not believe you. He will just think you are bluffing."

SCOTT: Did she say "what will happen," meaning Baker, "if he doesn't work it out?"

HILL: Yes; I think she did.

SCOTT: Then what did you say?

HILL: I think I told her that I was going to sue him.

SCOTT: Bring suit. Then she made the statement when you said you may have to bring suit. What did she say?

HILL: She said, "That is going to bring out everything involving Mr. Baker," and I said, "It probably will."

SCOTT: And did she then say anything to you about her own plans?

HILL: Yes; she said would I give her a week's notice before I sued if things were going to get really hot, and she indicated that she was there for one reason, to make more money than she could any other place.

Bobby Baker failed to heed the warning. Perhaps he had become by this time so drunk with the idea of his own power and influence that he just couldn't believe any Washington "operator" would be so crazy as to sue the Secretary to the Senate Majority. But Ralph Lee Hill was no Fred Black. On September 9, 1963, he lowered the boom; he sued Bobby Baker. And with that suit, the debris of the corrupt society blew sky-high in Washington and cast an ominous pall over the pure-white Capitol dome.

5

The next act belonged to Senator Williams. The Delaware legislator who is often called "the conscience of the Senate" had played a major role in exposing the mink coat–deep freeze scandals of the Truman administration, the vicuna cloth–Oriental rug gratuities of the Eisenhower administration, and he was now to fill within the Senate the role of the crusading district attorney prosecuting Bobby Baker.

The filing of Hill's lawsuit, specifying his $250 and $650 monthly payments to Baker and demanding $300,000 in damages for Capitol Vending for loss of the Melpar contract, stirred at first only a mild curiosity in the Washington press. Nobody had ever heard of Capitol Vending or Serv-U, and the original stories landed on inside pages. But, slowly, reporters began to dig. They found that Baker only recently had moved into his $125,000 mansion only a stone's throw from Vice-President Johnson's; they discovered that he made just $19,600 a year and his wife, Dorothy, records keeper of the Senate Internal Security Subcommittee, earned $11,757 a year. How, they began to ask, do you purchase and maintain a $125,000 mansion on a combined salary of only a little more than $31,000 a year?

Baker wasn't answering such questions. When Hill's suit was filed, he issued a blanket denial of all charges, then vanished into the inner sanctum of his Senatorial office and became unavailable to the press. This was the state of affairs when *Vend Magazine,* a trade publication, broke the first detailed analysis of the Bobby Baker case. It traced the phenomenal growth of Serv-U in just twenty months, the heavy bank loans made by Senator Kerr's Fidelity National to help bankroll it, and it reported that Bobby Baker, his wife, and Serv-U had floated a $746,000 mortgage on the flossy Carousel Motel in Ocean City, Maryland. *Vend* wound up its exposé with these words: "In view of the phenomenal growth of Serv-U over a 20-month period in a handful of plants owned by corporations doing billions of dollars of business with Uncle Sam, the question of any relationship between Serv-U and either of the Bakers needs an answer."

It had taken almost a month for affairs to percolate to this explosive stage. In that month, Senator Williams had been watching the cautious newspaper reports, and he had been doing some investigating of his own. By early October, he felt he had amassed sufficient information to justify an inquiry, and so on October 3, he called on Senate Majority Leader Mike Mansfield and dropped the whole Bobby Baker problem in his lap. Mansfield agreed that Baker should be questioned and asked Williams to contact the secretary, tell him the substance of the charges, and request that he meet the following day, Friday, October 4, with the leadership of both parties. Finding Baker proved not so easy; Bobby suddenly became the little man who wasn't there. Williams put through repeated telephone calls to Bobby's office and to the Democratic cloakroom. He left word for Baker to call back; Baker's office promised he would—but he never did.

The time for the Friday meeting came and passed—and still no Bobby Baker. Senator Mansfield now undertook the task of chasing down the elusive Secretary of the Senate Majority, and on Friday night he reported to Senator Williams that he had at last found and talked to Baker. It was agreed that Bobby should be asked to appear at a meeting of the joint leadership on Monday afternoon, October 7, at three o'clock. Again Bobby failed to appear. Senator Mansfield, arriving for the scheduled session in Senator Dirksen's office almost an hour late, told the leaders, as Williams later testified, "that Baker had come to his office just prior to the meeting and told him that he was not going to come down and answer any questions, but that instead he had tendered his resignation."

So quickly, under pressure, had the most powerful man in the Senate folded. It was a capitulation that seemed to scream there was an unholy lot here that could not bear close scrutiny in the light of day.

Senator Williams, taking this view, promptly introduced his resolution calling for a full-scale investigation. The agitated Democratic majority in the Senate, evidently taking the same view, named no special and vigorous investigative task force, but turned the inescapable chore over to the Rules Committee, headed by Senator Jordan and safely in the control of the Establishment.

Before the committee could dip its toes in these burning waters, however, there was a new eruption, a new sensation. A Silver Spring, Maryland, insurance man, Don B. Reynolds—portly, with thinning and graying hair, a moon face, a low, soft-voiced manner of speaking and a tendency to drop a polite "sir" into almost every sentence—decided to talk for publication. Just why Reynolds opened his mouth at this particular time remains one of the more intriguing mysteries of the Bobby Baker scandal, but open it he did in interviews with the press on the afternoon of that Friday, October 4, when Bobby Baker was making himself scarce to the most powerful figures in the U.S. Senate. And when Don Reynolds spoke, he rattled some of the loftiest rafters in the federal edifice.

Reynolds disclosed that Bobby Baker had been a secret partner in his insurance business since 1955. He declared that it was through Bobby that he had sold two $50,000 life insurance policies on the life of Lyndon B. Johnson. He charged that to get the business he had had to agree to buy $1208 worth of advertising time he didn't need on the Johnson-owned radio and television station, WTBC-TV, in Austin, Texas. And he insisted that, further to express his gratitude and to cement business relations, he had indulged at Baker's suggestion in some fancy gift-giving, bestowing high-priced Magnavox hi-fi sets on both Johnson and Baker, at a cost of $1260. He had even paid for the installation of the sets in the Johnson and Baker homes. For all of this Reynolds had some documentary proof, canceled checks for the radio time and canceled checks and invoices for the hi-fi sets.

Don Reynolds, like Bobby Baker, hailed from South Carolina, but he had had a much more promising start in life. He had had an appointment to West Point, but had flunked out. In June 1941 he graduated from the Foreign Service School of Georgetown University and entered the Air Force, where he rose to captain's rank by war's end. He joined the State Department and had overseas assignments in Germany and South Africa. There were allegations that he had dealt in black-market goods and had had questionable associations with women. He left the State Department, returned to the Air Force, was confronted with more allegations of black-market activities, resigned, and was honorably discharged. The innuendos concerning Reynolds' conduct all seem to have stemmed from his service in Germany, and about them Reynolds later said, "I did no more and no less than any American officer residing there."

Subsequently, in 1953, Reynolds testified before the Senate Internal Security Subcommittee in executive session about sex deviates in the State Department and the Air Force. He was later accused of having made unfounded allegations, but he insisted that everyone named by him had been "eliminated" from the federal services. It was at the time of this testimony before the Senate committee that Reynolds first met Bobby Baker.

A couple of years later, when he set up his own insurance business, Reynolds heeded the advice of a wise old veteran of the game who told him he ought to get as a partner someone who "was inclined toward either purely political or social life." Baker seems to have qualified on both counts, and, when Reynolds approached him, he agreed to become vice-president of Reynolds' agency and to buy ten shares of nonvoting, dividend-only stock at $25 a share. It was typical of Bobby Baker that he never paid for the shares and that they were never issued. And it was typical of him, too, that he afterwards listed these shares in his financial statements as being among his assets—and assigned to them a value of $5000.

Not all of these details came out immediately. Reynolds' first disclosures to the press had consisted of little more than the revelation that Bobby Baker had been his partner and that they had been involved together in insurance deals, including the writing of policies on Lyndon Johnson's life. These hints were enough to bring Reynolds an invitation to appear before Senate investigators in executive session; it was from this questioning, in November 1963, that word first leaked out about the purchase of air time on the Johnson-owned Austin station and the gift of the hi-fi sets to Lyndon Johnson and to Baker. In the brief interim between first and second disclosure, however, one cataclysmic event had happened: President John F. Kennedy had been assassinated in Dallas, Texas, and Lyndon B. Johnson had become President of the United States.

Word that Reynolds had blown the whistle in talks with Senate investigators quickly seeped out into the newspaper world of Washington, and the White House, by its sensitive and jittery reaction, seemed to indicate that it was aware of the leak. Calls began going out to newspapers from sources close to the White House in an effort to get them to kill or play down stories that were being prepared for publication. The Washington *Star,* a great capital newspaper, reported that it had been contacted personally by Abe Fortas, a Washington attorney who is one of the President's closest advisers, after it had asked the White House for comment on the stereo gift. Papers were warned that Reynolds was highly unreliable, and subsequently information detrimental to him was leaked from confidential Air Force and State Department files to columnist Drew Pearson. Despite this kind of pressure, newspapers printed the story of stereo gift-giving, and the Bobby Baker scandal achieved a new dimension of significance.

When Don Reynolds took the witness stand before the Senate Rules Committee on January 9, 1964, the full story came tumbling out. Reynolds' canceled checks and notes on which not even interest had ever been paid showed that, over the years, he had contributed some $15,000 to Bobby Baker's welfare because, as he testified, Bobby "was consistently trying to better my insurance business." Bobby, said Reynolds, always seemed to be needing money in the early years of their collaboration. ". . . he would get himself into binds and he would come to me and ask me if I could help, and sometimes I could and sometimes I could not."

The most significant instance in which Bobby looked out for the betterment of Reynolds' insurance business occurred in late 1956 or early 1957. Lyndon Johnson, then the powerful majority leader of the Senate, had recovered from a severe heart attack and was seeking life insurance that would be written at high, hazardous-risk rates. Baker tipped Reynolds to the prospect.

McLENDON: What individual did you speak to with reference to the possibility of selling insurance to Senator Johnson after Baker told you that the Senator was in the market?

REYNOLDS: He introduced me first of all to Mr. Walter Jenkins, that is, Bobby arranged for an appointment for me to see Mr. Jenkins.

McLENDON: And you saw him as a result of the appointment made by Baker?

REYNOLDS: Yes, sir.

McLENDON: Did Jenkins confirm that the Senator was in the market to purchase life insurance?

REYNOLDS: He would like for me to see what could be done, sir.

Walter Jenkins was the hard-driving administrative assistant to the then-Senator Johnson. He had been with Johnson since 1939 and was trusted with the most intimate details of Johnson's official and private life. His name had already received a brushing mention in connection with the activities of the Q Club and a few

months later was to leap into headline prominence as the result of
a morals arrest during the heat of the 1964 Presidential campaign.

After talking to Jenkins, Reynolds testified, he approached
various companies on the subject of insurance for Johnson, and
finally, in February 1957, he got the Manhattan Insurance Company to write a $50,000 policy on the Senator's life. Another
$50,000 policy was written shortly afterward. In 1961, just be-
fore the then-Vice-President Johnson left on a trip to Africa, an
additional $100,000 term policy was written. On all of these
policies Reynolds received commissions that initially totaled
around $5000, plus an annual 5 per cent on the premiums as they
were renewed.

About the time the first policy was being written, Reynolds
testified, he was informed by Jenkins that he had competition,
that a man named Huff Baines, a distant relative of the Senator,
was in the bidding for the policy and had offered to buy time on
the Johnson-owned television station.

McLENDON: Did you agree to meet that competition and purchase the advertising?

REYNOLDS: I made the statement consistent with having the
privilege of writing the insurance . . . that I would do my best to
purchase comparable advertising time. . . .

Reynolds had no use for television advertising in Texas, he said,
and so he scouted around to see if he could sell the $1208 worth
of time he was buying to someone who might be able to use it.
In this way, he hoped to recoup at least part of his loss. He finally
made a deal with Albert G. Young, president of Mid-Atlantic
Stainless Steel Co., who agreed to use the time trying to sell pots
and pans to the Texas folk over the Johnson-owned Austin station.
Texans weren't buying many pots and pans, however, and Reynolds only got back about $160.

Senator Curtis asked Reynolds why he had bought the time
in the first place.

REYNOLDS: Because it was expected of me, sir.
CURTIS: Who conveyed that thought to you?
REYNOLDS: Mr. Walter Jenkins, sir.
CURTIS: Where?

REYNOLDS: In his office, sir. . . .

CURTIS: Did you just happen to go down to his office?

REYNOLDS: No, sir. I was contacted by—whether Bobby or Mr. Jenkins' office, I do not remember, sir. But I went down to discuss it with him. . . .

CHAIRMAN JORDAN: May I ask a question there? Was there any question at that time of additional insurance being purchased?

REYNOLDS: No, sir. But I might state categorically that I hoped by doing this it would develop good will, sir, and the fact that should the occasion occur later, that they certainly would give me a primary consideration for further purchase of life insurance, sir —of my good will and intent, sir.

This was a hope that evidently was realized when the Johnson $100,000 term policy was purchased in 1961.

Midway between the 1957 and 1961 insurance purchases came the adventure in stereo gift-giving.

In the spring of 1959, Reynolds testified, Bobby Baker suggested to him that it would be a good idea if he gave a hi-fi set to Senator Johnson. There was much questioning about this, but the clearest account of the transaction developed in Reynolds' answers to Senator Robert C. Byrd of West Virginia, a Democrat whose hostility to any witness giving anti-Baker testimony is patent on the record. The colloquy between Byrd and Reynolds went like this:

BYRD: You are sure that it was at the suggestion of Bobby Baker?

REYNOLDS: Yes, sir. I supplied Bobby with a catalogue from the Magnavox Co., and he said that he had taken it for Mrs. Johnson to make a selection. I placed an order through the friendship or knowledge I had with the Magnavox Co., told them to ship it direct by air express to the Senator, sir. . . .

BYRD: He [Baker] made no explanation as to why you should send a hi-fi set to Senator Johnson?

REYNOLDS: I am trying to remember so as not to take it out of context. To the best of my belief and recollection that I had been drawing renewals on the contract and I hadn't been producing any return to the company. . . .

BYRD: Would you state again what you said about sending a catalogue out to Mrs. Johnson?

REYNOLDS: Yes. Bobby called me and said that the then Senator would like to have a stereo set, and he asked me what kind I could obtain to the best advantage, that is cost to me, and I told him the only manufacturer that I knew, sir, that I could depend on for top quality would be Magnavox, and I sent or took to Bobby's office a Magnavox illustrated catalogue.

Reynolds submitted invoices from the Magnavox Company showing that the set delivered to the Johnson home had been billed to him. If a copy of the invoice accompanied the delivery, as presumably it did, there should have been little doubt in the Johnson household as to the source of the gift. The bill for the installation had also been paid for—as another invoice showed— by Don Reynolds.

These records impelled Senator Claiborne Pell, Rhode Island Democrat, to question Reynolds.

PELL: Is this a matter of general custom in your industry when you write insurance policies of this sort; do you have other clients to whom you feel it incumbent to do the same or not?

REYNOLDS: I have never been asked by any other clients, sir, to do so.

PELL: But in this case the suggestion was made to you not by the client but by Mr. Baker?

REYNOLDS: The advertising time was requested by Mr. Jenkins. The stereo was by Bobby, sir.

The impact of this testimony was such that President Johnson was moved to make one of his rare comments on the Baker case. At a press conference in the White House on January 23, 1964, after he had finished discussing national issues, a reporter asked him, "How do you think things are going up on the Hill?" The President made a few brief comments on pending legislation, then said:

"There is a question also been raised about a gift of a stereo set that an employee of mine made to me and Mrs. Johnson. That happened some two years later [after the purchase of the insurance], some five years ago. The Baker family gave us a stereo set.

We used it for a period and we have exchanged gifts before. He was an employee of the public and had no business pending before me and was asking for nothing and so far as I knew expected nothing in return any more than I did when I presented him with gifts."

This explanation shifted the stereo gift from Reynolds to Baker, something that the records of the case simply do not support, and it obviously raised as many questions as it answered. Questions like: Is it common for a hired hand earning less than $20,000 to give the boss a $584 stereo set? Is this kind of thing done so often that it is not unusual and so raises no suspicion in the recipient's mind that some special favor may be sought? What kinds of gifts had Baker and Johnson exchanged previously? Were they in the habit of swapping presents of the magnitude of the stereo set? Naturally, no one was asking such questions.

Aside from the documentary record of checks and invoices that substantiated Reynolds' story, there were other checkpoints in his account. And, in the end, they all checked out.

Reynolds had testified that, when he discussed the sale of television time with Albert G. Young of Mid-Atlantic Steel, Young had wanted some confirmation that the arrangement would be satisfactory with the Johnson-owned TV station. Reynolds said he would have Walter Jenkins telephone Young. Young testified that he had, indeed, received such a telephone call from a man who identified himself as Walter Jenkins. The caller had confirmed the arrangement for the transfer of Reynolds' TV time, and Young had gone ahead with the deal. Democrats on the investigating committee sought solace in the fact that Young had never met Jenkins, didn't know his voice—and so the call might have been the work of an imposter. It was not a very logical or convincing rationalization.

The best witness, one might have thought, would have been Walter Jenkins himself. Republicans clamored to have him called, but the Democratic majority on the committee refused. Instead, they adopted the more cautious procedure of having Jenkins tell what he had to tell to committee investigators and then sign an affidavit attesting to the accuracy of their account of the interview. This tactic produced a most consoling version of events and enabled the Democratic majority in a report on July 8, 1964—a report prematurely labeled final—to cast doubt on Reynolds' charge that he had been pressured to buy advertising time.

Jenkins said he was "quite sure" Bobby Baker had known of Johnson's desire to purchase life insurance. He was "positive that he had never heard from any source" of a business connection between Baker and Reynolds. He had never been present at any conversation between Baker and Reynolds at which commissions earned by Reynolds had been discussed. And: "He [Jenkins] emphatically denies ever suggesting to Robert G. Baker or to Reynolds the LBJ Company [the TV company that was paying the Johnson premiums] should get any sort of rebate from the commissions earned by Reynolds." Jenkins did not deny that he knew Reynolds had purchased TV time, but he did deny "any knowledge of any arrangements by which Reynolds purchased advertising time on the TV station."

This seemingly emphatic repudiation of Reynolds' charge that his purchase of advertising time had been a force-put deal became less emphatic with the passage of time. Jenkins' arrest on a morals charge in the latter stages of the 1964 Presidential campaign was followed by his forced resignation from the President's White House staff. Jenkins vanished into a hospital, underwent psychiatric care for several months, and then was questioned once more by committee investigators after new charges by Reynolds had forced the committee to reopen its "closed" case. This time Jenkins' statement varied greatly from his previous affidavit.

His "emphatic" denials that he had ever suggested Reynolds buy advertising time and that he had "any knowledge" of how the purchase of advertising time came about were now replaced by this statement:

"During the time consideration was being given to the purchase of insurance through Mr. Reynolds, I received word from the LBJ Co. it would not be necessary to pursue the matter further because a local agent in Austin had become interested in selling the policies, and that he not only had been an advertiser on the radio and television stations for many years, but also had always related the amount of his advertising to the amount of his business done with the station.

"I am confident I communicated this information to Mr. Reynolds. . . ."

Jenkins said he then received word "that Mr. Reynolds wished very much to sell the policies and would also like to purchase advertising time in the event he sold them." Reynolds, Jenkins said, "offered to purchase advertising for the purpose of meeting the competition of the Texas agent. Certainly, I did not 'pressure' him to do so."

Jenkins may not have regarded this wily insinuation as "pressure," but it becomes quite easy, in the light of his statement, to understand how Don Reynolds became convinced "it was expected of me, sir," to kick back part of his commission in advertising time to the station that was paying the premiums. Here revealed at the summit, on the highest level in the land, were the ethics and business practices of the corrupt society.

6

July 22, 1962, was a memorable day in Washington. It was unforgettable at the time, and it was to become even more remarkable in retrospect. It was the day that Bobby Baker threw a big wingding to celebrate one of the most gaudy achievements of his flamboyant career—the official launching of his plush million-dollar Carousel Motel in Ocean City, Maryland.

The Carousel was located some 140 miles from Washington, but Bobby was determined to make it an oceanside rendezvous for the advise-and-consent set—and to launch it with a bash nobody would ever forget. Everybody who was anybody in Washington was to be invited—Senators, congressmen, members of their staffs, bankers, savings and loan executives, union leaders, even the queen of party-givers, Perle Mesta. And the guest of honor, of course, was to be Vice-President Johnson, "The Leader" to whom Bobby had given undying allegiance.

It might seem like a long trek from Washington to Ocean City for one day's carousal at the Carousel, but Bobby Baker arranged all with the idea of making the event simply irresistible. He hired six air-conditioned buses from the D.C. Transit System. He loaded them with champagne and pretty, scantily clad waitresses to serve the same. The buses picked up the elite of our nation at the Mayflower Hotel and then took off for Ocean City, champagne corks popping every mile of the way. By the time the bus caravan rolled into the new motel's semicircular driveway, the distinguished partygoers were floating on a plateau of high spirits and were raring to frolic with Bobby Baker, the millionaire motel mogul.

Such a heady mixture of potent liquor and lissom waitresses and page-one personalities made a big splash on the society pages of the Washington newspapers. But nobody seemed to ask the obvious questions: How was this miracle performed? How had it happened that Bobby Baker, an employee of the Senate, was suddenly making like a Conrad Hilton?

The lack of curiosity on the part of the Senate of the United States says much. With the high-swinging brawl that had launched the Carousel, Bobby Baker's suspicious affluence had been flaunted before the entire capital; perhaps the prevailing corruptions of our times are reflected in the simple fact that no one in authority seems to have thought it strange. It was as if everybody accepted the idea that this kind of thing happens every day of the week—and that, perhaps, may be the very point; perhaps it does.

So far as the record shows, just one participant in the gay celebration seems to have had misgivings. This was Mrs. Gertrude C. Novak, an attractive blonde who, with her builder-husband had started out in partnership with Baker in the Carousel. The specially chartered buses, the vintage champagne, the short-skirted, net-stockinged waitresses and the manner in which all this hospitality was lapped up by the distinguished guests stunned Mrs. Novak.

"The grand opening threw me," she told the New York *Herald Tribune* in one interview. "I definitely did not think he [Baker] would have that big a splash. It was all his idea. I felt uneasy. I've worked for the government fourteen years, thirteen of those with the Small Business Committee, and we don't ever accept a gift. I realized something was wrong. That is when I began to have a two-fold feeling about Bobby."

Except for the blindness sometimes caused by close friendship, Mrs. Novak, it would seem, should have had ample grounds for a "two-fold feeling about Bobby" long before. The Novaks, Gertrude and Alfred S., had been those close friends who had put up $12,000 of their own cash so that Bobby could take half the profits in the remunerative early-Magic deal. Later, they had gone with Bobby into the Ocean City motel venture, in the course of which Mrs. Novak had come to realize that Bobby always had impressive amounts of loose cash lying around in his Senatorial office. The story about how the Carousel came to be built and about the fat envelopes of cash Bobby contributed to it came out in Mrs. Novak's testimony before the Senate investigating committee.

The Carousel began as a modest gleam in the eyes of the Novaks and Bobby Baker. In 1959 the Novaks, Novak's brother, Donald, and Bobby Baker had purchased two blocks of land in Ocean City, one at 110th Street and one between 47th and 48th streets. They decided to build a motel on the 110th Street block, and their original plans called for a moderately priced ($350,000–$400,000) hostelry. But then Bobby Baker began to get grandiose ideas. He wanted to expand the number of units; he was set on including a fancy restaurant and nightclub, and the costs began to soar toward the $700,000 mark.

This was too rarefied a financial atmosphere for the Novaks, and the original one-third-each partnership was scrapped. Bobby Baker assumed one-half of the total burden, and Alfred and Gertrude Novak divided the second half with Donald Novak. Still the costs soared toward the million-dollar mark they were ultimately to reach, and Alfred Novak worried. On the morning of March 3, 1962, his wife found him in their garage with the car motor running. He was dead, officially ruled a suicide, a verdict the widow later contested.

Four days later, a hurricanelike storm swept the Eastern seaboard and a huge tidal wave engulfed the Ocean City waterfront, badly damaging the partly finished Carousel. About this time, while Mrs. Novak was grief-stricken over the loss of her husband, Bobby Baker and Ernest Tucker stopped by to offer condolences and to discuss business. Since Mrs. Novak was too distraught to handle the account books of the motel, they thought it would be a good idea if Ernest Tucker took over the chores she and her husband had been doing; Ernest also could administer her husband's estate for her, and she wouldn't have to worry. So it was arranged.

Mrs. Novak's financial affairs were still entangled with the financial affairs of Bobby Baker, however. They were still in partnership on the second block of Ocean City property, on which they were to pay $80,000 in installments over a five-year period, and Mrs. Novak's financial fortunes were bound up to great degree in the fate of the Carousel, into which she and her husband had sunk most of their money. In her testimony before the Senate committee, she described how these involvements gave her an insight into Bobby Baker's method of operation. There was a time in November 1962 when another payment was due on the second Ocean City lot and she did not have the money to meet it. Bobby told her to come over to his office; he would take care of everything.

McLendon: Tell the committee the circumstances, what occurred.

Mrs. Novak: Well, what happened there this particular instance, this payment of nearly 13—well, a little over $13,000 had to be made. . . . So he gave me cash of $13,300 this particular day, November 19, 1962, to deposit in our account.

McLendon: The Carousel account?

Mrs. Novak: No, the Alfred S. Novak account. From which, then, I had drawn a check in the exact amount due to make payment for this other Ocean City block, to Mrs. Freed, in Reading, Pennsylvania. . . .

McLendon: How did he give it to you—in a package, a bundle or what?

Mrs. Novak: Well, I put it in a bundle later, but it was on his desk. We had to count it out.

McLendon: Who is "we"?

Mrs. Novak: His secretary, Carole Tyler, and I counted it out.

McLendon: Did Mr. Baker instruct you and Miss Tyler to count the money?

MRS. NOVAK: Yes.

MCLENDON: Did he make any statement about where he got this money from?

MRS. NOVAK: No. He just told us the money was there, to count it, for me to deposit that, and write this check out. He had to leave the office to go on the Senate floor, because they were going into session. And he did not tell me where he got the money.

MCLENDON: Did you and Miss Tyler count it?

MRS. NOVAK: Yes, we did.

MCLENDON: What did you find?

MRS. NOVAK: Well, we found a little bit more money there than Mr. Baker said there was. So we put that—she put that money back into the file cabinet.

A deposit slip introduced into evidence showed that Mrs. Novak had indeed deposited $13,300 in cash on the day she said she had obtained the money from Baker.

This was not the only time, Mrs. Novak testified, that she found Baker practically floating in the green stuff. On April 11, 1962, he gave her another $2500 in cash; on November 2, 1962, another $2000 in cash; and on November 12, 1962, still another $12,000 in cash. Bank-deposit slips confirmed cash deposits of these amounts on these dates in the Carousel Motel account.

The last $12,000 payment was so unusual Mrs. Novak never forgot the circumstances. Baker was going to be out of town, and he told her to pick up the money from his wife at the office of the Senate Internal Security Committee. Mrs. Novak said a messenger from her office had to walk by the Internal Security office to pick up the mail, so she asked him to stop in and get an envelope from Mrs. Baker. "I assumed it was going to be a check," Mrs. Novak testified. But when the messenger came back with the envelope, "it was thick."

MCLENDON: It was money instead of a check.

MRS. NOVAK: It was cash instead of a check. It scared me to death, because I didn't much want a messenger or anyone else carrying cash. I would have gone over there personally, or had her deliver it personally. But Mr. Baker asked for me to pick it up from Mrs. Baker. Rather than my going, since our messenger was going right by the office, I had him pick it up. And there inside the envelope was $12,000 in cash.

Mrs. Novak testified that she never had any idea where Bobby Baker, the $19,600-a-year Secretary to the Senate Majority, got all this cash; this, she said, was never discussed. Bobby made some payments into the Carousel account by check, but every so often he would come up with these big wads of cash, usually in bills of $100 denomination. She was certain that she had picked up at least $31,000 or $32,000 in cash from Baker; and, since not all deposit slips were available, she agreed with Senator Curtis that the amount might have exceeded $45,000.

Even with all the $100 bills he could rustle up, however, Bobby Baker found it impossible to keep pace with the insatiable tendency of his Carousel to gobble up money. He had to finagle financing in impressive amounts, and when it came to finagling, the record says there were few to match Bobby.

Take the damage done by that March 1962 coastal storm. Bobby worked industriously—and successfully—to get the Senate to pass a special tax-break amendment that would permit storm victims to apply their losses to their 1961 rather than their 1962 income tax returns, giving them an immediate tax benefit. Then he sought the aid of the Small Business Corporation for a loan to recoup the storm damage to the Carousel. The SBA wanted proof that the owners had invested $160,000 in the motel in addition to the value of the land. So Bobby telephoned a contact of his at the American National Bank in Silver Spring (the same bank where all those cash deposits were being made) and arranged for a phony $100,000 loan for fifteen days. Bobby pledged he wouldn't take the money out of the bank; it would be deposited in a special account, and after fifteen days it would be the bank's again. But in the meantime Bobby would have a deposit slip showing $100,000 had been invested in the business. Hoodwinked, the Small Business Administration loaned the Carousel some $54,-000.

Even this kind of cash was relatively small potatoes compared to the Carousel's needs. More, much more, was needed, and so Bobby put the big touch on the Fraternity Federal Savings and

Loan Association in Baltimore. Mrs. Novak testified that Bobby told her he had "been good to them and they were returning a favor." They returned it in the kind of cash that speaks loudly of gratitude—first a loan for $270,000, then another for $90,000. It may possibly be of some significance that, attached to the first loan papers in the bank, was a note from Baker saying the Baltimore firm could open a new branch—one that had been turned down previously by the Federal Home Loan Bank Board.

By such means the Carousel was financed; by such means it opened and threw the gala party for all those notables from Washington. Mrs. Novak, who was working in the office, keeping the accounts, testified that she was terrified at the prospect of what the party would cost (she estimated $5000 to $6000), but Bobby kept reassuring her by saying it would be mostly on the cuff. "It won't cost us much at all to have this grand opening," he told her.

Evidently he miscalculated the generosity of some of his friends, for after the "grand opening," the grand bills began to pop in. Mrs. Novak would pass the bills along to Baker, calling them pointedly to his attention by saying, "Here is a bill for so-and-so much money on behalf of the grand opening." And Baker would scowl and shake his head and say, "They never should have sent that bill."

One bill never did show up. The vintage champagne and the liquor consumed at the "grand opening" apparently had been donated. As for the bills that were tendered, most of them were never paid. Typical was the D.C. Transit Company bill for $1324.48 for the buses; not only wasn't it paid—it didn't even appear on the Carousel's books as a debt. But a year later Bobby Baker popped up as a member of a committee soliciting donations to a $100-a-plate dinner in honor of the bus company's chairman.

Such wheeling and dealing gets one just so far; there usually comes a time, as in the case of Billie Sol Estes, when the operator wheels and deals himself into a cul-de-sac. This time approached for the Carousel at the end of 1962. Its accounts showed that, in its first six months of operation, it had lost $91,718.56. Such a loss, tagged on to all the backbreaking loans that had been floated to get the place built, made it imperative that the motel be sold—

and fast. So Bobby Baker went to work and arranged the deal. The purchaser? That big California vending-machine company with scads of money—Serv-U Corporation.

All of the assets of Bobby Baker's Carousel were transferred to Bobby Baker's Serv-U in a deal that left his one-time good partners, the Novaks, crying in the wilderness for their money. Mrs. Novak testified that she and her husband had sunk $63,789 into the motel. Donald Novak had invested $43,789. In the sale to Serv-U, they got back not a dime. All they got were Class B, nontransferable, nonnegotiable promissory notes, indicating that Serv-U might pay them sometime when it was convenient. The Novaks' notes were Class B notes because there was a Class A note that took precedence over theirs. Who held the Class A note? Bobby Baker and his wife, of course, and it was for $182,818.21. Bobby Baker had made certain that, if his Serv-U ever begins paying off on the Carousel, it will pay him off first.

7

There was more, much more, to the Bobby Baker story, but to tell it in detail would be almost repetitious. It was all cut from the same pattern. Like squirrels in a cage, the deals went round and round—the obvious influence-peddling, the stacks of $100 bills, the fees paid for no visible services rendered, the girls, the parties, the stock manipulations based on inside knowledge.

Some phases of the story must be capsuled, if only because the ties and associations of the Secretary of the Senate Majority, the most powerful man in the Senate, continued to be most revealing. One of the closest links was forged with Edward Levinson, the Las Vegas gambler who had so obligingly bankrolled Serv-U. Especially striking was one stock-money deal that connected in one chain Senator Kerr, Fred Black, Bobby Baker, Edward Levinson, and Benjamin Sigelbaum.

It began early in 1962 with a visit Fred Black paid to Senator Kerr. After having been introduced to the uncrowned king of the Senate by Baker, Black had cultivated the acquaintance, often showing up to play gin rummy with the Senator. On this occasion, between shuffles, Senator Kerr dropped a valuable hint: it might pay Black, he said, to look into the Farmers and Merchants State Bank in Tulsa, Oklahoma. This was now being reorganized, and stock purchased quickly could get one in on the ground floor, with the prospect of a handsome profit.

Black promptly borrowed $175,000 from the Kerr-McGee Fidelity National Bank and Trust Company. With this he bought 6400 shares of the Tulsa bank stock, which were put up with Fidelity National to guarantee the loan. Senator Kerr, Black testified, arranged the transaction, but the Senator did not know what later happened to the stock he had helped Black get.

Having acquired his bundle of stock, Black began to think of his friends. He decided at first to cut Bobby Baker in for half of the loot, but then he got to thinking about Ed Levinson and Benjamin Sigelbaum. "Mr. Baker and I decided," Black testified, "that as long as we had Levinson and Sigelbaum with us in Serv-U, that we would give them the same benefits on the stock— they could be our partner." Levinson, as a result of this decision, got 1500 shares of Tulsa bank stock, Sigelbaum 1600; and at the time Black testified, the shares had risen some $6 to $7 apiece in value.

In another bank deal, Bobby Baker was the scout who found the action. When the District of Columbia National Bank was chartered in 1962, the first new bank in the district in twenty-nine years, Bobby got himself cut in for 1500 shares. These he promptly split, 350 shares apiece, with Fred Black, Edward Levinson, and Benjamin Sigelbaum. It seems significant that, in a period in which gambling and racket interests were worming their way into control of a number of national banks—and looting some of them to the point of ruin—the gambling interests represented by Ed Levinson were invited into the banking business by no less a personage than Bobby Baker, Secretary to the Senate Majority.

Banking wasn't the only activity in which the eminent secretary fronted for the gamblers who had put him into business with Serv-U. In early 1963, Levinson became interested in expanding his casino operations into the Caribbean. Now, Pan American World Airways runs a number of hotels, with gambling casinos attached, in the Caribbean sun-and-fun spots on its far-flung routes. So Bobby Baker picked up a telephone and, fast as a jet takeoff, there were Ed Levinson and Bobby Baker sitting down to a luncheon confab with John Gates, chairman of the board of International Hotels Corporation, a subsidiary of Pan American. Baker explained to Gates, Gates later testified, that he had arranged the conference because Levinson was a good friend of his. In all, three conferences, all arranged by Baker's office, were held on the Caribbean casino deal; and though nothing came of it in the end, nobody could say Bobby Baker hadn't tried.

Just as close as his ties to the gambling interests of Las Vegas were Bobby Baker's relationships with the Murchisons of Texas. In one peculiar arrangement that drew a lot of attention, a Puerto Rican meat dealer decided he could make a profit by importing meat from a Haitian packing house owned by the Murchisons. But there had been some difficulty about standards of cleanliness in the Haitian packing house; it would have to be approved health-wise before its meat could be shipped into Puerto Rico.

The Puerto Rican entrepreneur came to Washington seeking help on this little problem; and, naturally, being in politics himself and politically wise, he sought out Bobby Baker. Baker steered him to the law offices of Webb & Law, the Murchison representatives in Washington; and almost before you could blink an eye, several things happened. The Agriculture Department pronounced the Haitian meat plant simon-pure; the Puerto Rican dealer got his license to import meat from Haiti; and Bobby Baker began collecting a fee for services rendered of a quarter-cent a pound on every pound of meat delivered.

Handsome as this was—and a quarter of a cent a pound can be pretty handsome when it is being paid on meat in million-pound lots—it didn't hold a patch to the deal that came Bobby's way when the Puerto Ricans became disenchanted with the Murchison– Haitian meat. The meat not only was tough, some of it was spoiled; and, even though it was nine cents a pound cheaper than meat imported from the States, the Puerto Ricans decided they wanted no more of it. A new outlet for the Haitian meat had to be found, and, fortunately, it was handy. A Chicago packer had

had some of the cheap Haitian product and wanted more; he agreed to take over the contract.

Before he did, however, there were certain matters to be arranged. The Chicago packer was advised that, if he was to be rewarded with Haitian meat, he would have to pay a "commission" to get it. After some haggling, he agreed to pay the demanded "commission" to the law firm of Tucker & Baker. The Chicagoan testified he had never heard of Tucker & Baker and didn't know who they were, but he was told they "were due a finder's fee for originally locating the buyer in Puerto Rico."

Thus Bobby Baker continued to collect his meat commission, though this time he had had nothing to do with finding and arranging the business. Not only that, under the new arrangement, *he was also being paid by the Murchisons!* A contract was signed guaranteeing him 10 per cent of the profits of the Haitian packing house up to a total of $30,000 annually. Now, if there is anything more pleasant than getting paid once for doing nothing, it is getting paid twice for doing nothing—and Bobby Baker obviously was in this delightfully happy situation.

The reek was a little too much even for the Senate probers. When they had Clint Murchison on the stand, they poked and prodded him about the Haitian meat deal. Counsel McLendon asked Murchison about the "peculiar transaction" by which Baker was getting paid on every pound of meat sold by the Murchison plant in Haiti. "I hardly consider it peculiar," Murchison said, a remark to make one wonder what, in the realm of business, might be considered peculiar. Murchison's explanation was that there had been "a problem of export," and "the problem" had been "mentioned" to Tom Webb.

"Webb suggested that he might be able to take care of it," Murchison testified, "and we agreed to pay . . . that the company would pay Webb some fee—I forgot what it was—I am sure that has been in evidence—if it were done, and subsequently he did negotiate it, he did it through a friend—working through a friend of Baker's, and apparently he felt because of that he should give some of the fee we agreed to give to Webb to Baker. That is the best information I have been able to get."

It would seem that the door had been opened to a lot of questions. How did the Haitian meat plant suddenly meet health standards so that its product could be shipped to Puerto Rico and the United States? Did Bobby Baker have anything to do with this? Was it just coincidence that American packers at this time were protesting about the competition of cheap, low-grade foreign meats—and couldn't get anywhere in Congress? Did Bobby Baker have anything to do with this? These were the kinds of questions that, naturally, weren't being asked. The Senate committee did try to figure just what the meat deal, double payments and all, meant to Bobby Baker. Some records seemed to be missing, but the committee estimated that, at the very least, Bobby Baker netted a regular $400 a month.

Baker made less, but still he picked up $2500 for the price of a telephone call in another Murchison merry-go-round delightfully entitled Sweetwater Development Co. Sweetwater involved experimentation with a process for turning salt water into fresh, and all of Bobby Baker's Murchison buddies were tied up in it. Robert F. Thompson, the Tecon tycoon who had taken the plunge with Bobby on Magic stock, was president of Sweetwater; Sweetwater's headquarters were located in the Dallas office of Thompson's Tecon, and its Washington "office" was behind the door of Webb & Law, the Murchison representatives. Sweetwater was formed in 1961, and its success was almost immediate. On May 1, 1962, it obtained a contract that ultimately was to bring it $119,000 from the Office of Saline Water in the Interior Department.

Though Army auditors frowned on the way regular Murchison expenses were loaded on Sweetwater so that they could be charged off to the federal government, Sweetwater led a charmed life, its prestige unaffected by such charges; and on April 27, 1963, it got a second contract for $151,000 that was later amended to $1,025,000, the kind of escalation that is not hard to take. It didn't seem to matter to anyone in government that federal auditors had frowned upon Sweetwater's being billed $1000 a month for the services of Tecon's Thompson; another $1000 a month for the part-time skills of Bedford Wynne, Dallas lawyer and Murchison partner in the Dallas Cowboys; and $1800 a month for office space in the regular office of Webb & Law, where Sweetwater's name wasn't even listed on the door. It would seem that Sweetwater was having a sweet time with Uncle Sam's money, but this seems to have shocked no one.

In any event, in August 1961, Bobby Baker telephoned Representative Emanuel Celler, the Brooklyn Democrat who is chairman of the House Judiciary Committee, and asked him if his law firm would like to perform a few services for Sweetwater. Celler had no objection—though, he insisted later, he made it clear from the start that his firm wouldn't represent Sweetwater in any dealings with the federal government. Nor did it, Celler said. He explained his law firm only investigated real estate leases for supermarkets Sweetwater was interested in in the North (the Army auditors had reported Sweetwater was engaged in nothing but government contracts), and he didn't think he had even known, Celler said, that Sweetwater was engaged in desalinization work. Anyhow, the congressman's law firm performed some services for Sweetwater from August 1961 to August 1962. It was paid $10,000, and a $2500 finder's fee, routine practice in the legal fraternity, Representative Celler said, went to Bobby Baker, Secretary to the Senate Majority.

The saga of Sweetwater and a lot else might never have come to light except for that persistent gadfly of the Baker investigation, insurance man Don Reynolds. The Democratic majority had closed out the case with what it labeled its "final" report in July 1964. It had concluded that there was really nothing to be done about Bobby Baker. He had wheeled and he had dealt, yes, but there was no evidence he had violated any specific conflict-of-interest statutes. The committee majority put it: "While the committee has no direct proof, it is a reasonable inference to be drawn from the evidence assembled by the committee that some of Baker's friends used him and his knowledge of legislative activities —they thought he was well worth cultivating."

With that gentle epitaph the Bobby Baker case might have died, except for Don Reynolds. The insurance man still had an ace up his sleeve, and he finally revealed it to Senator Williams. He declared that he had been the "bag man" for Bobby Baker in the transfer of $25,000 from Matthew H. McCloskey, contractor for the District of Columbia Stadium, to Baker for use in the 1960 Kennedy–Johnson Presidential campaign. McCloskey was a power in the Democratic party, a former treasurer of the national committee, and a onetime ambassador to Ireland.

According to Reynolds, the political payoff had been worked this way: He had written the performance bond on the $20 million D.C. Stadium for McCloskey's construction company. The premium on the bond actually had been $73,631.28, but he had written the invoice to the McCloskey firm—on the instructions of Baker, he said—for $109,205.60. The McCloskey company actually had paid him this amount. He had sent the proper premium to the insurance company for which he was the agent; he had kept $10,000 for himself for his services as a "bag man"; and he had dished out the remaining $25,000 in cash to Baker as it was needed during the campaign.

In support of this story, Reynolds again offered documents—the invoice for the premium, the invoice to the McCloskey company for $109,205, and a photostat of a canceled check showing the construction firm had paid the larger amount.

This sensational charge and its documentation kicked open all the closed doors of the Bobby Baker inquiry. On December 1, 1964, the Senate Rules Committee sadly reassembled, once more to hear Don Reynolds and to decide what the devil to do about him. Before the public session, the committee questioned Reynolds in private—and Reynolds, feeling, as he later stated, that the committee had tried to make him rather than Baker the target of its probe, unloaded accusations in all directions.

The full details of his testimony have not been revealed and almost certainly never will be. One source with access to the testimony described it as "so scandalous that it probably never will be made public in full." Reynolds lashed out with a variety of charges against Majority Leader Mansfield, Rules Committee Chairman Jordan, Senator Howard Cannon (D., Nev.), and Senator Smathers of Florida. He alleged that Vice-President Lyndon Johnson in 1961, during a tour of the Orient, had spent 150,000 Hong Kong dollars, counterpart funds, during a fourteen-hour shopping spree.

Reynolds furnished some other specifics. He testified that he had seen a card-file list of 100 to 200 call girls in a certain Capitol Hill office. The owner of the list, Reynolds testified, made girls available to visiting firemen. Mrs. Rometsch, he declared, was just one among a bevy of international beauties who included another German girl, a girl of Czechoslovak origin, and others.

Reynolds also claimed that, on one occasion, he had been shown "a little blue flight bag" filled with packets of $100 bills totaling $100,000. The go-between handling the loaded bag had told him, he said, that it was a payoff for a huge defense contract and that it was intended for a high official.

In addition, Reynolds charged that a Navy contractor who could not get certification for his equipment got a reversal of the Navy's decision easily after a woman principal in his firm took part in an orgy in New York with Washington governmental officials.

Reports from the closed session indicated that the Senators were flabbergasted by Reynolds' sweeping charges; and, when the hearing went public before the television cameras, there was no question that the committee majority was hellbent on discrediting Reynolds. Chairman Jordan, a perpetual sneer on his sharp-visaged face, grilled Reynolds fiercely, casting doubt on his entire testimony in the McCloskey matter because he had taken so long to produce it. Counsel McLendon charged bluntly that Senator Williams, the instigator of the Baker investigation, had lied when he said that he previously had tried to get the committee to look into the McCloskey-Stadium involvement. Senator Williams, reading from the record, hurled the lie right back and stalked out of the hearing room, telling the committee he refused to stay any longer and be insulted. Peppery Senator Curtis lashed at McLendon: "You have called Senators down when they are asking questions, and I resent it. And I resent the sandbagging of a colleague." The shillelaghs were flying all over the place.

When the smoke cleared, Reynolds' testimony was hard to discount, try mightily as one would. After all, his testimony on the performance bond was supported by documents, and the committee, frustrated, had to turn to McCloskey for an explanation.

The former Democratic treasurer was a burly man with a mane of snow-white hair and a pink complexion. He proved a combative, even arrogant, witness. Instead of being defensive, he went on the attack from the start. He dressed down Republican hecklers on the committee, told them he didn't intend to repeat his answers, and advised them, if they wanted to know what he had to say, they'd better keep awake. Reynolds, he charged, "hasn't told the truth once. Every time he tells a story he tells it different, and you know it."

"Now, Mr. McCloskey," began Senator Curtis.

"Now, Mr. McCloskey, your grandmother," McCloskey snarled right back at him.

The Republican committee members seemed rocked back on their heels by this display of aggressiveness, and McCloskey rumbled right on with his explanation like a great, big, burly bear rolling over a pack of hound dogs. Sure, he said, somebody in his firm had overpaid Reynolds $35,000. "Somebody goofed," he declared. Reynolds should have returned the money; it was dishonest of him not to have done so. The McCloskey firm was going to sue to get it back. "We have plans to recoup it, that's for sure," he declared.

McCloskey was casual about the picayune $35,000 error.

"We make goofs like that every once in a while," he told the committee. Once, he said, his firm made a $150,000 "goof" on the construction of a high school. Another time, his firm purchased a building from a railroad and only later found that $92,000 in taxes was outstanding on the property. "We sent a check," he said casually.

Unexplained was how a firm that made so many goofs, especially in such a routine matter as checking up on the taxes due on property it was buying, had managed to stay in business—and make millions.

8

In such fashion did the Bobby Baker hearings come to a close. Baker himself took the Fifth Amendment, refusing to answer all questions. So did Carole Tyler. So did Edward Levinson. So did Benjamin Sigelbaum. And so, in essence, did the Senate of the United States; for, with only a few exceptions, the Senate seemed relieved to accept Chairman Jordan's dictum "We are not investigating Senators."

There was some talk about the Senate's adopting stiffer codes for its employees, but not quite so much talk about a stiffer code for the Senators themselves. Senator Jacob K. Javits (R., N.Y.), supported by his colleague Senator Kenneth Keating, introduced one partial-disclosure bill. Senator Clifford P. Case, New Jersey Republican, drafted a tougher measure that would have compelled Senators—and every officer and employee of the federal government, civil or military, earning more than $15,000 a year—to make a full disclosure of his assets and financial interests. The Case proposal, which made eminent good sense in a world in which billions of dollars in contracts are at the disposal of the federal government, caused rumbles of shock and outrage among the Senator's colleagues. Senator Dirksen was a powerful and prominent figure who became incensed at this proposed invasion of his privacy, a deed that, he growled, would demote him to the status of a "second-class" citizen.

As for the Rules Committee itself, it concentrated fiercely upon the task of showing up not Bobby Baker but Don Reynolds.

In early March 1965, Chairman Jordan triumphantly brought forth a report which he labeled the FBI's answer to Reynold's secret charges. He indicated the FBI had investigated every one of Reynold's charges—and had found every one a spurious concoction. The implication was that Reynolds had lied, and Democrats muttered in their beards about the possibility of prosecuting him for perjury.

But a little further examination began to cast strange sidelights on the so-called FBI report. In the first place, the report did not carry the signature of J. Edgar Hoover, the all-powerful director of the bureau, and the Hoover signature is invariably affixed to reports the FBI labels its own. Further probing by newsmen showed that the FBI had not put the report together at all. It had merely questioned witnesses, and from the raw materials of this questioning, lawyers in the Justice Department had drafted the so-called FBI report. The procedure raised the possibility that a judicious selection of testimony had been made in arriving at the verdict so much desired by the Rules Committee majority—that testimony contributing to the desired end had been credited and harmful testimony ignored. And this, indeed, seems to be precisely what had happened.

Key Reynolds charges were discredited in this fashion: there hadn't been 150,000 Hong Kong counterpart dollars available in 1961 at the time of Lyndon Johnson's alleged shopping spree; American officials in Hong Kong averred only $37,642.75 had been on hand at the time. Fred Black, Edward Bostick, and Senator Cannon all denied Reynold's version of a party at which Black was supposed to have assured Bostick he could get Melpar a subcontract from North American Aviation. According to all of these principals, it never happened. So it went. In every instance, those accused by Reynolds repudiated his charge, and these multiple denials were accepted as irrefutable evidence.

No evidence that might have supported Reynolds was permitted to see the light of day. One especially glaring omission involved party girl Linda Morrison. Her name had figured prominently in Senator Scott's questioning of Bostick, and it had been threaded in and out of the record virtually every time girls and parties were mentioned. The underlying, though not very widely publicized, reason for these repetitious and tantalizing references to Miss Morrison was that some explosive tape recordings had been made by Richard L. Bast, a Washington private detective. Bast had been engaged in the investigation of a divorce case and had stumbled head-on into some of the high-life shenanigans of Washington. In a letter to Senator Scott on March 2, 1964, he revealed that he had recordings of conversations "with Miss Linda Morrison and a former female employee of the Senate Rules subcommittee." The tape recordings, he said, "reveal incredible activities" on the part of one Democratic Senator. "I can assure you, Senator, that Miss Morrison will not invoke the Fifth Amendment and will tell the complete truth," Bast wrote. In the light of this, it seems significant that Don Reynolds in his secret testimony months later should also mention Miss Morrison as one of those present at some of the wild parties he described. It would seem that Miss Morrison should have been a vital witness on the subject of Reynolds' credibility. A committee source said later that she was indeed questioned by the FBI, but whatever account she gave was not mentioned in the carefully edited report devoted to discrediting Reynolds.

The attack on Reynolds and the FBI investigation from which it derived produced one other intriguing item of intelligence. In questioning Elizabeth Shotwell, a secretary in Baker's office at the time of his resignation, the FBI learned that no steps had been taken to sequester the contents of Baker's office files. Carole Tyler, the FBI was told, had been permitted to remove from the files all material "she regarded as being personal." Common sense would seem to say that this oversight, if such it truly was, helped to sabotage the Bobby Baker inquiry from the very start.

The final picture that emerges from the Bobby Baker case is one of devastating contrasts: Bobby Baker, the accused, chipper and virtually unscathed going off into the setting sun to manage his multimillion-dollar Serv-U Corporation in California; Don Reynolds, the accuser, a man attacked, badgered and vilified, selling off most of his insurance business and turning into a virtual recluse, accessible only through his most intimate friends. In the contrast is capsuled the reward of the corrupt society—the palm that goes not to truth or justice but to place and power. Bobby Baker had dealt from the top, Don Reynolds from a much lower rung of the ladder—and Bobby Baker, in essence, had won.

He had won though a legion of fact had been stacked against him; he had won because he could not be permitted to lose. Again there is the devastating contrast that tells the story: on the one side, the soft, slow-spoken Don Reynolds, a man perhaps of speckled past and certainly unclear motivation, but a man who produced a documentary record to support his most serious charges and who, in the final showdown on the Texas TV advertising kickback, was corroborated in essence even by Walter Jenkins; on the other side, the august Rules Committee of the Senate, one of the great power complexes of the nation, palpably dragging its feet at every phase of the inquiry, refusing to investigate Senators, refusing to look into the activities of the call girls who spiced virtually every deal, and in the end going to desperate lengths to impugn the testimony of Reynolds, the accuser, while dealing with the utmost gentleness with Bobby Baker, the accused. As the conservative *New York Times* said, the committee in its final one-sided attack on Reynolds was "continuing to go to extraordinary lengths and to employ the most unusual tactics in its effort to close the lid on its inquiry into the affairs of Robert G. Baker." Why? Why unless guilt was so deep and so all-pervasive that truth, at any cost, must be strangled?

A year and a half earlier, before the inquiry had even started, *Life* magazine in its issue of November 22, 1963, had quoted "an old friend of Bobby Baker" as saying: "If Bobby ever told everything he knows, there wouldn't be any Senate left—Democratic *or* Republican." *Life* thought at the time that this opinion "overstates Baker's importance and underrates the Senate," but the sequel was to demonstrate that Bobby Baker's importance was not exaggerated nor was the explosive potential of his knowledge. It was a demonstration that serves well to cap this account of the corrupt society.

The Capitol of the United States still stands. Its needle spire still reaches to the sky, and the floodlights at night still gleam on the graceful curves of its majestic dome. But the white purity of its façade seems less soul-inspiring, the evening shadows seem to close in closer now: after all, Bobby Baker dwelt and dealt there.

9

In Conclusion

THESE PAGES HAVE pictured the ethical collapse of a civilization, the kind of collapse that occurs when man embraces delusions that are at war with realities. The central fact of modern life is that this is the age of the mass society, of the computer and automation, of overproduction and overabundance. It is a society that is entirely new, vast, complex and different; and it cannot be managed, as we are endeavoring to do, on eighteenth-century concepts. This does not mean that those concepts were not valid in their time; it does mean that an eighteenth-century virtue may well become a twentieth-century vice.

In past centuries, man struggled to produce, to tame a hostile environment, to wrest from it sustenance for himself and perhaps a slightly better life for his children. His was an uphill battle against scarcity, ignorance, primitive ways. On this continent, he cleared a wilderness, turned it into fields and farms, and made it habitable and productive beyond the dreams of the first explorers. It was the kind of contest for survival that naturally produced the traditional American ethic, essentially the Protestant ethic, of honesty, hard work, thrift, and sacrifice. It bore social labels like *rugged individualism* and *free enterprise* and *laissez faire*.

These were concepts that in their time and place had some relation to the realities of life. But what becomes of rugged individualism in the world of the mass society? Of free enterprise and laissez faire in the world of power complexes in which a single corporation may dominate an entire industry and "administer" prices? To ask such questions is to expose the gap between myth and reality.

If myths did not hurt, this might not matter, but the truth is that they do. A man embracing a myth is a man unable to cope with reality. And the reality today is that the world of scarcity—the world of all our yesterdays—has been suddenly and magically transformed into the world of overproduction and overabundance. The problem today is not to produce enough food for man to eat, but to limit production and store the glut that still threatens to inundate the market. The problem is not to make enough automobiles and washing machines and television sets but to dispose of them. Not the fulfillment of genuine needs but the creation of want and consumption has become the problem.

Viewed in this context, certain elements in the life around us become clear. We are trying to run all the intricate industrial machinery, all the massive power complexes of the latter twentieth century, on the structure of an eighteenth-century private-profit ethic that is an anachronism in the oncoming age of cybernation. To channel all of the enormous power and resources of the twentieth-century technological society toward the goal of "free enterprise" and private and corporate profit is to create a social system at war with the vast majority of its members. To maintain such a system, even precariously as we have been maintaining it, means indulgence in phony practice and hypocrisy. The boundless capacity of machines, outstripping scarcity and need, creates a crisis of overproduction—a crisis that we endeavor to meet, in order to maintain the profit structure, by deliberately shoddy products and the quick obsolescence that guarantees the periodic return of buyers to the market. We prop up the entire structure by discarding the old Protestant ethic of sacrifice and thrift and the ingrained responsibility that went with it; and we replace it with the tawdry badge of "borrow, spend, buy, waste, want."

The society that results is not a responsible society, not a stable society; it is inevitably a society in pursuit of the meretricious and the unreal. And it must remain so as long as we cling with the fanaticism of religious bigots to the shibboleths of *free enterprise* and *rugged individualism* and *laissez faire,* the delusions that prevent our grasping the realities of our time.

The plain fact is that the world of the mass society cannot be administered on the basis of old-line free enterprise or old-line capitalism. The tremendous forces that have been unleashed—the forces that are herding the vast majority of us onto the payrolls of gigantic corporations, that will soon concentrate 80 per cent of us in metropolitan centers—cannot be allowed to remain the exclusive property of a relatively small management class and their chosen retainers. The bounties must be spread and shared.

To say so much is not to embrace Karl Marx; it is rather to appeal to common sense. Marx had no vision of this age; the forces unleashed by the technological revolution outdate him as much as they outdate the myths of free enterprise. But it stands to reason that these tremendous forces cannot be allowed to thunder purposelessly across the human landscape. They must be controlled and made to serve social purposes. If prices are to be administered, a virtual imperative in this technology, then they must be administered for the over-all good of the mass society, not for private corporate greed. If machines and automation are to do the work of man, it would seem clear that they must not be allowed to discard man—that their benefits must not be hoarded by a managerial oligarchy, but distributed throughout the mass society. The elephants, bloated now to enormous size, must not be allowed to dance among the chickens.

If they are permitted to perform such a macabre rite, then all becomes and remains pretty much as it is today, a racket. The chief goal in life, man's only hope, lies in getting a grip through "inside" knowledge, favoritism, espionage, blackmail—any and every device—upon some handle of the mass power structure. In such a society private greed rules and dominates, for there is no other viable ethic. Man displaced, man dwarfed, realizing that all that counts is to grasp a power lever, can turn in this climate in only one direction—*against* the social order. In this perspective, it is perhaps not so hard to understand that bank clerks become swindlers, executives turn to embezzlement, cops turn to robbery.

As long as the private-profit ethic persists as *the* goal in the mass society, this utter corruption of ethics must be expected to continue and to intensify. The sybaritic life at the top, as illustrated by the Bobby Baker scandal, will become even more than it is today the hallmark of a Romanesque decline.

All of this is clear handwriting on the wall, especially when one realizes that we are today only in the infant years of cybernation, the wedding of machine brains to machine skills in the displacement of man. The ultimate problem, almost certainly, has been little more than sketched for us by the relatively toddling steps we have taken down the new road in the past two decades. Gerard Piel, publisher of *Scientific American,* pointed out in one symposium that, in the decade from 1950 to 1960, the Gross National Product increased between 70 and 100 per cent—yet "the factory labor force remained almost constant." He stressed that the era of cybernation had only begun to affect white-collar jobs and middle management, areas in which it will be especially devastating, and he argued that the early impact had been "concealed somewhat by the expansion of population" and the increased demands inevitably resulting from it. In the future, he saw the inevitability of an "enlarging gap between the employed labor force and the more rapidly increasing size of the labor force as a whole."

Senator J. William Fulbright, certainly one of the more brilliant intellects in politics, has written: "As a result of the rapidly spreading automation of the American economy, the traditional mechanism of distributing purchasing power through employment and income is breaking down. In essence, our ability to generate economic demands is falling steadily behind our ability to increase the supply of purchasable goods and services. It may be that the growing disequilibrium is so profound as to be irreversible by government policies in support of education, economic growth and full employment. If so, we shall eventually have to devise new ways of providing income to those who cannot be put to gainful work."

Gerard Piel, in a summary that drew a contrast between past and future, put it this way: ". . . I think we could sum up the difference between the side of the water-shed in human history that we are talking about and the side we are moving into in the following terms: In the society of scarcity, one man's well-being could be increased only at the expense of other men's well-being. It is plain that the society of abundance presents us with entirely the opposite situation, in which one man's well-being can be increased only through the increase in the well-being of all others." Piel hopefully looks to a new age that would "relate people to people, not people to things."

The Great Society about which President Johnson talks has clearly become an attainable reality in our day. Whether it will ever be achieved depends in great measure upon the ability of the American people and their system to come to grips with the reality of life in the mass society. This means inevitably a stronger role for government, a much stiffer regulatory role to curb some of the more buccaneering excesses of the present private power structures. I would think and hope that this would not result in a governmental collectivism to replace the kind of corporate collectivism that has come to dominate so much of our present lives. The genius of the American system has been its flexibility, its adaptability, its success in borrowing from diverse philosophies and molding all into a middle-way democratic government and society. This would suggest a pattern that would see much more control and regulation of business than we have today, much more planning and programming to harness the enormous technological forces that have been released to serve the welfare of the entire mass society; but it would suggest at the same time the retention by business and the public of vital fluidity and freedom, check reins against government's becoming a dictatorial force.

The achievement of such a system, infinitely complex, based on broad understandings and accommodations, poses an almost superhuman challenge; but it is a challenge that must be met. If we are ever to achieve the Great Society, we must reconcile the well-nigh irreconcilable—the overweening power of the mass society with the individual needs and freedom, the individual dignity and welfare, of man. At the heart of our dilemma lies this dichotomy: power and freedom, man responsible to the mass yet achieving through the mass individual liberty and stature. On the resolution of this issue depends the future. The forces of the mass society can work infinite evil or infinite liberation. They can be used to free man for greater and nobler endeavors, or they can be used, as they are largely being used today, to make him a pawn, a cog, in a vast and impersonal power complex against which, seeking his own, he instinctively rebels, instinctively fights—and so turns with alarming frequency *against* society. The choice is between a liberated and more ethical society on the one hand, a racket-ridden and corrupted society on the other.

Notes

CHAPTER I

THIS BOOK DOES not contain detailed footnotes for specific statements, but I shall indicate in these chapter notes the sources on which I have relied for major incidents and facts.

The story of Douglas Johnson was told by the Associated Press in two nationally syndicated articles on March 11 and April 21, 1961. Nelson Algren's letter to Johnson is taken from a copy he sent to Carey McWilliams, editor of *The Nation*.

For an account of the corruption of legislatures in the 1880's see Theodore Roosevelt's autobiography. The Norris quotations are taken from *Fighting Liberal, the Autobiography of George W. Norris* (Collier Books, 1961).

The quotes from Chief Justice Warren's speech are reproduced from a copy of the text; see also *The New York Times*, Nov. 12, 1962.

For statistics on the dwindling farm population and the concentration of business power see the 1962 edition of *Statistical Abstract of the United States*, issued by the Bureau of the Census and published by the U.S. Government Printing Office. See also *All Honorable Men* by Walter Goodman (Little, Brown, 1963); *The Organizational Society* by Robert Presthus (Knopf, 1962); and a column by Sylvia Porter in The New York *Post*, Sept. 19, 1962.

The Lynd quotations are from "Our 'Racket' Society," *The Nation*, April 25, 1951.

For the events of July 6, 1962, see *The New York Times*, the New York *Herald Tribune*, the *Daily News*, and the New York *Post* for the following day.

The Eric Fromm quotes are from "Our Way of Life Makes Us Miserable," *The Saturday Evening Post,* July 25 and August 1, 1964. The Joseph Wood Krutch quotes are from a guest editorial, "The New Morality," in the *Saturday Review.*

CHAPTER 2

This chapter owes a great debt to *The Gentlemen Conspirators* by John G. Fuller (Grove Press, 1962); to Walter Goodman's *All Honorable Men;* and to articles in *The Wall Street Journal* and *Fortune* magazine. Especially important in revealing the attitudes of many of the executives involved were the *Journal*'s articles of January 9, 10, 12, and 13, 1961, and *Fortune*'s two-part probe-in-depth, "The Incredible Electrical Conspiracy," by Richard Austin, in the April and May 1961 issues.

For accounts of the court proceedings and sentencings, see *The New York Times,* February 7 and 8, 1961; *Newsweek,* February 20, 1961.

Testimony developed before the Kefauver committee made virtually daily stories in the press during April and May 1961. Burens' testimony may be found in *The New York Times,* April 25, 1961; Burke's and Stehlik's in *The Times* and the New York *Post,* April 27, 1961; Loock's in *The Times, The Wall Street Journal* and the New York *Herald Tribune,* May 12, 1961. Other important phases of the testimony appear in *The Times* in the April 18, April 20, and May 5 issues.

For an analysis of the importance of TVA's role, see column by Marquis Childs, the New York *Post,* March 6, 1961.

For the union side of the electrical controversy, see a two-page editorial spread in the *UE News,* February 27, 1961, and a booklet, "The Public Plunderers," by James B. Carey, president of the IUE, and published by the union.

Acounts of the treatment of the jailed executives may be found in *The New York Times,* February 11, 1961; the New York *World-Telegram and Sun,* February 16, 1961. The Reverend Mr. Gibson's quote is from *Christian Century,* November 8, 1961.

General Electric's attitude was reflected in its public relations newsletter headed "The Turning of the Tide," April 27, 1961, in which appear liberal quotes from Cordiner's address to GE stockholders at their annual meeting.

A series of running stories in the press has dealt with the settlement of the damage suits. See *The New York Times,* July 28, 1962, for account of first settlement; the New York *Herald Tribune,* June 3, 1964, on the Philadelphia utilities case; *The Wall Street Journal,*

May 14, 1963, on U.S. Supreme Court decision on suits prior to 1956; the *Herald Tribune,* April 30, 1964, for Phillippe's statement to GE stockholders on the likely total cost to GE.

For stories on the government's attempt to get GE to sign a consent decree not to cut prices to ruinous levels see *The Wall Street Journal,* June 12, 1961, and *Business Week,* June 17 and 24, 1961.

On continued identical bidding, see the New York *Post,* April 8 and May 3, 1961, and *The New York Times,* May 3, 1961.

The *Value Line Investment Survey* article is in the *Congressional Record* for April 12, 1961, pages A2422–A2424.

For two excellent editorials on business ethics, including quotations from the report of the Cordiner task force, see The Washington *Post,* January 4 and 5, 1961.

The *Playboy* symposium appeared under the title "Business Ethics and Morality," in *Playboy,* November 1962.

After this chapter was written, on August 31, 1965, Judge Wilfred Feinberg in New York Federal Court assessed triple damages totaling $16,873,203 against General Electric and Westinghouse as a result of the price-fixing conspiracy. The suit had been brought by Ohio Valley Electric Corporation and Indiana-Kentucky Electric Corporation, both firms charging they had been gouged in prices charged for steam-turbine generators. Judge Feinberg, after a two-month trial that amassed more than 5,000 pages of testimony, held that GE and Westinghouse had participated in a twenty-year-long price-rigging conspiracy that lasted from 1939 until the federal government's anti-trust action in 1959. A recapitulation showed that 1,912 civil anti-trust suits had been filed in the wake of the criminal-court action. Of these, more than five years later, 719 still remained to be disposed of throughout the country. Legal sources estimated that total damages that would ultimately be assessed against all the firms involved in the price-rigging would probably run to more than $500 million. Even before Judge Feinberg's ruling, it was estimated the conspiracy had already cost GE more than $225 million and Westinghouse $110 million. At the same time, on another wing of the "administered price," price-rigging front, the nation's major steel companies were being fined a total of more than $725,000 for rigging prices on a wide range of steel products. In these cases, however, no executives were sent to jail, and no civil damage suits had been filed.

CHAPTER 3

The *Harvard Business Review* survey formed the basis of a two-part article, "How Ethical Are Businessmen?" which appeared in the July and August 1961 issues.

For call-girl disclosures, see *Advertising Age*, February 2, 1959; Sara Harris in *Cavalier*, April 1959; Michael Marsh in *Labor*, as reprinted in *The Gazette and Daily*, York, Pa., April 3, 1959.

Norman Jaspan lectures frequently to business groups. In addition to the texts of some of his speeches, I have relied here on the book *The Thief in the White Collar*, written by him in collaboration with Hillel Black (Lippincott, 1960).

For articles on industrial espionage, see two-part series by Don Molinelli, the New York *Daily News*, April 30 and May 1, 1958; three-part series by Selwyn Raab, the New York *World-Telegram and Sun*, December 5, 6, and 7, 1962; *Business Week*, November 25, 1961, and November 10, 1962, *The New York Times*, October 29, 1964, and *Business Week*, October 31, 1964; article by Jack Smith on the work of Harvey Wolfe, the Los Angeles *Times*, February 11, 1962; and article on the Aries judgment in the New York *Herald Tribune*, November 28, 1964.

Quotes of Freeman speech are from the Chicago *Sun-Times*, October 16, 1958.

On the society of waste, see *Business Week*, May 5 and June 16, 1956; "Recipe for Prosperity" by Kenneth Burke, *The Nation*, September 8, 1956; *Newsweek*, January 8, 1962, and January 15, 1962.

CHAPTER 4

See "Truth in Packaging" by Senator Philip A. Hart, *The Nation*, June 29, 1963. Also Parts 1, 2, and 3 of the hearings on Packaging and Labeling Practices before the subcommittee on antitrust and monopoly of the Senate Judiciary Committee, 87th Congress, U.S. Government Printing Office, 1961 and 1962.

For details on the great highway-robbery scandal and the story of Massachusetts corruption, I have relied on "Super-Graft on Super-highways" by Stanley Meisler, *The Nation*, April 1, 1961; "Highway Robbery," by Rep. Jim Wright, *The Saturday Evening Post*, Nov. 30, 1963; a transcript of the David Brinkley telecast obtained from NBC; "Dirty Money in Boston" by Charles L. Whipple, *The Atlantic Monthly*, March 1961 (this issue also contains the full text of Judge Wyzanski's final analysis of the Worcester case testimony); "Scandals Pock Construction Landscape," *Engineering News-Record*, Jan. 4, 1962; "Political Whirlwind Trails Bay State Scandal," by Charles L. Whipple, The Washington *Post*, May 20, 1962; "Chasing Down Corruption," by Michael Liuzzi, *The Christian Science Monitor*, March 3,

1962; and an exceptionally detailed three-part series by Anthony Lewis in *The New York Times,* June 19, 20, and 21, 1961.

The Kennedy tax-reform proposals are contained in the "President's Tax Message," submitted to Congress by Secretary Dillon May 3, 1961, Hearings of the House Ways and Means Committee, U.S. Government Printing Office, 1961. See also Volume I of House Ways and Means Committee Hearings and Volume I of Senate Ways and Means Committee Hearings, both printed by U.S. Government Printing Office, 1961.

For other material on the expense-account proposals and what happened to them, see the New York *Herald Tribune,* May 4, 1961; James Reston in *The New York Times,* July 22, 1962; Sylvia Porter in the New York *Post,* Aug. 5 and 6, 1963; *The Nation,* Sept. 15, 1962; Murray Kempton, in the New York *Post,* Aug. 30, 1962; Associated Press article on Senator Douglas' no-tax-for-millionaires revelations, Oct. 17, 1963; the New York *Herald Tribune,* Feb. 8, 1964, on retention of the oil depletion allowance; *The Nation,* Sept. 28, 1964, for article by Senator Lee Metcalf (D., Mont.) on the stock-option racket.

My account of Wright Patman and his battle on the foundation tax dodge is based on my own interviews with Patman and an earlier article I wrote, "The Big Gyp," *Saga,* October 1964.

CHAPTER 5

An excellent early study of the Billie Sol Estes case appeared in *Fortune,* July 1962, under the title "Estes, Three-Sided Country Slicker."

For colorful background on Pecos, see "The Predicament of Pecos, Texas," by Fletcher Knebel in *Look.*

For accounts of the Henry Marshall murder mystery, see the New York *Post,* May 9, 1962, and July 12, 1962; and *The New York Times,* July 20, 1962.

Other excellent accounts of the Estes affair may be found in *Time,* May 25, 1962, and *Newsweek,* May 28, 1962.

For accounts of testimony developed in the Texas inquiry, see a running series of almost daily stories in *The Wall Street Journal* from mid-May to mid-June 1962.

Full accounts of testimony developed in the congressional inquiries appeared, again in almost daily articles, in *The New York Times* and the New York *Herald Tribune* during June, July, and August 1962.

Final conclusions on the case and verbatim quotes of much of the pertinent testimony are contained in the reports of the House and

Senate Committees on Government Operations, U.S. Government Printing Office, 1964.

For two good accounts of Billie Sol Estes in Abilene see article by Donald Janson in *The New York Times,* August 16, 1964, and one by Finis Mothershead of the Associated Press in the Washington *Sunday Star,* September 27, 1964.

Another good summary of the case may be found in *Facts for Farmers,* published by Farm Research, Inc., New York, in the issue for June 1962.

For accounts of the windup of the Estes case, see *The New York Times,* November 8, 1962, for his conviction in Texas; the New York *Herald Tribune,* January 30, 1965; and *The National Observer,* Feb. 1, 1965.

CHAPTER 6

This chapter owes a great debt to Meyer Weinberg's *TV in America, the Morality of Hard Cash* (Ballantine Books, 1962). It is the best and most complete account of the quiz-show scandal that I have found.

For the development of the quiz-show scandal as reflected in the press, I have relied mainly on files of *The New York Times* and the New York *World-Telegram & Sun.* The months of August and September 1958 are important for the early developments, the demise of *Dotto,* the Stempel affidavit in the *World-Telegram & Sun,* and the subsequent uproar. For accounts of the congressional hearings, the issues of October 6–13, 1959, and November 2–7, 1959, are especially important.

An excellent brief article on the ethical rot and corruption exposed by the quiz-show scandal is "The Rigged Society" by Murray Hausknecht in *Dissent,* winter issue, 1960.

A good study of public reaction to the Van Doren episode is to be found in "Van Doren as Victim: Student Reaction" by Gladys Engle Lang and Kurt Lang, in *Studies in Public Communication,* University of Chicago, summer issue, 1961.

For accounts of the pleadings and sentencings, see *The New York Times* and the *Daily News* May 9, 1961 and January 18, 1962.

See the New York *Post* January 25, 1962, for an account of what happened to some of the headline figures in the scandal after the worst had blown over.

Jack Gould's account of the reasoning of the FCC examiner in the Barry–Enright radio-license-renewal case may be found in *The New York Times* May 9, 1963.

CHAPTER 7

The quotes on the TV scandal in relation to the fixed society are from Murray Hausknecht's *The Rigged Society,* mentioned in the preceding chapter's notes.

For sources on the cheating problem and scandals, see: Los Angeles *Mirror,* Dec. 1, 1961, for account of Bancroft Junior High survey; *The New York Times,* Jan. 30, 1965, and *The Times* and New York *Herald Tribune,* Feb. 4, 1965, for accounts of the Air Force Academy scandal, also *The National Observer,* Feb. 1 and 15, 1965; for accounts of the Rider College scandal, see the New York *Post,* March 15, 1961; for the doctor-licensing scandal, see the New York *World-Telegram & Sun* and *The New York Times,* Nov. 15, 1962. The Philip Jacob survey of colleges was reported in detail in the *Insider's Newsletter,* April 9, 1962.

In dealing with the problem of office morality and the white collar thief, I have relied extensively on two books—*The Operators* by Frank Gibney (Harper, 1960) and *The Thief in the White Collar* by Norman Jaspan with Hillel Black (Lippincott, 1960). I have used in addition a wide number of other sources, principally: "What's Happened to Morality in the Office?" by Warren C. Stevens, *Modern Office Procedures,* February 1964; text of Jaspan's speech, "Internal Control of Fraud and Embezzlement," given to the American Management Association, Jan. 25, 1962; "Embezzlers, the Trusted Thieves," *Fortune,* November 1957.

For details on shoplifting see: "Shoplifting: Our White-Collar Scandal" by Don Wharton, *The Reader's Digest,* April 1963; the columns of Sylvia Porter in the New York *Post* for June 14, 1963, Dec. 23, 1964, and Feb. 5 and 8, 1965; on bank thefts, see "The Boom in Bank Robbery," *Fortune,* January 1960.

The cop-burglar scandal has received its fullest treatment in Ralph Lee Smith's *The Tarnished Badge* (Crowell, 1965). The excerpts used here were taken from Smith's article "Cops as Robbers" in *The Nation,* Feb. 1, 1965. For other details on the cop-robber scandal see: "Cops as Robbers" by Roscoe Fleming, *The Nation,* Oct. 21, 1961, an account of the Denver case. Other key articles on the Denver situation may be found in *The New York Times,* Oct. 3, 1961, and the New York *Herald Tribune,* Aug. 28, 1961. A summary of police scandals throughout the nation, written by the Associated Press, was carried in the Washington *Post,* July 23, 1961. For accounts of the Nassau scandal, see the New York *Post,* Aug. 7, 1963, and the *Daily News,* Aug. 14, 1963. Articles on the Bristol, Conn., police scandal appeared in *The New York Times,* Oct. 8, 1964, and the New York *Herald Tribune,* Oct. 11, 1964.

CHAPTER 8

For this account of the Bobby Baker case, I have relied primarily upon the voluminous record, Hearings Before the Committee on Rules and Administration, U.S. Senate, 89th Congress, U.S. Government Printing Office, 1964 and 1965.

An excellent pocket-book account of the Baker case is G. R. Schreiber's *The Bobby Baker Affair; How to Make Millions in Washington* (Henry Regnery, 1964).

The best early reporting job on the Baker case was the article *"Scandal Grows in Washington"* by Keith Wheeler in the November 22, 1963, issue of *Life* magazine. This is especially valuable for its insights into Baker's role as errand boy for the Senate Establishment and for its accounts of call-girl partying.

The day-by-day newspaper accounts are too voluminous to be listed in detail, but I shall try to indicate some of the more important sources. For an excellent wrapup account, focusing on the many unanswered questions on the Baker affair, see the three-page article, "The Fallen Angel," by Paul Hope and John Barron in the Washington *Sunday Star,* January 10, 1965.

For accounts of Elly Rometsch, the Quorum Club, and call-girl activities in Washington, see the New York *Post,* October 28, 30, and 31, 1963; the *Daily News,* October 30 and 31 and November 3, 1963; the New York *Herald Tribune,* October 28, 29, 31, 1963; *The New York Times,* October 29, 1963.

Bobby Baker's background and the duties of Secretary to the Senate Majority were developed in "The Strange Case of Bobby Baker," *U.S. News & World Report,* Feb. 10, 1964. See also "How Baker Turned Access into an Asset," *Business Week,* Feb. 8, 1964. Baker's finances were dealt with in "The Fast Rise of Bobby Baker," *U.S. News & World Report,* Feb. 3, 1964.

For some of the ethical issues posed by the Baker case, see "The Senate Shocks a Senate Prober," by Cabell Phillips, *The New York Times Sunday Magazine,* August 9, 1964.

McLendon's view that Bobby Baker was the most powerful man in the Senate was expressed in an article by the Chicago Daily News Syndicate, March 1, 1965; see the New York *Post* of that date.

A good word portrait of Fred B. Black, Jr., and the role of "the Washington operator" may be found in The Washington *Post,* May 10, 1964.

Accounts of Walter Jenkins' second affidavit, conceding he mentioned advertising to Reynolds, may be found in *The New York Times* and the New York *Herald Tribune,* February 25, 1965.

The Celler fee issue was discussed in articles in *The Times, Herald Tribune,* and New York *Post,* January 27, 1965.

For some description of Reynolds' secret testimony, see the New York *Journal-American,* December 4, 1964, and for accounts of the so-called FBI report and criticism of it, see Ted Lewis' "Capitol Stuff" column in the *Daily News* and the article by Dom Bonafede in the New York *Herald Tribune,* March 4, 1965. See *New York Times* editorial of the same date.

Other accounts taking a critical look at lapses in the Rules Committee inquiry may be found in an article by James Deakin, St. Louis *Post-Dispatch,* Dec. 13, 1964, and Dom Bonafede, New York *Herald Tribune,* March 7, 1965.

Details of the Bast–call-girl involvement are from photostats of Bast's letters to Senator Scott and the committee in my possession.

Accounts of how little Bobby Baker seems to have been affected by it all may be found in the New York *Herald Tribune,* March 7, 1964 and March 14, 1965.

CHAPTER 9

Gerard Piel's quotes are from a symposium, "Jobs, Machines and People," held under the auspices of the Center for Democratic Institutions, Santa Barbara, Calif., 1964.

Senator Fulbright's quotes are from *Old Myths and New Realities* (Random House, 1964).

Index

[*345*]

PACE COLLEGE WESTCHESTER
LIBRARY
Bedford Road, Pleasantville, N. Y.
914 ROgers 9-3200

Books may be borrowed for two weeks.
Identification card must be presented each time
books are borrowed.
A charge of 5 cents is made for each day a book
is overdue.
A charge of 25 cents is made for each day a reserve book is overdue.

 PRINTED IN U.S.A.